The Anti Money Laundering Complex and the Compliance Industry

In contrast to other strategies of tackling security phenomena, the battle against money laundering has assigned an important task to private organisations. Private actors form the basis of the anti money laundering (AML) approach since they are responsible for detecting and reporting transactions that may be linked to money laundering. This has resulted in the development of new professional groups, such as compliance officers, or AML officers, working within financial institutions to implement AML legislation. As a result, the battle against money laundering has led to the creation of an AML complex, consisting of the activities of private and public actors carrying out regulatory, monitoring, reporting, investigatory and judicial tasks.

On the other hand, however, fighting money laundering implies the active involvement of an entrepreneurial market, the compliance industry, providing services and tools in support of the fight against money laundering. This industry stimulates compliance and AML investments by providing monitoring systems, blacklists, training and advice to corporations that are obliged to implement the AML legislation. The compliance industry provides an additional service to AML regulation, in which AML compliance is marketed as a product for sale.

Financial institutions, the focus of the empirical research that forms the heart of this book, can be seen as go-betweens; making part of the AML complex on the one hand, buying services from the compliance industry on the other hand. The Belgian compliance officer, an obligatory function in each Belgian bank, functions as the central actor in this book, and as such serves as a case study of the implementation of European and US guidelines. This professional group has not been the subject of study before in Belgium. Inside the walls of financial institutions, an impressive compliance apparatus continuously checks our transactions, deposits and financial movements.

This study gives a first insight into the functioning of this system and shows that the cooperation in the fight against money laundering is inherently linked to problems of public and private partnership, intrusions of privacy and questions of proportionality.

Antoinette Verhage holds a PhD from the Department of Penal Law and Criminology at Ghent University, Belgium.

Routledge studies in crime and economics
Edited by Peter Reuter *University of Maryland, USA*
Ernesto U. Savona *University of Trento, Italy*

The Anti Money Laundering Complex and the Compliance Industry

Antoinette Verhage

 Routledge
Taylor & Francis Group

LONDON AND NEW YORK

First published 2011
by Routledge
2 Park Square, Milton Park, Abingdon, Oxon OX14 4RN

Simultaneously published in the USA and Canada
by Routledge
711 Third Avenue, New York, NY 10017

Routledge is an imprint of the Taylor & Francis Group, an informa business

British Library Cataloguing in Publication Data
A catalogue record for this book is available from the British Library

Library of Congress Cataloging in Publication Data
Verhage, Antoinette, 1977–
The anti money laundering complex and the compliance industry /
Antoinette Verhage.
p. cm.
1. Money laundering–Prevention. I. Title.
HV6768.V468 2010
332.1'7–dc22
2010039673

ISBN: 978-0-415-60076-7 (hbk)
ISBN: 978-0-203-82848-9 (ebk)

Typeset in Times
by Wearset Ltd, Boldon, Tyne and Wear
Printed and bound by TJI Digital, Padstow, Cornwall

Contents

Figures and table

Figures

Table

Preface

This book embodies the results of a four-year PhD study, which was initiated by my promoter asking the question: who are these compliance officers and what do they do?

I had conducted research into public–private policing before and the compliance officer seemed an interesting function to look into more closely. A recent study in France (Favarel-Garrigues *et al.*, 2008), had also revealed that there is more to compliance than you might think at first glance. And indeed, after a while, a new world of compliance, transaction monitoring, reporting, know your customer (and much more) opened up, leading to the decision to dedicate my PhD study to this intriguing subject. To date, compliance officers are a mystery occupational group and highly unrepresented in research. I hope that this book will not only fill this void, but will also open up the minds of criminologists in their conceptualisation of policing and public order.

The book is compiled of nine chapters, each of them based on one (or two) article(s) that was written in the course of this study. The combination of these articles in this book results in an encompassing overview of this subject, focusing on a new domain. As part of this study was carried out during the financial crisis of 2008, the topicality is even more pertinent.

Most of the chapters are based on empirical data, both survey data and interviews that were conducted with the leading figures of this study, the compliance officers, but also with other people functioning in the AML system.

Compliance officers all over the world are faced with the same challenges and encounter identical problems. Although European regulation has resulted in a streamlining of AML and compliance issues, also American and Australian compliance officers will recognise the dilemmas of their Belgian colleagues in this study. Furthermore, the AML system and its effects have been under scrutiny since its emergence, in an international sense. Academics from all over the world have questioned the effects and have asked themselves whether the end justifies the means. This book will therefore not only be relevant to Belgian readers, but will be of interest for everyone involved with or interested in the AML system everywhere. Although compliance officers are very difficult to find (they are working hidden and quasi-anonymously behind the large and often impressive entrances of banks), once they are found, they are very interesting and intriguing conversation partners.

I therefore sincerely hope that this book will also inspire other researchers to study this interesting professional group. I can certainly recommend it.

Acknowledgements

This is the publication of my PhD, a four-year-long process of trial and error that was supported by many people. This also implies that writing an acknowledgement is not that easy: where to begin? I would like to start by thanking the members of the exam committee and the Dean of our Law Faculty for their willingness to be a part of this PhD trajectory. Some of the members of the exam committee were also part of my guidance committee and have witnessed the entire route: Marc Cools, Brice De Ruyver and Bob Hoogenboom; thank you for being critical and inspirational, each from your own perspective.

Second, many thanks to the editors and publishers who published results of my research, and allowed the republishing of some of these articles in this book, and the (anonymous) reviewers for their constructive comments. These comments were very helpful in providing insight and giving depth to the discussion. Petrus van Duyne and Jackie Harvey, thank you for providing room for both thought and for publication. During my research, I was given the opportunity to travel to several other countries which allowed me to test my research hypotheses and discuss results with colleagues. I think this is also the right place to thank the Crimprev and GERN network (and specifically Joanna Shapland), for its inspirational gatherings. I would also like to thank the FWO (Fonds Wetenschappelijk Onderzoek Vlaanderen) for its support of this study.

Without those many compliance officers this book could not have been written. Many of you do not realise how interesting your job actually is. Thank you for investing your time in this study, even in times of crisis. Of course also the other respondents were indispensible for this research, such as police respondents and members of the compliance industry. Febelfin should also be thanked as it supported the survey in the first phase of this research.

Thanks also to the publishers that granted me the permission to republish parts of the published articles: Maklu, Boom, Springer, Wolf Legal Publishers and Emerald. Also many thanks to Routledge (Thomas Sutton and Simon Holt) for their enthusiasm with regard to this project!

Within our research group Social Analysis of Security, writing a PhD is not a lonely task. Preceded by a number of shining examples and together with 'fellow sufferers', the road to a PhD is less arduous than expected. Jutta, Lieselot, Stefanie and Lieven, thank you for your help in stressful times and for taking my mind off things when needed. Thanks also to all friends who remained interested and concerned during the past four years, but also before and after.

My promoter, Paul Ponsaers, deserves a special appreciation. Paul, your qualities as a mentor, supporter and critical reader have been priceless, not only during those four years, but ever since I started at Ghent University and to this very day. Thank you for your inspirational commitment, for asking the right questions and just for being there. I sincerely hope that you will continue to do so.

Growing up in a family full of genuine and loving interest in each other, with two 'little' brothers as enthusiastic supporters, and a firm 'Zeeuwse' ground, has been a privilege. Pa and Ma, thank you for believing in me and for providing me with an invaluable guide for the rest of my life.

And finally, Frank, how to thank you? Maybe for those conversations in which you showed me the other side of compliance, or simply for giving me elbow-room. But also for all the good times together. With you as my tower of strength, I'm sure that the best is yet to come.

1   Introduction

Whoever fights monsters should see to it that in the process he does not become a monster.

(Nietzsche, 2009)

Introduction

When de' Medici 'founded' the first bank on the benches of the Florence market over 600 years ago (Ferguson, 2008), they could hardly imagine the role that financial institutions would play in the future, nor could it be inferred that financial institutions would become one of the big brothers of the twenty-first century, reporting their own clients to the authorities in case of suspicious transactions or attempted money laundering.

The role of banks in anti money laundering (AML), although inevitable in the battle against this type of crime because of their central and crucial position in financial markets, has taken the shape of an encompassing and above all very intrusive system. Surprisingly, criminology has given relatively little attention to this system since its emergence in the late 1980s. This is remarkable, not only for the extent of its invasion into personal spheres and the subsequent privacy issues that arise from it, but also for its immensity. After all, the AML system is – quietly – activated whenever a bank transaction is carried out, cash is deposited or bills are paid through online banking. Financial institutions, as gateways to the financial system, to economic power and possibilities, are considered to be one of the major vehicles for money laundering and therefore also represent an important means to prevent this type of crime. In the past ten years, the investment of this sector in the prevention of money laundering has been increasing rapidly.

Today, 'compliance' and 'anti money laundering' are terms that make part of a semi-universal language that has been developed since the late 1980s. After all, money laundering, the 'process in which assets obtained or generated by criminal activity are moved or concealed to obscure their link with the crime' (IMF, 2004), has increasingly received attention during the last twenty years, from both policy-makers and international organisations. This criminal phenomenon is depicted – first by the US, but quickly followed by the UK and Europe – as a major threat to society and its economy. As a result, the battle against money laundering has become an international concern and – as some claim – a convenient motive for policy-makers to implement far-reaching regulations and guidelines. Fighting money laundering is a national (cf. for Belgium see the National Security Plan of the Belgian Police, 2008–2011) and international priority (on the level of the European Union, the US and international bodies like the OECD and IMF) and has been so for over two decades. During this period, we have witnessed a growing apparatus of legislation, regulation and guidelines on an international level. This battle not only focuses on the prevention of money laundering as a crime in itself, but is also used as a means to identify the perpetrators of predicate crimes being the origin of the crime monies to be laundered.

The input and effort that is demanded from public and private actors in the prevention and detection of money laundering is rather high (Commission of the European Communities, 2009). As a result of international and national initiatives that were taken in the fight against organised crime and money laundering, we are currently witnessing the development of two parallel angles around the fight against money laundering and its predicate crimes: a legislative, regulative angle, designed to prevent and detect money laundering on the one hand, and an intrinsic commercial position towards anti money laundering, stemming from a self-protecting reflex by financial institutions, aspiring to protect themselves against regulatory and reputational risks. These developments will be referred to respectively as the *anti money laundering complex* and the *compliance industry*. Between these separate and yet intertwined perspectives, we see private financial institutions, straddling both worlds. These private institutions are on the one hand a part of the AML complex, through the employment of inspectors who need to enable the institution to comply with the regulation: the *compliance officers*. On the other hand, however, these financial institutions purchase services from the – non-financial – compliance industry to support their implementation of AML measures, and are in this sense sponsors of the compliance industry.

The compliance officer, responsible for the implementation of AML legislation and reporting of potentially suspicious transactions, symbolises a part of this private investment in anti money laundering. As a bank employee, responsible for the implementation of governmental objectives, he finds himself trapped between crime-fighting objectives and commercial goals. The duality of the involvement of private partners in the AML complex and the vastness of the system induce a closer look at the functioning, values and perceptions of actors within this system. This was the starting point of my PhD study (2006–2009) which is embodied in this book.

Research questions

This research set itself the objective of gaining insight in the compliance function of financial institutions, based on the central hypothesis that the AML complex and the compliance industry are two parallel constructions, both working in the same domain, but on the basis of different objectives and motivations. These differences in motivation may not only result in differential attitudes and working methods, but also reveal the dilemmas that actors within AML are dealing with.

The *AML complex* consists of the activities of private and public actors, carrying out regulatory, monitoring, reporting, investigatory and judicial tasks. The objectives of the AML complex are prevention, crime fighting and law enforcement, and it is based on government regulation.

The *compliance industry*, on the other hand, is an entrepreneurial market providing services and tools in support of the fight against money laundering. This industry stimulates compliance and AML investments by providing monitoring systems, blacklists, training and advice to corporations that are obliged to implement the AML legislation. The compliance industry provides an additional service to AML regulation, in which AML compliance is marketed as a product for sale.

Financial institutions perform a pivotal role between these constructions, adding to and interacting with both the complex and the industry. As go-betweens, they are continuously looking for a balance between the interests that derive from each structure: commercially oriented – within an entrepreneurial environment – or crime fighting and prevention. Based on this dual role, the complex and industry were studied from exactly this viewpoint. Starting from the compliance function in Belgian financial institutions, we intended to answer three questions: (1) how do these constructions function; (2) which interactions do we see between both; and (3) how does the compliance function fit into this perspective?

At the start of this research, we hypothesised that within the AML complex adverse attitudes are present, as different actors with dissimilar backgrounds are united. The outsourcing of government tasks to the private sector results in a

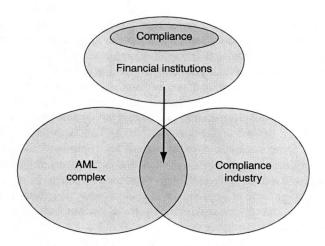

Figure 1.1 AML complex–compliance industry.

paradoxical role for financial institutions. After all, the financial institutions' core business can clash with the monitoring task that is imposed by AML legislation; it is not always in a commercial interest to refuse customers or end client relationships. Looking into these potential contrasting interests can lead to an increased insight into the position of financial institutions and the norms they uphold, and to a view on the feasibility of imposing a surveillance function on private corporations. On the other hand, we also recognise interests that stimulate compliance within banks. Out of concern of risk management and foremost reputation protection, AML compliance can be encouraged. Regulatory sanctions also play a role in this respect, and serve as the stick in case of non-compliance.

The compliance officer bridges both worlds. In his/her role as inspector of employers, colleagues and clients, his function inherently implies a duality. The compliance officer is a relatively recent actor within AML; in Belgium this function was only implemented in 2001, as a result of a regulatory obligation. The compliance officer is therefore a new and recent profession that has some analogies with policing and private investigation. The compliance officer actually polices the money and determines the input of the AML chain, through his or her reporting duty to the FIU (Financial Intelligence Unit).

Research scope

In every research, choices need to be made and some paths cannot be taken. This allows for a detailed focus in research, but inevitably implies that certain areas will remain unstudied. In this research, we have defined the research scope by focusing on three domains. Our choices will be outlined shortly.

First of all, in an international sense, this study is limited to the Belgian compliance officer, working within the Belgian system. However, I am convinced that the issues which the Belgian compliance officers are confronted with, are quasi-universal. Compliance officers all over the world have to make judgements on a daily basis whether to report a client or not and have to analyse the extent to which a transaction can be considered as 'normal'. Compliance officers all over the world are faced with the same dual position: working as a bank employee, but sometimes having to make decisions that may harm the bank in a commercial manner. This was also confirmed by research in other countries (for example Levi, 1997; Levi, 2001; Favarel-Garrigues *et al.*, 2008; Harvey and Lau, 2009). Regardless of the specifics of the legislation, the bottom line is the same. Of course, differences in legal system and requirements for compliance officers exist and are sometimes crucial to the AML system. On the other hand, system problems are also discussed as universal. For example, feedback from the authorities to the private sector can be seen as minimal in most European countries, as shown by a recent study commissioned by the European Commission. The same study concluded that reporting institutions within Europe also question the efficiency and effectiveness of the system. This is partly due to the lack of transparency and know-how with regard to the outcome of AML policy

(European Commission, 2008). The daily dilemmas may therefore very well be relatively convergent.

Second, in view of the AML reporting system, we must note that this study is limited to financial institutions, excluding other reporting institutions, based on both feasibility and their role within the AML approach. Although studying the reporting behaviour of other institutions would have been interesting, financial institutions were the first to institutionalise a formal compliance function for the AML task.[1] Furthermore, within the reporting system, financial institutions not only report the highest sums to the FIU, their reports were also those that are most often sent to the public prosecutor's office (in 2005, almost 75 per cent of all reports to the public prosecution were based on reports by financial institutions (CTIF-CFI, 2006)). Banks therefore represent an important actor within AML. Today this finding still holds. In 2008, financial institutions reported 4,034 suspicious transactions to the FIU. Although financial institutions today make up only 21 per cent of all reports to the FIU (see Chapter 8), reports stemming from banks have the highest percentage of 'subsequent reports' that are sent by the FIU to the public prosecutor's office (64.7 per cent of all files), and are worth 79.3 per cent of the total amount of money that is considered as 'criminal' in all reports to the public prosecutor's office (CTIF-CFI, 2009). We assert that financial institutions are involved in the battle against money laundering in a threefold manner: first, they are a commercial institution, aiming to present themselves as reliable and trustworthy towards their stakeholders. This implies implementing solid AML and compliance policies to show the outside world that they are taking these matters seriously. Second, the financial institution also acts as an inspection agency, having to monitor and verify (trans)actions of their customers and employees. Financial institutions are put in a position that may lead to conflicts of interest (Naylor, 2007) between their obligations towards the authorities on the one hand and responsibilities towards clients on the other. And third, banks themselves are monitored by regulators as they are also potential offenders.

A third limitation to this research is the fact that compliance was narrowed down to anti money laundering. First of all, we must make clear that 'compliance' may refer to a number of initiatives taken by corporations to make sure that they are abiding rules (Hutter, 1997), which can relate to a broad area of regulations, such as environmental or labour issues. 'Compliance' in the present study, however, is used in a more strict sense and implies the implementation of the integrity policy within the financial institution, concentrated on the topic of money laundering. A compliance function within a bank combines, next to anti money laundering, also other domains, including for example privacy legislation and insider trading. Anti money laundering, however, not only represents the basis of the compliance function (through the Law of 11 January 1993) and still makes up for a large part of the daily activities of compliance officers (as was also confirmed during the interviews and in the survey), but also is the most relevant part of the compliance function to study from a criminological point of view. The AML task, after all, implies prevention and detection of a criminal activity, which in itself is of interest for criminologists. In this sense, obligations of compliance – or AML officers – have several similarities with policing. As part of their duty is to make sure the bank acts according to the rules, we witness the emergence of a type of 'policing' within a private organisation ('policing the enterprise', in other words). In this context, we also observe some parallels with private investigation services, operating within corporations to investigate fraud and crime by employees (Hoogenboom, 1988b; Cools, 1994). These parallels, combined with the specific position of the compliance officer within a bank, result in an intriguing function in which several interests are at stake.

Methodology

Phasing

In this four-year research we used a multimethodological approach (Ponsaers and Pauwels, 2002; Bijleveld, 2005), implying a combination of quantitative and qualitative traditions. Both methods are complementary and may provide supplementary data. This decision was based on two grounds: first of all, we were moving in a research domain that had not been subject to criminological research in Belgium before, and we therefore had to take into account that a large investment was needed in order to make a first exploration of the sector. Second, the combination of several methods seemed the most efficient way to deal with potential access problems.

Every research consists of a technical research plan (Billiet and Waege, 2003). This study was divided in five phases, but we must note here that these phases were not as strictly defined as they may seem below. Actually the phases melted into one another – specifically the interviewing phases – which inevitably resulted in overlaps. The first phase – the literature study and document analysis (twelve months) – consisted of an exploration of the compliance domain and was carried out by means of studying literature and documentation on the domain of financial institutions and money laundering.

In a second phase, we carried out a number of exploratory interviews with a limited number of gatekeepers of the compliance field: compliance officers of the large banks in Belgium, the financial institutions' umbrella organisation and AML consultants. Based on this information, combined with the information from the first phase, a web survey (standardised questionnaire) was developed. As contact addresses of compliance officers were either not available or, if available, protected for reasons of privacy, we were not able to send the survey directly to the compliance officers. However, the umbrella organisation for the financial sector, Febelfin, was willing to help us by sending the survey to all of their compliance contacts within the Belgian banks.[2] A reminder was sent twice (Dillman, 1991). This resulted in the spring of 2007 in seventy-four filled-out questionnaires, which were analysed by use of SPSS (a statistical software package). The web survey allowed us to reach a larger amount of respondents at the same time, mapping their views and characteristics (Dillman and Bowker, 2001), and gave us the necessary basic information on which we could found the following phases. Despite the shortcomings such as low response rates, coverage errors and technical problems related to web surveys (Dillman and Bowker, 2001), we are of the opinion that the use of a web survey had several advantages. It allowed us to reach a relatively large number of compliance experts in a short period of time. The goal of this web survey was to get a first impression of the backgrounds of compliance officers, their opinions and views on AML regulation, cooperation and information exchange, but also to map different compliance practices.

The subsequent in-depth interviews (phase 3) built on the results of the survey and could give more context to the results. Again, being compliance officer is a delicate profession and this became clear when we started looking for contact information: names or addresses are not publicly available. Compliance officers were contacted through telephone calls to general information telephone numbers, and via general e-mail addresses. In combination herewith, we also made use of the snowball method: at the time of an interview, we asked respondents who they would recommend for an interview. In this phase maximum diversity was strived for, which implies that we contacted both large, medium- and smaller-sized banks, with the view of gaining insight into a broad array of compliance functions. In this phase, we interviewed twenty-three compliance officers (eleven large banks, seven medium-sized banks and five small banks). The interviews lasted on average 1.5 to 2 hours.[3] Additional observations of three AML courses for bank employees also took place. Apart from the interviews with compliance officers, other actors in the AML complex were interviewed to get an idea of their perspectives, practices in and opinions on anti money laundering and compliance. We interviewed respondents from the police services, both at a federal and an international level (six respondents), the regulator and the FIU (three respondents). The selection of regulatory and law enforcement respondents was based on their expertise with regard to the subject. We can summarise our sampling as a combination of snowball or chain sampling on the one hand and purposeful sampling on the other hand (Patton, 2002). Six interviews were conducted with respondents from the compliance industry. All thirty-two interviews were analysed by means of MAXQDA (VERBI, 2007), a software program for text analysis.

Once the results of the first two phases were written down in articles, we decided to send these documents to some of our respondents, for a 'field test'. In combination with this test, we also carried out three more interviews in April and May 2009 with two compliance officers of large banks (both respondents were already interviewed in an earlier phase) and a member of the compliance industry, in order to assess the effects of the current credit crisis on compliance and AML.

Methodological remarks

By combining both an exploratory, quantitative approach with an in-depth qualitative method, we were able to get both an overall and a specific view on the compliance sector. Acquiring an overall view was indispensable at the start of this research. We would not have been able to ask the same questions during the interviews, without relying on the results of the questionnaire. Second, the results of the questionnaire gave us the opportunity to enter into a discussion with our respondents with regard to specific observations that we made during the analysis of the survey results. The interviews were crucial in providing a qualitative, in-depth context for the survey results, and in gaining insight into more 'sensitive' subjects, such as AML reporting and investigation. However, as always, we must be aware that the discourse that our respondents have applied, always implies a certain bias (Liedtka, 1992). Awareness of this bias also implies calculating in the fact that high-educated, professional respondents, within a professional setting (such as compliance officers), will not be inclined to completely speak their mind with regard to sensitive subjects of discussion. The use of a combination of research methods (the multimethodology that we referred to earlier) is one challenging way of tackling this bias (Crane, 1999). We actually did notice that results from the interviews were able to nuance or contextualise the survey results.

A second manner to factor in 'social desirability bias', is by interviewing respondents from different services (public and private) that have different outlooks on the phenomenon, which allows for a cross-checking of the answers that are given, which we have done. Third, we have looked for objective sources on the functioning of AML, such as judicial files/statistics, or FIU statistics. In both cases, we did not succeed in accessing this kind of information. With regard to judicial files and statistics, we had to conclude that statistical information that is available often lacks details and remains relatively unclear. With regard to FIU statistics, we could only make use of the statistics that are published in the annual report, as the FIU did not give us permission to analyse their own, more detailed data. This kind of information would have made a verification of the functioning of the AML complex and the reporting duty of financial institutions more profound.

We can state that the warnings in literature that the private sector is very difficult to reach and that the use of secondary data is more easy, did not apply to the present study. Once the right 'entrance' was found, a sector emerged that seemed receptive to the research and willing to talk about the issues that occupy them on a daily basis. One of the banks even invited us to their in-house training on AML, and also the umbrella organisation supported this research in the first phases. Furthermore, the compliance sector is quite small, which implies that word travels fast.

Ultimately, we can only conclude that the timorousness of criminologists to study this sector seems unfounded and are convinced that other research in this field should be applauded.

Overview

The next chapters of this book discuss the results of this PhD research. The second chapter focuses on research into corporations in general and discusses the different approaches and methods that are applied in these studies. After this view on methodology and other research in this domain, we will focus on the origins of the battle against money laundering and the effects thereof on policies and practices. We will explain how the AML complex has arisen and how the compliance industry has taken shape. The fourth chapter subsequently discusses the first empirical results of the PhD study, giving an idea of compliance officers' perceptions of their activities in anti money laundering. In Chapter 5 we will discuss the functioning of the AML complex – looking at both the compliance officers and at the public and private partners that form this complex. Chapter 6 subsequently focuses on the investigation tasks of compliance officers, and on how 'suspicious transaction monitoring' and reporting is carried out in practice, which decisions need to be made regarding the investigation of suspicious activity, but also in a more broader sense how the opportunities, difficulties and hindrances for the execution of a compliance task within a commercial setting are carried out. The purpose of Chapter 7 is to discuss the rise and growth of the 'compliance industry' by looking at the reasons why this industry became such an important element in the battle against money laundering. In Chapter 8, we try to give an idea of the efficacy of the (Belgian) AML system, looking at the output of this system in terms of prosecutions and convictions. And in the concluding Chapter 9, we will try to position the AML system on a continuum of crime control approaches, explaining that while we are policing the money, basic rights such as due process and privacy may be violated.

2 Methodology in studying corporations
Breaking out of the tunnel vision[1]

Introduction

Even though for some criminologists corporations are extremely intriguing and fascinating actors, up until today research on them remains rather marginal. Criminological attention on 'the corporation' was instigated by Sutherland. He stated, in 1940, in the first lines of his article on white collar crime:

> This paper is concerned with crime in relation to business. The economists are well acquainted with business methods but not accustomed to consider them from the point of view of crime; many sociologists are well acquainted with crime but not accustomed to consider it as expressed in business.
>
> (Sutherland, 1940)

The quote dates from 1940, and emphasised the void between business studies and sociology by referring to crime committed by businesses. The aim was to reform criminology by arguing that crime by 'business and professional men' (Sutherland, 1945), is a subject criminologists should study. And apparently with success, as forty years later it was stated that an 'international community of white collar crime scholars has been established' (Braithwaite, 1985).

Nevertheless, we have established that corporate crime, although it has gained more attention, still remains a niche in criminology. In spite of the 'corporization of the world during the twentieth century' (Braithwaite, 2000), criminology courses in universities and criminological handbooks show an under-representation of corporate crime (Lynch et al., 2004). It still appears to be difficult to get funding for research in this field (Simpson, 2003). The ratio of articles on ordinary crime as compared to those on white collar crime in criminological journals is 10:1 (Lynch et al., 2004). These comments lead us to suggest that although the topic of white collar crime has resulted in increased knowledge of corporations and crime, the corporation within criminology has remained a marginal actor.

Furthermore, within an already underexposed field of study in criminology, corporations are mainly represented in a one-dimensional sense: as perpetrators. Once the corporation becomes the subject of criminological attention, this attention is quasi-restricted to corporate *crime* and the negative role corporations may have in society. We argue however that corporations are not only interesting for criminologists when they commit offences. There are other capacities in which corporations intersect with criminological concerns. After all, corporations not only commit crime and as such are regulated and supervised, they are also victimised by crime, and take up tasks in the field of crime prevention and crime fighting. In our view, criminological consideration of corporations encompasses these four perspectives: the corporation as perpetrator, subject of supervision, victim and crime fighter.

In this chapter, we will discuss the criminological relevance of corporations and the role of the corporate world in its relations to crime in general. After elaborating on the relatively modest criminological attention paid to corporate involvement in offending, experiencing, preventing and fighting crime, we will look for reasons and motives for this lack of criminologist interest for the corporate world. We will relate this to methodological issues in studying corporations – more specifically the difficulty in gaining access to the corporate world. Without pretending to be exhaustive, we will discuss examples of qualitative research that have tried to fill this void and succeeded in surmounting these methodological difficulties. To conclude, we will try to learn some lessons from the methodology deployed.

Corporations in criminology: perpetrator, subject of supervision, victim or crime fighter

Traditionally, criminology has been principally concerned with public, social and economic order through a vision of governmental monopoly on preserving these orders. This world view, reflected in appointing the police as the main actor in the domain of (public) security provision, has dominated criminological research agendas and curricula for decades (Ponsaers and Snacken, 2002). The core of criminological attention is still made up of the penal segment of security policy, such as the police, judiciary, criminal procedures, etc. (Croall, 2001). But as society changes, criminological focus should also adjust. Nowadays, more and more focus is placed on other actors within a broader domain of security. Regulatory agencies have taken up a part of governance, but also private policing agents have secured their place in the criminological field. The landscape of security is no longer as neatly arranged and structured as one would like it to be (Hoogenboom, 1994; Bayley and Shearing, 1996; Garland, 2001; Zedner, 2006). And the question is whether this has ever been the case.

The 'new regulatory state' (Braithwaite, 2000) has resulted in the decreasing relevance of traditional criminological studies, pushing criminologists in new directions. New risks, and thereto related new styles of governance, in the sense of risk control mechanisms and activities in preventing, detecting and punishing crime, deserve criminological attention. One of these fields is the corporate world and its experiences with crime and crime control. Corporations have become increasingly important within society as their influence and power has grown, which has resulted – apart from an increased apparatus designed to control and inspect corporations (M. Cools, 2005) – in a rise in their involvement in crime (both as a perpetrator and as a victim) and crime control.

Corporations are an essential subject of study in their role as offender and victim on the one hand, and as a partner in crime control on the other hand. This versatility of corporations makes them not only an interesting and fascinating field of study, but also a valuable source of knowledge and know-how. After all, knowledge on how corporations either prevent or deal with crime, the information they gather during their activities and investigations, and the responses to criminal activities they develop, may be instructive for the public policing services and other authorities.

This does not imply that criminology has not contributed at all to studying corporations and the way they are involved in crime at large. The starting point for the interest in corporations can be found in the concept of white collar crime, a concept that has awoken interest in the corporate world. As a result of the attention paid to white collar crime, 'criminology came out of the sewers' (Ruggiero, 2000) and the corporation as a perpetrator became the subject of research.

Corporations as perpetrators

Ever since corporate crime[2] was placed on the research agenda, several studies have focused on companies, businesses or organisations as perpetrators of different forms of financial (and other) crime. Almost sixty years after the 'invention' of white collar crime (Sutherland, 1949), we can state that corporate crime no longer completely escapes the attention of criminologists the world over. The scope of studies of criminal corporations, can be summarised under the denominator 'organisational criminology' or 'corporate criminology'. In addition to criminology and sociology, other disciplines have also become engaged in studying the concept of 'corporate wrongdoing', such as legal and political sciences or management and economics (Geis, 1993).

The legacy of Sutherland

Although corporate crime has received relatively more attention during the last decades, in comparison to traditional crime it remains a subordinate part of the criminological agenda (Hoogenboom, 2001). Research into corporate perpetrators is still under-represented in criminology, compared to 'regular' perpetrators of crime (Simpson, 2003). Opinions about this viewpoint diverge, but according to a recent review of criminological literature this under-representation persists: although some criminologists are indeed working on the issue of white collar and corporate crime, overall 'the discipline continued to pay little attention to these serious, harmful activities' (Lynch et al., 2004). This situation persists even though several authors have emphasised the fact that one is more likely to be victimised by a type of white collar crime than by street crime (Punch, 1996; Russell and Gilbert, 1999).

Several reasons can be put forward to explain the lack of criminological interest in corporations as criminal actors. Van de Bunt, for example, states that the modest attention given to corporations and their relations to crime requires a mental shift in the way we think about organisations. Corporations are respected in society, which implies that it is hard to believe that these organisations 'can also be criminals who may cause considerable damage to the public interest' (van de Bunt, 1993). However, it is not only the 'trustworthy' image of corporations and the attitude towards the business world that have put a brake on research in this field. For years, the focus of traditional research has been on the more conventional forms of crime. Some state that this may be due to an over-emphasis on 'regular' criminological subjects: 'criminological attention for business has always been marginal. Criminology was traditionally concerned with "nuts, sluts and perverts", those on the fringes of society' (Cools and Haelterman, 1999). Levi suggests that this tunnel vision may be due to funding opportunities for scientific research, but also mentions the lack of access to this specific world:

> many criminologists have been heavily engaged in the drugs, policing and corrections debates – where most of the research money is – and the fact that sophisticated adult offenders for gain are less readily accessible and less touched by the populist politics of law and order than are juveniles or petty persistent offenders or violent criminals.
>
> (Levi, 1998)

Research on corporate crime

Others have given overviews of research on corporate crime, and we refer to their work for an impression of this research (Braithwaite, 1985; van de Bunt, 1992; Croall, 2001; van de Bunt and Huisman, 2004, 2007). However, some important studies need to be mentioned with regard to *empirical* research. One of the leading researchers in this field is Braithwaite. He succeeded in developing a more structural approach to corporate crime (Braithwaite, 1984; Ayres and Braithwaite, 1992; Fisse and Braithwaite, 1993) and showed that qualitative research in this field is possible, by interviewing managers, executives and (former) employees. Clinard and Yeager carried out file analyses in 1980 and in a subsequent piece of research, Clinard (1983) interviewed retired managers on corporate ethics and rule observance. Regarding empirical research in the Dutch-speaking regions, we should mention Punch (1996) van de Bunt (1992; van de Bunt and Huisman, 2004) Huisman (2001) Huberts (Huberts *et al.*, 2004) – although Huberts conducted research into law-breaking governments, not corporations – and Vande Walle (2005) who conducted an empirical research into conflict management regarding consumers in the pharmaceutical sector.

Corporations as a subject of supervision

The second role of corporations is related to the context in which they operate. Earlier we referred to the new regulatory state, which implies that corporations themselves are subject to supervision and inspection. This external supervisory context, made up of police services, inspection agencies, regulators, judiciary and other institutions, has been studied increasingly in recent decades. One of the reasons for these studies is that official data may give a more reliable view of corporate behaviour (mainly as a perpetrator, but also as a victim or a crime fighter). A second reason for these studies is the problematic accessibility of primary information on corporations. By studying secondary data and information sources of more accessible institutions the difficulty of gaining access to the primary source – as we will explain later – is circumvented (Lascoumes, 1986). Furthermore, researchers may gain a more adequate understanding of institutions 'by examining the work of other officials in the system' (Skolnick, 1975).

The supervisory context is built upon penal law and special laws, the latter regulating specific areas such as social security, environmental issues, tax, etc. On each level of this chain, information can be gathered regarding corporate behaviour (such as police data, judicial statistics, inspection files, etc.). Attention in this field has focused on the regulatory agencies, mainly because these services can provide relatively significant quantities of information on corporations. Regarding corporations, business regulatory agencies or inspection services have grown to be 'more significant law enforcers than the police' (Braithwaite, 2000). Contrary to research on policing, which can look back on a lengthy tradition (Skolnick, 1975; Fijnaut, 2001), the subject of inspection and supervision by other agencies was neglected by criminology until the late 1980s (Willemsen *et al.*, 2008). In this period a greater interest was taken in the role of business regulatory agencies and governmental agencies performing policing and regulatory tasks (Braithwaite, 2000). Well-documented examples are mainly found in the areas of environmental and occupational safety. Kagan and Scholz interviewed in the late 1970s regulatory officials, inspectors, directors of enforcement agencies and managers of regulated firms (such as steel foundries and automobile assembly plants) regarding enforcement strategies with regard to subjects such as workplace safety, health regulation, pollution regulation, etc. (Kagan and Scholz, 1984).

However, important work has been done, such as that by Grabosky and Braithwaite (1986a;, 1986b; Braithwaite *et al.*, 1987) who made an inventory of regulatory agencies and their practices in Australia. In the same year, in France, Lascoumes (1986) described the way in which financial crime is controlled by different agencies. Hawkins studied the style of regulation and the practice of inspectors in the early 1980s (1983, 1984) and, more recently, Hutter (1997, 2000) studied occupational health by interviewing workers, as did Gray (Gray, 2006).

More specifically for the Netherlands and Belgium, we refer to Kellens (1974), who analysed fraudulent bankruptcies by use of (among other things) analyses of judicial files in the late 1970s. More recently, Ponsaers (Ponsaers and De Cuyper, 1980; Ponsaers, 1983; De Baets *et al.*, 2003; Ponsaers *et al.*, 2003) made an inventory of the current landscape in inspection and regulatory agencies and the processing of their files by the public prosecution service in

Belgium. Keeping in mind that one of the motives of studying regulatory frameworks lies precisely in acquiring knowledge on corporate behaviour, it is no surprise that a number of researchers working in the field of corporate crime or victimisation, are also working on regulatory issues. Huisman, van de Bunt and van den Heuvel are examples (van den Heuvel, 1993; Huisman and Niemeijer, 1998; Fijnaut and van de Bunt, 2000; Huisman, 2001; van de Bunt and Huisman, 2004). Another manner by which we can gain some insight into the practices of private institutions is the work of Van Duyne. He has also dedicated some of his work to the analysis of files of police services and financial intelligence units (FIUs) regarding anti money laundering activities of private institutions (for example, van Duyne and de Miranda, 1999). However, in spite of an obvious increase in criminological attention given to regulatory agencies, there still is a lack of empirical research into practices of inspection services and other supervisors (Ponsaers and Hoogenboom, 2004).

Corporations as victims

An under-researched domain

Corporate victimisation has been the focus of even less attention in the criminological field (Gill, 1994). Criminological interest has focused mainly on the corporation as an offender (M. Cools, 2005). A clear indication of this lack of scientific interest in corporate victimisation, is the fact that the first national victim survey among businesses was not carried out until 1990. The 1990 victim study by van Dijk and Terlouw in the Netherlands showed that businesses suffer considerable damages as victims of crime. Moreover, victimisation percentages are higher than those of households (van Dijk and Terlouw, 1996). In 1994, the ICBS, an international survey on victimisation of corporations, was conducted. This allowed for a comparative view and also pointed out that businesses often become repeated victims of the same crime. The survey showed that the main offences corporations fall victim to are theft, fraud by personnel and burglary (van Dijk and Terlouw, 1996). Apart from scientific surveys, a number of private firms also carry out surveys among corporations to assess the extent and nature of the crimes they fall victim to. PricewaterhouseCoopers' Global Economic Crime Survey is one of them. In 2007, the fourth survey was carried out and showed that 43 per cent of all corporations in the survey has fallen victim to a form of economic crime that had significant impact on the corporation in the past two years. More than 75 per cent of these crimes are committed by persons external to the company (PricewaterhouseCoopers, 2007). Crimes affecting businesses are, for example, asset misappropriation, accounting fraud or corruption and bribery. These surveys show that victimisation of corporations is considerable, and makes us wonder what justification there is for such minimal criminological interest. In spite of the fact that these issues are of great concern for employees specifically and businesses in general, criminological interest in workplace crime remained negligible until the 1990s (Gill, 1994).

Explanations for this lack of interest could be the absence of figures on victimisation – as stated above – until the second part of the 1990s, which resulted in the invisibility of these types of crime. A second justification may be related to the problems in gaining access to corporations, a topic that we will discuss in the following paragraphs.

Current research on victimisation

Despite these problems, several scholars have made attempts to put victimisation of corporations on the criminological agenda. Henry (Henry and Mars, 1978; Henry, 1983) carried out empirical research into 'managerial justice', based on statistics from corporations, complemented with postal questionnaire surveys sent to personnel managers of British manufacturing companies and interviews with managers and employees (Henry, 1994). As a result of his research, insight was gained into the practices and procedures of corporations in relation to disciplining and punishing crime and resolving conflicts within the company. Mars, an anthropologist and co-author of the first book, was also active in this field of research but focused mainly on crime at work. Often, he collected his data through participant observation. For his PhD, in the 1970s, he spent eighteen months on the docks, analysing pilferage by dock workers (Mars, 1972, 1982, 2001, 2006). Gill studied commercial robbery of commercial premises and presented a first view on the perceptions of robbers and the prevention of robbery of enterprises (Gill, 1994). He interviewed a large number of robbers and asked them for their motives and practices. Furthermore, a survey of staff of a retail company in 1993 studied the prevalence of victimisation in the workplace. The survey showed that 11 per cent of the staff had been physically assaulted, and 50 per cent reported verbal abuse (Beck *et al.*, 1994). This again showed the relevance of research in this area. In 1998, a survey of businesses was carried out in the UK in relation to victimisation of criminal offences, resulting in an overview of business sectors and their experience with crime (Gill, 1998).

In the Dutch-speaking region, empirical research on these subjects was quasi-absent until the 1990s. Cools was the first to study employee crime and the reaction of corporations to this type of crime in his PhD research in 1993 (Cools, 1994). Cools interviewed managers and executives on employee crime and made an analysis of the files on decisions made inside corporations when they are confronted with these types of crime. In this sense, his research presented a first insight into the corporate approach regarding victimisation, private investigation and private justice. On a methodological level, this research showed that it is actually possible to access corporations and collect information on 'sensitive' topics within enterprises.

Currently, victim surveys have recognised corporate victimisation, which provides us with an idea on the amount and extent of victimisation experienced by corporations. However, a number of fields remain open for study. Examples are the impact of crime and victimisation on businesses or the influence and extent of fear of crime within the corporate world (Hopkins, 2002). More knowledge on the risks corporations perceive and their assessment of victimisation is needed in order to understand corporate attitudes towards crime and their investments in crime prevention.

Criminology has shown slightly more interest in the approach adopted by corporations to prevent victimisation. Regarding both internal and external crime, specific actions can be taken by corporations to prevent themselves from being harmed. As far as internal crime is concerned, we refer to the studies on employee crime, as discussed above. The phenomenon of external crime is perhaps difficult to handle for corporations as facts on the issue are hard to come by. This brings us to the crime-fighting tasks of corporations, which will be discussed in the following section.

Corporations as crime fighters

When it comes to studying the corporation not as an offender, but in its role in the *prevention or detection* of crime, as a partner in the law enforcement chain, we can see an almost total lack of criminological interest. Research in this field of activity remains scarce (Ponsaers, 2002a; Ponsaers and Hoogenboom, 2004; Cools, 2006), although the impact of these private actors in law enforcement on the level of crime prevention, detection and sometimes even punishment is not to be neglected. Their activities often take place relatively out of sight of traditional research, and therefore remained quasi-unnoticed in the world of criminology.

Corporations can be involved in crime control in several ways. On the one hand, an organisation may have crime control or prevention as its core business, such as private security services or private investigation companies. On the other hand, private organisations can be employed in the prevention or detection of crime, even though this is not their core business. This implies that corporations are compelled to make a contribution to the fight against crime. Examples of the latter are supermarkets incorporating an investigations department, companies with in-house guarding services or banks establishing AML departments.

Private policing – crime fighting as core business

In the 1980s and 1990s criminological interest in private policing or private security emerged as a research domain. The first study to draw attention to the plurality of policing was probably that of Shearing and Stenning in the early 1980s on the increasing private security sector in Canada (Shearing and Stenning, 1980). Hoogenboom studied private investigators in the Netherlands (Hoogenboom, 1988b), and Johnston described the involvement of non-public or quasi-public organisations in crime control (Johnston, 1992). These early studies focused on the 'policing' tasks of private corporations, looking for similarities with traditional police services such as security guards or alarm services (Kempa *et al.*, 1999). Later, more emphasis was placed on the 'fragmentation' (Johnston, 2003) or pluralisation of policing (Hoogenboom, 1994; Bayley and Shearing, 1996; Jones and Newburn, 2002), stressing the diversity of actors in the landscape of non-policing agents. Other empirical studies on private policing and their activities were carried out by Button (2007). These studies showed that private police forces had been emerging and taking over the domain that was allegedly reserved for public policing. In some countries, the amount of private police agents even outnumbered the public police (Grabosky and Braithwaite, 1986a).

These examples illustrated a lacuna in criminology: as criminologists had been focusing on 'old state institutions of police-courts-prisons' (Braithwaite, 2000), they had failed to address other crime-fighting institutions. It soon became clear that these private and emerging forces deserved criminological attention and, moreover, that criminology could benefit from insights into the corporate world and management expertise (Hoogenboom, 1999).

The last decade has shown an increased scientific interest in the private provision of security (Cools, 2004), in the broadest sense; in Belgium, studies by Boon (1993), Van Outrive *et al.* (1995) and Mulkers and Haelterman (2001), have made a first attempt to enter the world of private security and guarding, followed by a more recent empirical research by Cools and Verbeiren (2004), while Cools *et al.* (2005) also studied private investigators. In the Netherlands, Hoogenboom was the first to draw attention to this private aspect of policing (1988b, 1994), followed by Eysink Smeets and Etman in 2001 (Klerks *et al.*, 2001). Empirical research into private security corporations, however, remains rather limited.

Crime fighting – but not as a core business

Next to the spectrum of private security providers, private organisations can also get involved in fighting crime, although their core business is completely distinct from fighting crime. These corporations are forced – either by their victimisation or by regulation – to take on a role in crime control and crime fighting and are a part of the larger 'policing' picture. An example of such crime-fighting tasks by non-security companies is the engagement of (financial) institutions in the battle against money laundering which requires them to investigate and report suspicious transactions to the authorities (Verhage, 2009g). These corporations adopt a law enforcement role with regard to their employees, their clients or to other corporations, and work in a quasi-police-like paradigm, by checking and investigating crime. The role and activities of several corporations with a core business in anything but security, has received little or no attention from criminologists, and their activities are often overlooked. Of course, activities of private investigative departments have been studied, but mainly with a goal of dismantling unlawful practices and breaches of privacy. As a result very little information exists on how they actually perform their daily tasks (M. Cools, 2005). To put it in other words: 'business as usual' is often omitted from criminological research, let alone when specified for ethical or deontological issues. Looking at other disciplines, we come to the same conclusion: empirical research, for example on how banks implement corporate governance, is quasi-absent (Heremans, 2007). One of the explanations for this lack of criminological concern for private actors' involvement in the penal chain, is the assumption that criminologists are more interested in the 'spectacular forms of corporate crime and much less in how organisations as such emerge and develop' (Lippens, 2003). Organisational criminologists are more interested in the 'crime' than in the 'organisation' part of organisational criminology. By this Lippens implies that criminologists often forget about normal, day-to-day life in organisations, and instead react to scandals occurring in specific companies. As a result, we miss a lot of information on what is going on inside companies 'day in, day out, out of sight, in everyday settings and contexts' (Lippens, 2003). Certain questions remain unasked and therefore unanswered: 'What is their vision of ethical or lawful business? What do they say about business ethics and ethical behaviour? How do they imagine ethical business practice?' (Lippens, 2003).

Is this a topic which criminologists should study? We think it is. The corporate world is of criminological relevance, not only for its power – hence its potential damage – or for its quantity (van den Heuvel, 1998) but also for the degree and mode of input, investment and potential impact it has on the level of prevention and investigation of crime. These activities are obviously relevant for criminologists. The functioning of these private actors does not lie beyond the criminological domain: on the contrary, studying the actual practices of these partners in crime prevention and detection can reveal potential lessons to be learned by 'regular' law enforcement agencies and vice versa. After all, a more transparent attitude from private sector companies on their methods and practices may lead to possibilities for an exchange of ideas.

After this brief overview of the corporate involvement in crime, victimisation and crime control, and its relevance for criminology, in the following section we aim to discuss a few of the explanations for the small amount of empirical research in this domain of criminology.

Methodological explanations for tunnel vision?

The focus of criminology on traditional crime, victims and crime fighters, and the late acknowledgement that non-state actors play a role in policing have led to a kind of criminological tunnel vision. But apart from these factors there are also some methodological reasons for the restricted research into corporations in general. Empirical research, in which new information is gathered about or within companies, remains scarce in spite of the growing interest in this field shown by criminology.

Corporate characteristics

In general, the limited aptitude of corporations for empirical research, whether concerning crime, victimisation or crime fighting, is attributed to the (assumed) characteristics of corporations. Corporations are judged to be closed entities, a non-transparent domain in society, which leads to invisible crime and victimisation rates. 'Many businesses are secretive – particularly about strategy and data that ostensibly might be valuable to competitors – and zealously guard access to sensitive regions' (Punch, 1996). Several characteristics, typical of corporations in a commercial setting, are said to prevent corporations from actively engaging in scientific research.

First, the official statistics, often used in criminological research on 'traditional' crime, are mainly based on police records, which seldom include crime related to corporations (both corporate crime and employee crime) (Croall, 2001). Victim surveys rarely include these crimes and statistics provided by the industry itself are not always reliable. This results in a lack of statistical information, making it more difficult to gain a rudimentary insight into the criminological basics of corporations.

Second, the domain of corporate criminology is perceived as a highly complex and technical field (Croall, 2001). Studying economic crime, fraud, auditing, etc. not only demands an investment by the criminological researcher in economics, management or fraud techniques, but also requires making oneself familiar with management jargon, organisational structures and philosophies. Criminologists have a hard time adapting to the jargon, and sometimes lack the background for understanding corporate culture (van de Bunt and Huisman, 2004). Still, the authors moderate this gap between criminological background and the corporate world, by stating that the same gap will be present in research into, for example, delinquent immigrants (van de Bunt and Huisman, 2004). The same authors state in 2007 that, although organisational crimes are often considered to be complicated and technical, this is not always the case. On the contrary, these crimes are 'not necessarily technically complicated or hard to judge from a moral point of view' (van de Bunt and Huisman, 2007). However, a different mindset is required, as research into organisations is different from 'regular' research. Here it is not the individual that that is focused on, but the organisation, in which the individual plays a supporting role (van den Heuvel, 1998). Within traditional criminology, the individual perpetrator is the main focus of research, while corporations 'fall outside the scope of criminological imagination' (van den Heuvel, 1998).

A third explanation, and related to the second motive, is the access problem or, in other words, the difficulty of gaining access to primary data. This problem seems particularly present in research into the crime-fighting role of corporations. Also outside criminology, empirical research on the way in which corporations fulfil this role is either scarce – specifically in areas such as business ethics, corporate social responsibility and corporate governance (Crane, 1999; Marschan-Piekkari and Welch, 2004) – or limited to surveys or other types of quantitative research. The 'access problem' will be discussed more in detail in the following section.

'Getting a foot in the door'

In this section, we discuss some of the methodological reasons for this hesitancy in studying corporations and discuss the choice between a quantitative and a qualitative approach in studying organisations.

One of the explanations for the focus on crime in organisational criminology, may be the lack of access to the field (Lippens, 2003). By access we imply both the willingness of corporations to cooperate, and 'the opportunities available to find empirical data (real-world data) and information' (Gummesson, 1991). This more practical problem has been discussed by several authors as one of the main problems in researching corporations (Geis, 1993; Cools, 1994; van de Bunt and Huisman, 2004). These difficulties apply not only to the criminological researcher, but also to researchers from other disciplines. First we will concentrate on criminological literature which, as we stated before, mainly focuses on corporate *crime* research. Most of the methodological problems in studying organisational crime, however, also apply to other types of research in relation to corporations.

In general terms, access includes both initial (getting a foot in the door) and continued (staying inside) physical access. One of the recommendations for gaining access to corporations is to identify 'gatekeepers' and 'informants', both essential figures in research (Gummesson, 1991). Gatekeepers are those who can help inside the corporation and introduce the researcher into the setting. Informants are individuals from that sector who can provide necessary and useful information, and are able to refer to other useful people within the field.

Initial access is said to be specifically problematic in studying corporations (van de Bunt and Huisman, 2004). It was once stated that it's more difficult to enter a multinational than to enter a young gang of delinquents (Bovenkerk, 1998). Simpson states that researchers need to convince the 'guardians at the gate' of the research problem, which means 'just getting a foot in the door is often a major accomplishment' (Simpson, 2003). Geis stated in 1993 that only a few researchers had succeeded in gathering information on these subjects at first hand (from the companies themselves), and it appears as though his observation still holds (Geis, 1993). Gaining access to corporations is more than a challenge (Cools, 1994), as corporations are sensitive to reputational harm and potential breaches of confidentiality.

But not only criminologists run up against this problem of gaining access. Other disciplines also warn us of the fact that doors are very likely to remain closed for research. Several methodological handbooks regarding business studies or the sociology of organisations make note of this problem, stating that access to companies is one of the main problems in doing research: entering the organisation is either prohibited or non-response is very high (den Hertog and van Sluijs, 2000). The 'Handbook of qualitative research methods for international business' states that we still do not really know how organisations react to changing moral demands (Marschan-Piekkari and Welch, 2004). This is partly due to the 'number 1 challenge' of the qualitative researcher: the problem of gaining access to firms (Gummesson, 1991). This lack of access can arise for several reasons: the sensitivity of the research subject or issues to be studied, the lack of 'clear organizational pay-off' (Liedtka, 1992) for companies, an unwillingness to invest time and efforts in research, or the avoidance of reputational risks. If corporations don't have a direct interest in cooperating, they will not be eager to do so. For criminologists, the problem in gaining access is even larger as they are unfamiliar with the corporate world and not aware of the internal mechanisms within corporations (the 'ins and outs').

Still, gaining access is not the only problem, as even when the corporation grants access to the researcher, restrictions may be imposed as to which results may actually be published. Researching companies, some state, is 'done by permission' (Marschan-Piekkari and Welch, 2004), which can have an impact on the way in which research is carried out and, by consequence, also on the potential results. After 'entering' the company, this does not mean the battle is won: a number of new problems arise. There are restrictions as to which people you are allowed to talk to and what kind of information they may give you (Simpson, 2003). Information may be biased, especially since the researcher is dealing with 'clever, conspiratorial, and secretive managerial deviants' (Punch, 1996). The researcher needs to be aware of the company culture and dynamics, learn to understand the corporate language and what is actually happening (Gummesson, 1991). And even when access is granted in one company, this does not mean access will be granted in the next company: the story repeats itself.

Consequences of access problems

Use of secondary data

In order to circumvent the problem of gaining access, researchers can decide to use secondary data in order to study corporations. Secondary data may include governmental information (such as the regulatory agencies we discussed above), publicly accessible company information such as annual reports, media coverage, or information gathered in other research (meta-analysis).

Cowton suggests that more use should be made of secondary data since primary data are either inaccessible, costly or biased (Cowton, 1998). Van de Bunt and Huisman state that the majority of researchers trying to study organisational crime, opt – precisely because of problems related to accessing the field – for the use of 'second-hand information: data from regulatory agencies and media-coverage' (van de Bunt and Huisman, 2004). Examples of secondary data are scandals, the media, public inquiries, police investigations and stories by whistle-blowers (Punch, 1996). Using secondary data can be interesting and certainly useful in certain cases – such as the use of court files or the current extensive coverage of financial scandals. However, they may entail the risk of being biased and incomplete, although some state that the same comment can be made about primary data (Cowton, 1998). Still, primary data are of great importance in getting a clear view on the reality within corporations and their views, perceptions and motivations. Even though with primary data (such as interviews) a researcher is always dependent on the story the respondents want to tell, and the amount of information respondents are willing to provide, the bias is likely to be smaller in primary information as compared to secondary data.

Predominance of quantitative data

Another consequence of the difficulties in gaining access to corporations/primary data is the predominance of quantitative methods for studying corporate issues. Traditional research methods may be more difficult to apply which implies that qualitative methods are more appropriate in studying organisations (Ponsaers and Ruggiero, 2002a). In some cases, a mix of both quantitative and qualitative methods is called for (Ponsaers and Pauwels, 2002; Bijleveld, 2005). Nevertheless, a brief view on business ethics research shows that quantitative methods are applied more often than qualitative approaches. Robertson examined articles in the Journal of Business Ethics in 1993 and concluded that empirical business research was dominated by survey methodology (Robertson, 1993), and more than ten years later Marschan-Piekkari and Welch came to the same conclusion (Marschan-Piekkari and Welch, 2004). Cowton also notices this with regard to empirical studies on business ethics, stating that this may be due to the fact that questionnaire surveys are quick and easy to use (Cowton, 1998). He adds to this that it is questionable whether this is the most appropriate way of studying this subject, as 'interviews, for example, may provide greater depth, although access may be "formidable"' (Cowton, 1998).

Even though a number of quantitative attempts have been made to study ethics and cultures within organisations, these were heavily criticised regarding their assumption that they were able to study culture as a concrete, definable phenomenon (Marschan-Piekkari and Welch, 2004). Crane states that the majority of research in business ethics (a subject closely linked to some of the criminological research subjects regarding businesses) is carried out by use of quantitative methods, which is not very suitable for researching morality in business (Crane, 1999). Moreover, in 1990, 81 per cent of all available empirical studies on morality issues in business was based on survey data only (Crane, 1999).

Qualitative methods are more time-consuming and possibly more difficult, as they are based on the willingness of the researcher to develop 'an understanding of organizational context' (Liedtka, 1992). Nevertheless, these methods are considered more likely to enable a more holistic approach, allowing the researcher to study the phenomenon in its context (Marschan-Piekkari and Welch, 2004). Qualitative methods, such as interviewing, participant observation and document analysis, permit the researcher to discover a domain, particularly when very little research has been carried out in this specific field. Developing a questionnaire is not easy when almost no information is available on a subject. Interviewing can be a useful approach to explore a research hypothesis and to get to know the field. Furthermore, interviewing allows for a more in-depth research, particularly when the research concerns 'sensitive' subjects, such as business ethics or rule-breaking (Liedtka, 1992). However, which method is most appropriate depends on the research question and the research that is to be carried out (Crane, 1999). Although for some fields, qualitative methods may be more appropriate, in view of the sensitivity of subjects, the complexity of processes, or the difficulty in assessing decision-making processes (Liedtka, 1992), a combination of qualitative and quantitative methods may provide the researcher in a relatively new field of study with the necessary information. Surveys and questionnaires can serve as a basis on which further research can be founded, and can be used to acquire the first view of a sector or a phenomenon. In a subsequent, more qualitatively oriented method (interviews, participant observation) these quantitative data can be tested. A multimethodology seems most suitable for these fields of study (Ponsaers and Pauwels, 2002). Although quantitative methods are of great importance in this domain, we aim to discuss primarily the qualitative studies that have been carried out regarding private organisations. The main reason for this is to gain insight into the manner in which researchers have found their way into organisations and were able to carry out their research. A piece of qualitative research (by means of interviewing or observations) may be more difficult to carry out in this respect, as it may be more threatening and more pervasive than a questionnaire. To show, however, that it is not impossible, and to make clear that (some) organisations may even be welcoming to scientific research in their domain, we chose to discuss some examples of successful criminological studies in the next section.

Some examples of gaining access

In this section, several recommended methods for gaining access to the field will be discussed and we will illustrate some methods which (qualitative) researchers have successfully used in order to 'get a foot in the door'. Although many authors refer to the problem of gaining access, we rarely read about studies in which access was completely denied: this is probably because these studies never get published for reasons arising from lack of information. Punch however discusses two studies in which access was problematic; both researchers had to make a number of attempts before they could convince organisations to cooperate (Punch, 1996). In these cases, corporations decided to cooperate after extensive lobbying (for example, one of the researchers was turned down by thirty-six corporations before gaining access), informal contacts and adjustments to the research proposal (Punch, 1996).

Corporations ... receptive to research?

Many authors refer to the problem of gaining access to corporations, and quantitative methods may result in a partial insight as response rates for several business studies are judged to be lower than for other subjects; some authors refer to rates as low as 12 per cent (Hoogenboom, 1988a) or 23 per cent (Henry, 1994).

This does not mean that researchers should be discouraged completely. On the contrary, there are some hopeful remarks. Van de Bunt and Huisman emphasise that the lack of access should not be overestimated (van de Bunt and Huisman, 2004). This is illustrated by the fact that a number of researchers do succeed in accessing corporations for, for example, interviews on (ethical) decision making

(Liedtka, 1992). However, in the Dutch-speaking regions, only a few criminological researchers have actually succeeded in gathering information from corporations themselves or as a result of empirical research (Cools, 1994; Hoogenboom, 1994; Huisman, 2001; Cools *et al.*, 2005; Rosenthal *et al.*, 2005; Vande Walle, 2005). Although most authors include only a short section on their methodology, we can infer from their publications some of the problems that had occurred at the start of their research, or, on the contrary, some recommendations that are valuable to researchers in the same field. Braithwaite's study will be discussed first, because of its status as an eye-opener in empirical research into corporations.

The first and most obvious example of this is Braithwaite's study of the pharmaceutical industry. In the appendix of his famous book on corporate crime, Braithwaite describes how he managed to get interviews with corporate executives (Braithwaite, 1984). He states that he arranged the interviews by telephone; no letter was sent to the executives. He did send letters for interviews in other countries, but received almost no replies. It seems that a direct way of contacting corporations is more successful than a more formal approach. In his interviews, he was rather clear about his research. He emphasised his sociological background, rather than the fact that he was a criminologist. Once executives had agreed to an interview, he told them that he worked for the Australian Institute of Criminology. Braithwaite describes how, once he successfully started interviewing, he made use of the snowball method to gain access to other corporations. Mentioning someone's name appeared to be very helpful in contacting other companies. Furthermore, he makes clear that the interviews also had an advantage for the respondents, as he could share information with the respondent about how other corporations deal with similar problems.

When starting the interview, he did not emphasise the guarantee of anonymity and confidentiality, as this would 'put respondents on their guard' (Braithwaite, 1984). However, when appropriate during the interview, the anonymity was ensured, and ultimately all interviews were treated anonymously regarding the respondents and the companies. With regard to the structuring of the interview, after having used a checklist for the first interviews, subsequent interviews were carried out without this list. Braithwaite concludes his description of 'getting a foot in the door' by stating that the most important lesson he learned was the significance of learning how the industry works, as this prevents the interview from turning into a marketing talk (Braithwaite, 1984).

Research in the Netherlands and Flanders

In the Dutch-speaking regions, empirical research on corporations, from a criminological point of view, is very limited. We will discuss a number of these studies, selected on the basis of originality or the specific target group, hoping to learn from the methods they have applied.

Hoogenboom, one of the first to draw attention to corporate security provision in the Dutch-speaking regions, interviewed private corporations with a security task, such as guarding services, private investigation services and trade information bureaus (Hoogenboom, 1988b). In the methodological explanation of the research, Hoogenboom emphasises the advantages of interviewing in relation to surveys. He states that the low response rates in surveys, in view of the research subject, calls for a more qualitative approach. He refers to response rates between 12 and 30 per cent (Hoogenboom, 1988a). In his PhD research, Hoogenboom again makes use of this interviewing technique, in interviews with management and executive staff of investigative organisations (Hoogenboom, 1994).

Cools, in his PhD research in 1993, interviewed managers and executives (Cools, 1994). In explaining his access to the field he states that the gatekeepers he interviewed were colleagues. At the time of his PhD he was working for an in-house guarding service within a large enterprise and could make use of his contacts within the field. This made the introduction to the field more or less redundant and allowed for a more informal entrance (Cools, 1994). This observation emphasises the need for a well-informed 'insider' who can introduce the researcher into the corporate world. However, this does not imply that all doors are automatically opened. In explaining his methodology, he specifies a response rate of 60 per cent on his request for an interview, all chemical, metal or textiles corporations. The corporations in the service industries (banks, insurance companies) that were approached for interviews, all refused to take part in the research. Cools explains this by stating that this sector is more dependent on its reputation, and will not be inclined to talk about employee crime in this respect. This sector is shielded from the outside world and little is known about their experiences with guarding services or internal conflict management. The file analysis of 2,524 files that was carried out in the framework of the same research, also provides a first and therefore very valuable understanding of the private justice practices in the corporate world.

Huisman also made use of interviews (within a larger framework of the case study methodology) in his research on violations by corporations (Huisman, 2001). During the interviews, a checklist with points of interest for the interview was used. In his preface, Huisman discusses the enhanced openness of corporations. 'Apart from one or two respondents, and sometimes with a slight mistrust, most respondents were receptive to talking about the sensitive subject of breaches and observance of the law' (Huisman, 2001). How he succeeded in contacting these corporations is not discussed in his publication. This is regrettable as Huisman managed to reach a large number of respondents, and it would have been useful for future research to know how he succeeded in convincing his respondents to cooperate.

Vande Walle conducted interviews in the pharmaceutical sector. In her publication, she examines the problems and advantages of interviewing corporations. She describes every step of her empirical phase, including gaining access to the corporations. First of all, she states that umbrella organisations, which were a source of access in Braithwaite's study in 1984 (Braithwaite, 1984) were actually more of a hindrance to access. Furthermore, the umbrella organisation will be more protective of the sector than a corporation, as a part of this sector, may be (Vande Walle, 2005). Braithwaite describes the way in which contacts with these umbrella organisations caused the research project to be spread like wild-fire through the sector, which emphasises the need to prepare interviews with these organisations. However, Vande Walle nuances this; she was never confronted with this 'spreading of the news', and states that none of the corporations were informed of the research prior to the interview. During the first contact with the corporation, she did not emphasise her criminological background, but did not lie about it either. In her research, the snowball method, which was considered successful in Braithwaite's research (Braithwaite, 1984) did not advance her contacts with the pharmaceutical sector. The most direct way of contacting corporations (telephoning them without sending a letter in advance) seemed to be most productive. Only four out of twenty-two corporations refused to cooperate.

Kees Cools also needs to be mentioned here as his research has shed a new light on corporate governance and codes of ethics. Studying corporations from a mere economic point of view (as an economist, not a criminologist), he interviewed CEOs and directors on the consequences of financial scandals for companies (K. Cools, 2005). His research is important as he not only gained access to higher management of corporations, but also convinced them to speak to him on 'sensitive' topics.

The final example of gaining access to private corporations is the PhD research of Ronald van Steden. In his research (van Steden, 2007) on the growth of private security in the Netherlands, he made use of a multimethodology, by carrying out a mail questionnaire survey (although with a low response rate), in combination with statistical information and interviews with experts and practitioners. The respondents were selected by use of snowball sampling (van Steden, 2007). It is important to note that in his research, none of the approached persons refused cooperation.

Is a tunnel vision justifiable?

We can no longer state that corporations are structurally neglected in criminological research. Currently, the knowledge gap is no longer as large as it used to be and a number of criminologists are broadening the scope of research. However, 'corporate criminology' remains a niche in criminology when compared to research on, for example, policing or juvenile delinquency.

The reasons for this niche, as we discussed above, can be found in a 'tunnel vision' on the one hand and in methodological issues on the other hand. The tunnel vision consists of criminologists neglecting corporate behaviour, victimisation and activities in crime control, while emphasising traditional parties in crime, crime control and punishment. Methodological issues, on the other hand, impair the possibilities for studying corporate actors, although these issues should not be exaggerated. True, official crime figures often lack the corporate side of the story, and gaining access may be more challenging when it comes to studying corporations. But is Punch still correct in assuming 'that we are perhaps dealing with institutional regions that are unresearchable by conventional, and ethical means' (Punch, 1996)?

We are more hopeful, and research (as we described above) has shown that it is far from impossible. We hope to have made clear that studying organisations is not doomed to fail. In spite of all the warnings, the difficulties in gaining access to corporations should not be exaggerated, and there is no point in discouraging researchers who want to study this domain. Of course, it probably will be less easy to reach the right respondents in a short period of time, and sometimes you will need to go off the beaten track. But with the necessary efforts it may be possible to develop 'normal' (criminological) relationships with corporations, as they routinely exist today with police services or the judiciary. A researcher has to invest time and put in the effort and there is no guarantee that these efforts will pay off. But considering the research that has been carried out, we can conclude that we can no longer speak of a hermetically closed world of corporations.

We can only applaud research in this field, since acquiring qualitative data is crucial in gaining some insight into this area of crime control. When private organisations are considered by the authorities as a partner in a crime control chain, this implies that criminology also needs to recognise them as an object of study. This could not only result in a cross-fertilisation between public and private types of crime control methods; more research can also enhance methodology in studying crime, victimisation and crime control. We therefore hope that by means of more research, the criminological tunnel vision opens up into a broad criminological horizon.

3 Money laundering and the social reaction

A battle instigated by power motives?[1]

Introduction

Money laundering is the transformation of money in order to give illegal money a seemingly legal appearance. In a purely legal sense, money laundering 'can consist of nothing more than depositing the proceeds of crime in a domestic bank account' (Levi, 2001).

Money laundering takes place on the threshold between the legal and the illegal/informal economy, although the boundaries between these two are partly artificial (Brown and Cloke, 2007; Vande Walle, 2008). After illicit money has passed this threshold, it will be 'formalised' and behave as 'normal' money. As such, money laundering is functional for both the formal and the informal or illegal economy; it allows for a legal use of money stemming from the informal/illicit economy in formal financial markets – stimulating precisely this informal/illicit economy – while the 'normal' behaviour of money results in financial flows in the financial market (Brown and Cloke, 2007). As a result of this legal use of money in the formal financial market, money laundering leads to power accumulation and is as such distinguished from other (traditional) types of crime. After all, the money launderer can gain economic power by taking up a position in the legal market, based on illegitimately acquired finances. Money laundering will hence result in an increase in power in the *legal* sphere.

Money laundering as 'power crime'

Ruggiero describes the concept of 'power crime' as crime committed by states, companies, financial institutions and other powerful organisations:

> Perpetrators of power crime are offenders who possess an exorbitantly exceeding amount of material and symbolic resources when compared to those possessed by their victims. Power crime should be located against the background of differentiated opportunities which are offered to social groups. Social inequalities determine varied degrees of freedom whereby individuals are granted a specific number of choices and a specific range of

potential actions they can carry out. (..) The greater the degree of freedom enjoyed, the wider the range of choices available.

(Ruggiero, 2007, p. 165)

There are two dimensions of power related to money laundering. To begin with, in order to speak of money laundering, the money needs to be 'earned' in the illegal economy by means of criminal acts, which often implies the use of violence or pressure in an illegal sense by which power is acquired. This power is subsequently transformed into 'legal' power by converting the money from illegal into seemingly legal revenues. By lifting the money over the border between the illegal and the legal, a new type of power is created: the ability to make (lawful) use of the acquired money in the world of legal corporations, investments and opportunities. This implies a rise in possibilities and as a result more potential to gain influence in the legal world. As long as criminal entrepreneurs are operating solely in the underground economy, their ability to operate on the legal market is hampered by the illegal source of their revenues. However, the moment they are able to launder these illegal revenues (thereby transforming illegal into legal funds), they will be able to utilise these funds in the legal economy, which implies the accumulation of economic power in two senses. Not only will this result in a growth in economic influence, but also in a strengthened position on the legal market. The legal market also allows for the use of legal mechanisms, available in that market. While operating in the underground economy, these mechanisms remain beyond the reach of criminal entrepreneurs, who will have to resort to other strategies, procedures and instruments, for example, illegal violence. After having successfully entered the legal economy, the state apparatus provides the means to exert and accumulate power in a legitimate way.

When we compare this power accumulation with a 'typical' crime, such as burglary, we soon see that the latter is a crime aimed at making money in a survival economy; burglars state that the reasons why they steal vary from either 'to survive, to live, to live a more luxury life', or to 'pay for my addiction'. Young burglars also remark that they get a kick out of a burglary, that a successful burglary results in a rush of adrenaline. The power motive is not present in the discourse of burglars: burglary is a 'job', something you do for a living (Verwee *et al.*, 2007). The ability to enhance legitimate power through burglary is quasi-absent, as these perpetrators predominantly remain in the illegal sphere. The ultimate dream of the burglar seems to be to succeed in a kind of treasure hunt, in the 'jackpot', the unattended tremendous 'score'. But ... every burglar knows that this happens extremely rarely, or perhaps never. There is no calculus, no power plan, in the long run of a career as a burglar.

The profits in money laundering

The question is to what extent gaining power in the economic sphere is actually a specific goal of money laundering? The US Department of State identified the power motive of money laundering in the following terms: 'Money laundering is now being viewed as a central dilemma in dealing with all forms of international organized crime because financial gain means power' (US Department of State, 1998). As we will discuss later, this rationalisation was one of the motivations to start the battle against money laundering in the 1980s: the fear of policy-makers about a growing criminal power group in the legal economy, with far-reaching influence on formal corporations and politics. In other words, what was feared was the criminalisation of the legal economic activities (Naylor, 2007). Although there is much debate about the reality of these fears, Naylor states that they have never been proven to be true or realistic.

According to Masciandaro, the economic function of money laundering can be found in the transformation of potential to effective purchasing power (Masciandaro, 1999). As the revenues of underlying criminal activities cannot be employed directly in the legal sphere for consumption, investments or savings, the origins of these revenues need to be disguised. It is precisely this transformation into *effective* purchasing power that leads to an augmentation of lawful economic power. This does not imply that *all* proceeds of crime are laundered; on the contrary, only a part of criminally earned money will be laundered for use in the legal economy, namely those parts of the proceeds of crime that perpetrators wish to invest or save (Levi, 1996). In several cases, much of the criminal revenues will be spent 'on the fast life, on cars, boats and home improvements, or kept in cash form or jewellery and other "movables" which can readily be transported overseas and is not bulky' (Levi, 1996). The analysis of several court cases on money laundering and civil forfeiture proceedings reveals that, along with the opening of foreign bank accounts and the purchase of art works and antiques, expensive lifestyles are the major ways of disposing of criminal proceeds. Defendants allegedly spend their money on fur coats, hotel bills, holidays or expensive clothing (Kennedy, 2005). These cases show that criminal entrepreneurs are not only driven by an irrational impetus to achieve power, but also by the desire to display that power in the form of *status*. The will to stand out and the desire to show strength are part of the incentive.

This implies that the money that actually will be laundered is money that is required to be used in a formal way, such as 'savings from crime, transfers of payment for criminal purchases, and deposits of savings from crime committed overseas' (Levi, 1996). Persons who engage in money laundering do this to avoid punishment and to be able to benefit from their profits through investments and consumptions in the legal economy (Stessens, 2000; Levi and Reuter, 2006). Naylor agrees on this point, adding that the reasons behind money laundering may either be the pursuit of security on a longer-term basis (including the wish to leave wealth to one's heirs), or the will to apply criminal methods to legal businesses in order to make even more profit (Naylor, 2007). The latter is an 'emergency scenario' (Naylor, 2007), as this would imply increasing power through legal instruments, but knowledge of how this scenario is realistic is limited due to lack of empirical evidence. Several authors warn of the stimulating effect that money laundering may have on crime: the rise in economic power makes crime more worthwhile (Unger, 2006), or in other words, it makes sure that crime does pay.

In this sense, money laundering also impedes legitimate corporations in their daily business. After all, by entering the formal economy, organised crime can make use of all possibilities in the upper world, resulting in unfair competition towards other corporations (Ponsaers, 2009). For example, if organised crime groups are allowed to buy property with criminal money in order to launder the proceeds of their crime, this could result in higher property prices and an unbalanced market. The legal status of financial means makes it possible for launderers to act as investors and buyers on the formal market, which may enhance criminal activities.

Following Gresham's law, bad money would drive out the good money (Coggan, 2002). The anti money laundering complex is designed to limit this power accumulation. The mobilisation of (among others) financial institutions, as one of the power players in society (Morris, 2009) and one of the gatekeepers to the formal economy, makes the system even more encompassing.

Suendorf, who studied several cases of money laundering, states that the profit motive is not the only reason for entrance into the legal economy. Illegal operations and the development of professional forms of money laundering are made possible thanks to the availability of legal corporations, some of which can also guarantee high living standards to launderers or even spurious forms of retirement funds. Rarely do such investments completely lack illegal objectives, or simply aim for integration into the legal sphere (Suendorf, 2001). In other words, money laundering is not only an expression of a never-ending desire for power and influence, but is also a means to feel 'safe' or comfortable. To summarise: by laundering criminal proceeds, launderers secure their illegal businesses on the one hand, and their personal future on the other. Money laundering acts, therefore, as an insurance policy.

Although research has shown that burglars sometimes state that they hide the money in order to build up a reserve for the future (Verwee *et al.*, 2007), and as such the same insurance-thinking is present, the intertwining with the legal world of businesses and corporations is completely absent in the use of the profits from burglary. Burglars do not aim for a place in the legal economy nor do they want to build an 'empire' by perpetuating their crime. On the contrary, they hope to consolidate their place in illegality: it is exactly this illegal sphere that allows for the continuation of their activities.

Costs

Alongside the advantages of money laundering, there are also some negative aspects: the laundering in itself is a costly method – the cost of money laundering is estimated at around 50 per cent of the amount of money that is to be laundered (Unger, 2006). Operations may take time, as sometimes complex procedures are put in place and, at each stage of the money laundering process, there is a risk of detection. Furthermore, as soon as the money is successfully laundered, taxes need to be paid. Taking these side effects into account, van Duyne concludes that money laundering 'is only applied when needed' (van Duyne, 1997). His observation is based on the fact that laundering, on the one hand, requires certain skills which are not always available, and on the other hand, it is both risky and costly. Therefore, people will only choose to launder their proceeds when all other options are unavailable. Taking all these negative aspects into consideration, why would people choose to launder their illegal proceeds, unless other than pure financial issues are at stake?

Some specific types of crime that precede money laundering may well be inherently linked to the pursuit of power and influence in the legal economy. After all, criminals can also choose to remain in the illegal economy, thus avoiding the risks and costs incurred when entering the formal economy. The quest for economic power and influence in the formal sphere may be more typical of crimes such as fiscal fraud or swindling than of drug-related crimes or prostitution. The ability to make use of both the legal and illegal economy, combined with the intertwining of legal and illegal activities, provides the 'business criminal' with benefits transcending the mere benefits generated by illegal actions.

Dutch empirical research has shown that organised criminals are not as interested in the domination of the economic and political arena as has long been assumed.

> Most criminals are not interested in generating economic and political power in the Netherlands. They fancy a certain life style and are somewhat 'addicted' to the luxury that comes with it. They like to live on the edge, but they are not particularly interested in becoming a relevant economic or political factor.
>
> (Nelen, 2004)

The Dutch 'organised crime monitor' points out that organised crime perpetrators make use of existing flows of goods and money, but do not control or aim to control infrastructures, for example, in the transport or financial sectors. They do, however, use these sectors to commit crimes and to invest dirty money (Kleemans *et al.*, 2002). However, there are controversial views on this point: some authors explicitly warn about the infiltration of organised crime in the legal economic or political spheres (Williams, 1994). As the researchers of the organised crime monitor observe, this situation is different in countries such as the US or Italy, where such infiltration has been documented (Kleemans *et al.*, 2002). Not surprisingly, this rationale was used in the Belgian implementation of AML in the early 1990s: 'Money laundering is a necessary result of a number of crimes that provide advantages for their perpetrators and is an important driving force for the development of crime, not only nationally, but also internationally and even globally' (Belgian Senate, p. 1). Van Duyne states, in this respect, that it is not organised crime as such, but 'organised business criminals' that are most successful in investing their crime money in the upper world economy (van Duyne and de Miranda, 1999). They are able to invest their illegally earned money in their own enterprises, which results in an increased potential for gaining economic power and influence. This observation leads us to the assumption that gaining power in the illegal economy and transforming this power to enhance one's economic position in the legal economy (by making use of money laundering) could be a feature of a specific category of crime and criminals.

The business criminal and money laundering

Adopting the concept of power crime, we established earlier that money laundering is a crime that produces power. Laundering illegal proceeds of criminal activities allows for integration in the formal economy, which leads to an increase in economic power, but also to a feeling of comfort and security through the disguising of the criminal origins of wealth. By laundering illegal funds, criminal entrepreneurs become real players in the formal economy, which enhances their opportunities for cooperation and partnership in the world of legitimate business. In the specialist literature we find little information on the consequences of money laundering in relation to the power position of criminal groups (Nelen, 2004). There are, however, some examples of legitimate groups that try to strengthen their position through money laundering. In these cases, we actually speak of organisational crime rather than of organised crime.

Take, for example, the Lernout and Hauspie (L&H) case that received a great deal of attention in the Belgian press during 2008. L&H is a Belgian company, providing speech-processing technology services. L&H developed its market position and, by December 1999 its annual turnover added up to $212 million; it employed almost 2,000 people and was represented in forty different countries (*De Standaard*, 24 December 1999). The company was applauded and praised for its entrepreneurship until, in September 2001, the *Wall Street Journal* published an article in which it was announced that the SEC (Securities Exchange Commission) had launched an investigation against it. This announcement resulted in a massive sale of L&H stocks and finally marked the decline of the company, which was accused of fraudulent bookkeeping and false sales figures. After the first media impact in 2000, the year in which L&H was dismantled, the second flow of media attention came when the court hearings for this case started in 2007 and official claims were made against L&H for swindling, fraudulent accounting, market manipulation, and abuse of company assets, but also for money laundering (*De Standaard*, 22 July 2006). L&H allegedly used front men and front companies in order to be able to manipulate its accounts and to cover its losses. Falsified accounts generated high stock prices, and after the discovery of the fraudulent manipulations, huge debts were uncovered (Vande Walle, 2002), which ultimately victimised a large number of parties. As the trial started, hundreds of people brought civil actions against L&H (*De Standaard*, 23 May 2007), including Dexia Bank and KPMG (*De Standaard*, 23 October 2007) who are on trial themselves. Dexia even started a website, claiming its innocence in the L&H case (www.dexia.be/lhsp). This type of crime symbolises the use of money laundering methods within formal economic spheres, methods which are not aimed at accessing the legal economy, nor at the 'washing' of illegally earned money, but mainly at the maintenance and expansion of economic power within the formal economy itself. L&H used front companies to keep up the appearance of a highly successful company, thus making its revenues seem higher than they were in reality. These front companies made artificial profits that were registered as real ones, but were also used as a framework to launder company assets (Vande Walle, 2002).

Another example is the famous BCCI case (Bank of Credit and Commerce International) that caused an uproar in the 1980s. In this case, the bank was actively involved in money laundering schemes. The BCCI admitted facilitating (among other things) money laundering, bribery and tax fraud, and was found guilty of several criminal offences. The role of the BCCI bank was proactive: the financial institution assisted the disguising of criminal revenues, enabling criminal clients to accumulate economic power, and reinforcing its own power in the process. Passas and Groskin summarise in the following way the function of institutional support in money laundering: 'The more powerful the actors who employ the services of international financial institutions, the greater is the institutions' ability to court attention, purchase influence and outspend control agencies' (Passas and Groskin, 2001).

These characteristics of money laundering have resulted in a very typical approach to this phenomenon. The fact that money laundering may lead to increased power relations in the formal sphere may well be one of the reasons why the AML battle has become this encompassing. In the following sections we will discuss the growth of the AML fight on an international level and focus on how this was implemented in Belgium.

International origins of the fight against money laundering

The battle against money laundering finds its origins in the United States in the late 1980s, with the criminalisation of money laundering in 1986 (Pieth and Aiolfi, 2005). Contrary to the rhetoric surrounding the 'follow the money strategy' (fighting organised crime), the interests underlying the implementation of legislation and regulation against money laundering are not as uniform as they may seem. Several documents refer to the 'war on drugs' as the major force behind the AML legislation,[2] but this was not the only push factor for the invention of – what later became – a global 'security quilt' (Levi, 2002), focused on the prevention of what is referred to as 'the flow of money from the illegal into the legal financial sphere'. Moreover, when analysing the years in which the AML movement started, we see several other interests that support the commencement of this AML complex.

The war on drugs

In order to understand these diverging interests, we need to go back to the US in the 1980s, the period of 'Reaganomics': a deregulation of the economy and a tough-on-crime policy (Hawdon, 2001). In this period, the concerns over the profitability of crime and, more specifically, drug crime, rose. The US government was concerned about the increasing threat of organised crime – personified by the mafia – and the threat of infiltration in both the legal economy and at the political level (Van Heuckelom, 2004). Large sums of money were said to be in control of criminal elements, the underground economy was expanding widely (Naylor, 2007), and policy-makers concluded that traditional methods were no longer effective in fighting these forms of crime (Thony, 2002). A picture was drawn in which mafia-like organisations were trying to take over formal economic and political spheres, profiting from a growth in the cocaine market (van Duyne *et al.*, 2005). Hawdon states that this period can be characterised by a moral panic regarding the 'war on drugs' (Hawdon, 2001) – in fact the same rhetoric that was used by Nixon, when he used the war on drugs as a key issue in his election campaign in 1968 (van Duyne and Levi, 2005).

This underground economy was said to be growing considerably, leading to a fear among policy-makers for the infiltration into and abuse of the formal economy through the proceeds of drug crime. Images of money laundering destabilising the economy and carried out by organised criminals who are planning to take over companies and financial institutions, thereby infiltrating the world of the formal economy, are not only historical: also more recently we still see this kind of argument (Aninat *et al.*, 2002).

These concerns resulted in the US in the Drugs Trafficking Offenses Act and the Money Laundering Control Act of 1986, through which money laundering became a criminal offence. The idea behind this new legislation was twofold: first, policy-makers were convinced of the fact that crime should not pay. Second the 'follow the money' philosophy, focusing on seizure and confiscation of crime-money was identified as the best way to 'hit them where it hurts most' (Nelen, 2004). This philosophy is rooted in the concept of the perpetrator as a *homo economicus* (Van Overtveldt, 2007), aiming at the realisation of specific goals, such as wealth, health or social status (Kleemans, 2001). Compliance with regulation should therefore be achieved through deterrence and deterrence experiences (Wikström, 2006). Although in those days little was known about either the phenomenon of organised crime, or about the methods to identify flows of money (Naylor, 2007), and the deterrent effect of sanctions and punishment were questioned (Kleemans, 2001), this was the approach that was adopted. Findlay (1999) refers to this emphasis on confiscating the proceeds of crime as the 'new industry of crime control'. As traditional crime prevention and repression methods no longer seemed to be effective, policy-makers stated that this type of organised crime needed an appropriate approach. The approach of transnational crime should no longer be limited to jurisdictional borders, and civil punishment seemed to be more effective (Findlay, 1999).

Financial interests

Parallel to these increasing governmental concerns, the 1982 financial crisis again pointed out how vulnerable the economy is. Central banks took steps to protect the economy. One of the initiatives they proposed was the prevention of money laundering (Helleiner, 2000). In their view, money laundering, apart from a profitable way to use illegally gained money in the legal economy, also has an impact on a broader macro level. To be more specific, it disturbs the normal flow of money within the financial system. In this view, the unpredictable money flows entering the legal financial system as a result of money laundering, allegedly impact on the overall volume of money circulating within an economy (Bartlett, 2002). These monetary volume changes supposedly disrupt the economy and have an influence on inflation, interest rates and exchange rates. Next to these concerns, money launderers, when they actually invest their illegally earned proceeds in the legal economy, also have an advantage in relation to the other (legal) players on the economic market as they are able to invest their illegally earned money in the formal economy; money laundering therefore results in unfair competition (Van de Werdt and Speekenbrink, 2008). As central banks are responsible for ensuring a balanced monetary policy (Hazlitt, 1979), they also have an interest in ensuring that this balance is not disturbed by unstable and destabilising flows of money.

Central banks had already been united in the Basle Committee since 1975, but based on these concerns they engaged in the battle against money laundering and presented a circular in 1988 on 'the prevention of criminal use of the banking system for the purpose of money laundering' (BCBS, 1988). In this circular they explained how banks can become victimised by money laundering, which can have several disturbing impacts, ranging from reputational damage, loss of public confidence in banks, or material damage as a result of fraud. The circular presented a statement of ethical principles for banks, based on customer identification, compliance with laws and regulation and cooperation with law enforcement. Although private banks had previously been able to avoid stricter regulation on money laundering under the show of dishonest competition (Naylor, 2007), when the Financial Action Task Force (FATF) was founded in 1989, and issued the forty recommendations in 1990, such regulation could no longer be averted.

The EU directive in 1991[3] introduced these AML standards to the European sphere, aiming at the coordination and cooperation of anti money laundering, but also indicating several obligations for all partners in the framework of a preventive approach of money laundering. These obligations referred to, inter alia, the identification of clients, the implementation of AML procedures and the duty to report suspicious transactions. Subsequently, member states were obliged to implement these European guidelines.

Reputational interests

Besides the legal framework surrounding anti money laundering, several initiatives were taken by the banking sector to protect itself from fraud and from being used as a mechanism for criminal purposes. Self-regulatory initiatives related to corporate governance and reputation protection were put in place. The

Wolfsberg group is one of many examples. This group of internationally orientated large banks developed a number of principles, the Wolfsberg principles (2000), which serve as a voluntary code of conduct for banks worldwide. These principles aim to harmonise compliance, AML regulations and KYC (know your customer) rules, and encourage banks to exchange information on these subjects (Pieth and Aiolfi, 2005).

Apart from this initiative, the banking sector itself has extended the AML policy by forcing other banks to implement these measures in order to enable them to stay in the market (Helleiner, 2000). Banks that do not follow this legislation are known in the sector and are seen as less stable and less healthy. Reputation is stated to be one of the most important factors in the financial sector and can therefore be used as a mechanism to put pressure on the sector. In particular the large, international banks, working with many clients, government institutions and international organisations, are very much aware of the reputational and regulatory risks related to poor AML standards (Levi, 2005). In other words: taking AML measures can also serve as a marketing tool. The question is to what extent the AML paradigm is still taken into consideration by the financial institutions when implementing compliance measures.

The irony of the implementation of AML measures is, in fact, that banks are as such not harmed by allowing money laundering (passively or by rendering services). Money laundering in itself does not damage commercial interests or pose any financial risks. Therefore we can hypothesise that without legislation, penal law enforcement and the accompanying reputational hazards, a commercially oriented bank would not be likely to prevent money laundering: criminal money is 'cheap' money for banks as these clients probably won't ask too many questions and will not try to grasp all discounts. The harm derives from the fact that laundering is prohibited. There is an AML legislation put in place which results at least in reputational harm when a bank gets caught money laundering, or – even worse – is seen as associated with terrorist financing.

Since the AML battle has now put severe strains on banks, the reputational risk (and, following from this, the impact on profit-making) has become too high to take. The emphasis on the allegedly detrimental effects money laundering may have on a social and economic level has resulted in raised expectations from the legislator as well as from the public at large (as a result of the emphasis on corporate governance, ethical businesses, etc.), who expect banks to obey these rules. As a result, money laundering has become one of the liabilities a bank has to deal with. But it is one with a high visibility effect which does not need to correspond fully with reality. This is endorsed by findings from the survey of PricewaterhouseCoopers in 2007: 12 per cent of all companies involved in the survey perceived money laundering as a high risk to their organisation. However, only 4 per cent of these companies actually reported having experienced incidents related to money laundering (PricewaterhouseCoopers, 2007). The perceived threat of money laundering (or rather, the perceptions of its negative derivatives like reputation damage) is therefore higher than the actual occurrence.

Furthermore, in its 2009 Global Economic Crime Survey, Ernst & Young state that the (perceived) risk of money laundering victimisation by companies has increased during the current financial crisis. Companies now estimate their risk of victimisation as higher than during times of financial stability (Ernst & Young, 2009). Of all the companies in the E&Y sample that experienced fraud in the year previous to the survey (30 per cent), 12 per cent reported falling victim to money laundering in the past year – money laundering even takes fifth place on the incident list of financial crimes. This illustrates both the perceived impact of money laundering – the 'threat images' of money laundering (Van Duyne *et al.*, 2005) and the awareness of companies with regard to the incidence of this crime.

Banks have a significant interest in preventing any association with money laundering (or terrorist financing, an ever-larger reputational risk since 2001). Reputational damage could not only lead to losing customers (as the credit crunch has shown, trust of the general public can be lost quite quickly, leading to bankers publically apologising for their mistakes (*De Standaard*, 28 April 2009)), but also, and most importantly, to the loss of trustworthiness with regard to other banks – and the current crisis has shown how important trust between financial institutions actually is.

The war on terror

After 9/11, AML initiatives were lifted to a more severe dimension. After the war on drugs, now the War on Terror is a reason to implement far-reaching measures on anti money laundering as terrorist financing is added to the AML legislation. Before 9/11 governments had tried to implement client profiles and 'know your customer' regulation. But this was stopped by the lobby of the banks and privacy lobbyists (Levi, 2002). The Patriot Act, however, implemented in the aftermath of 9/11, overruled these objections and introduced the possibility for information exchange between banks, but also enforced a larger access to that bank information for police and judicial services. Levi states that it would have been very unlikely that measures as intrusive as customer due diligence would have been accepted this silently without the attacks on 9/11 (Levi, 2002). Moreover, not only were more comprehensive regulations introduced, the War on Terror also increased budgets for police and judicial services and broadened their competencies (Kochan, 2006). Banks chose to intensify their checks and procedures, as any association with terrorism financing could have disastrous effects (Kochan, 2006). The FATF (Financial Action Task Force) developed specific guidelines for financial institutions to enable them to detect terrorist funding and the emphasis now shifted from drug-related crime to all serious forms of organised (international) crime (Gouvin, 2003) and terrorism.

The Belgian implementation of AML legislation

After the elaboration of the international framework surrounding money laundering above, we will now focus on the Belgian implementation of the AML complex. The Belgian approach to AML, based on the European approach as adopted in the EU Directives of 1991, 2001 and 2005, consists of both a repressive and a preventive/proactive method. Since the implementation of the EU Directive of 1991[4] in Belgian law, the Belgian AML system consists of both a repressive and a preventive pillar; the repressive approach involves the confiscation of the proceeds of crime, while the preventive pillar has introduced a monitoring and reporting obligation for private institutions. The latter – the reporting mechanism for (public and private) institutions – is the subject of this research.

Belgium implemented the European guideline by means of the Law of 11 January 1993 on the prevention of the use of the financial system for money laundering. This AML legislation formed the starting point of the creation of the Belgian AML complex. This law provides a preventive approach to money laundering and, in overall terms, implements the obligations of the EU Council Directive. In practice, this means that several organisations and/or persons (in 2006, 30,500 to be exact) are obliged to report suspicious transactions to an institution that was also founded by the law of 1993: the Belgian Financial Intelligence Processing Unit (CTIF-CFI).[5] Although at first only financial institutions were subject to this law, gradually non-financial institutions were also charged with this obligation (such as casinos or lawyers). For specific types of institutions, such as financial institutions, this reporting mechanism has been detailed in legislation and regulation.

The CTIF-CFI was installed as an administrative (and not a judicial) organisation to enable this institution to work independently and autonomously. This special status is based on the role it should fulfil as a filter of reports to the police and the public prosecution. In this respect, the CTIF-CFI can rely on an extensive professional secrecy, enabling it to operate with the strictest confidence to both sides (reporting institutions and police or judicial services).

The judicial follow-up is carried out by the magistrates and police officers who are employed by the FIU. Their involvement also guarantees access (by proxy) to all necessary information (police and judicial records) required to investigate any report received by the FIU. If the FIU decides that there is enough reason to suspect that (attempted) money laundering has taken place, it will report this to the public prosecutor, who will make subsequently decide on further investigation or dismissal.

The Belgian legislator initially limited the amount of predicate crimes out of concern not to burden the financial institutions excessively and the discussion that took place with regard to the rules of discretion and non-interference that are usual when doing business with banks as a client.[6] The Belgian government has searched for a compromise between the 'good functioning of the financial system'[7] and the efficacy of the judicial system regarding serious types of crime. These considerations show that the Belgian legislator was aware of the impact of this reporting system on the financial institutions as a whole, and did not want to burden the banks excessively.

The AML complex in Belgium comprises both public and private organisations, cooperating to prevent and investigate the laundering of crime-money:

(federal) police and public prosecution, the Belgian Financial Intelligence Processing Unit – FIU (CTIF-CFI), the COSC (Central Office for Seizure and Confiscation) and the supervisor of the Belgian financial sector, the CBFA (Banking, Finance and Insurance Commission). Besides the framework built by the authorities around anti money laundering, private organisations make up a large part of the AML chain since they are obliged to report suspicious transactions to the CTIF-CFI. These organisations are listed in the Belgian AML legislation[8] and can be either financial organisations (banks, insurance companies, investment companies, etc.) or non-financial organisations, such as lawyers, guarding companies or casinos and dealers in high-value goods. Private actors are a part of the AML complex as they are supposed to contribute to the prevention and detection of money laundering, but also represent the beginning of the AML chain.

The compliance officer as the centre of AML implementation in banks

In this research the focus lies on the task that financial institutions fulfil in the AML complex. This focus is based on several observations: this sector is one of the largest providers of reports to the FIU and the bank sector is known for its large investments in trying to comply with the AML legislation. Moreover, the credit institutions take up a unique place in AML legislation and implementation as they are legally obliged to appoint one of their employees as responsible for the implementation and application of the AML law, the compliance officer.

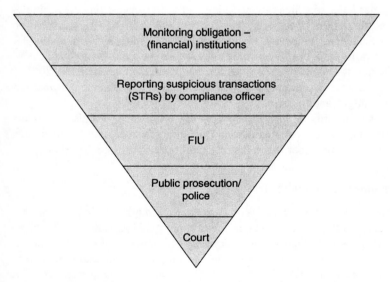

Figure 3.1 The AML chain.

The basis for this compliance officer can be found in the legal obligation to appoint:

> [...] one or more individuals who will be responsible for the implementation of this Law in their organisation. These individuals will be in charge of establishing procedures for internal control and information management in order to avert, detect and prevent transactions related to money laundering and terrorist financing.
>
> (Law of 11 January 1993, article 10[9])

The explanatory memorandum[10] specifies that this 'individual' should have 'a proper hierarchal level', chosen from the members of the management. They will be held responsible for the enforcement of the obligations resulting from the AML law. If deemed necessary, a procedure should be developed with regard to tracing and centralisation of information, adapting in-house control procedures to the legal obligations, and for the filing of reports to the FIU. The AML legislation of 1993 does not specify the statute of this 'individual', but these articles in the law do lay the foundation of the subsequent formalisation of the compliance function.

During the 1990s (in spite of the Law of 1993), the practice of reporting suspicious transactions remained rather arbitrary. For the financial sector, this gave rise to regulatory action. The supervisor (the CBFA) chose to detail the legal obligation to report suspicious transactions in 2001 (CBFA, 2001b) and obliged financial companies to install a specific function that (among other tasks) supervises compliance of the bank, staff and clients with AML guidelines: the *compliance officer*.[11]

This circular letter specifies this 'individual in charge' by adding AML implementation to the powers of the 'compliance function' (CBFA, 1997), a function that had existed since 1997 within financial institutions entrusted with the implementation of procedures for fiscal fraud prevention. As from then, 'each financial organisation is obliged to have at least 1 compliance officer' (CBFA, 2001a). Moreover, the compliance function is the only function in Belgian banks that has been legally obliged and specified.

The circular not only defines the concept of compliance, but also considers the areas of competence, responsibilities (including those of the board of directors and the executive board) and the statute of the compliance department.

The compliance function in theory

'Compliance' is defined by the Belgian regulator as 'the actual implementation of the integrity policy of the financial institution' (CBFA, 2001a). The compliance function is described as an 'independent function within the organisation, aimed at investigating and advancing observance of regulations related to the integrity of banking' (CBFA, 2001a). This is a rather broad domain, and this impression is supported when examining the domains related to integrity. These are listed in the circular of 2001, and include: AML, prevention of fiscal fraud, insider dealing, privacy legislation, deontology, transaction in financial instruments, etc.

The compliance department is expected to take up a role of coordination and initiative with regard to rule observance by the institution. Implementing AML procedures is only one of the many duties of a compliance officer, as the circular also mentions a number of other specific tasks related to integrity policy: formulate guidelines for employees, development of procedures and codes of ethics, training and enhancing the awareness of employees, establishing and reporting incidents, investigation of rule violations, monitoring transactions, client screening, give advice on new products, follow up on legislation, developing a deontological policy within the organisation, etc. The regulator allows for a delegation of specific money laundering tasks to AML officers in practice, but this does not alter the fact that, ultimately, the compliance officer is responsible for the AML policy; a full outsourcing of the compliance function is not allowed.

A number of years later, in 2007, this circular letter was partly converted into a legal obligation.[12] The compliance officer then became legally responsible for the implementation of AML procedures and the execution of these procedures within the financial institution.

Compliance, or literally 'observance' is the key issue in the involvement of private actors in the battle against money laundering and refers to the extent to which private actors are able to fulfil the demands that are imposed on them by AML legislation and regulation. The compliance officer is at the heart of the AML investments by financial institutions and therefore represents an important actor in the complex. These compliance officers are also active in other countries and are referred to in literature as 'banking detectives' (Kochan, 2006, p. 283), 'integrity watch-dogs' (de Bie and Carion, 2001, p. 4), or 'financial deputy sheriffs' (Levi, 1997, p. 17).

In a nutshell, the compliance officer will check transactions made by staff and clients, give training to staff and superiors, investigate clients' backgrounds when necessary and make reports to the FIU whenever a client or a transaction seems suspicious or could be related to money laundering or the financing of terrorism. In order to fulfil this task, the compliance officer makes use of several tools, such as software, specific programs and information providers.

Arising from their function and duties within the financial institution, the compliance officer has a dual position. His or her first responsibility is to safeguard the 'integrity of the bank' by applying the policy on integrity within the institution (CBFA, 2001a). This comprehensive job description results in compliance departments carrying the responsibility for an array of issues related to integrity in the broader sense (privacy regulation, insider dealing, prevention of fiscal fraud, conflicts of interests), among which anti money laundering is just one of the many other tasks to carry out (Nivra-Nyenrode *et al.*, 2007; Verhage, 2009g). The application of this integrity policy ought to enable the compliance department (the department within the bank working on compliance-related issues, headed by the compliance officer) to protect the bank from reputational or other damage. On the other hand, in practice, compliance tasks may clash with the commercial objectives of a bank: in certain cases, compliance departments have to make decisions that interfere with commercial objectives, typical of financial institutions. The regulator was aware of this duality and tried to establish a framework which should allow for an independent mandate. The position of the compliance officer should be supported by providing specific guarantees: a compliance officer ought to be able to work independently from commercial entities, 'monitoring and stimulating compliance with the rules regarding integrity of banking by the institution' (CBFA, 2001a). The source of inspiration for the protective measures was found in the Basle guidelines (BCBS, 2005): the compliance department should occupy an appropriate statute within the financial institution, which ought to be secured by a compliance charter. This charter is supposed to specify reporting lines, implying that compliance departments should be positioned directly under a member of the board of directors which should not only allow for free information flow between compliance officers and the higher levels within the bank, but also for an appropriate hierarchical position with regard to employees

Second, there are a number of incompatibilities (no combination with a position in internal audit services, or commercial posts) and a prohibition on the outsourcing of compliance tasks (although a company is allowed to obtain expert advice). These rules are installed to certify the independence of the compliance function, as a compliance officer needs to be able to carry out tasks and investigate files independently and autonomously. The charter not only establishes this independence, but also needs to assure credibility and authority. This is why the charter needs to be approved by the management (Thierens, 2004).

Although the regulator has taken steps in the right direction, these regulations do not exclude every contradiction or clash between compliance and commercial employees. After all, as the compliance officer is also a bank employee, it may be very difficult to act counter to the wishes of the directors and the bank's interests. Essentially, a compliance officer carries out governmental tasks, but is paid by the bank and works within the framework of the financial institution.

Room for discretion

The Belgian AML legislation is rather broad, and does not specify in detail in which cases banks are supposed to report transactions (i.e. clients) to the FIU. More precisely, the law states: 'when the institutions know or suspect that a transaction is connected to money laundering or terrorist financing, they will notify the FIU, before the transaction is carried out' (art. 12, Law of 11 January 1993). Article 20 specifies that any report should be made 'in good faith': 'no civil, penal or disciplinary claim may be instituted and no professional sanction may be executed with regard to the institutions that have provided information in good faith'. Both articles more or less confirm that there is room for discretion in deciding whether or not to report a transaction to the FIU. After all, to be able to assess whether a report is made 'in good faith', a compliance officer is supposed to have at least a preliminary insight in the case, which itself excludes the possibility of an automatic reporting system.

As such, the Belgian AML legislation is based on the principle of 'intelligent reporting': banks are supposed to report 'any transaction which they suspect of money laundering' (Spreutels & Grijseels, 2001). This implies that there are no objective indicators for reporting to the FIU: banks are supposed to develop their own standards on the basis of which they decide to report (contrary to, for example, the system that existed until recently in the Netherlands, where banks were supposed to report cases involving transactions above a specific amount (MOT, 2006)).

In 2007, a number of indicators were introduced to enhance uniformity in reporting (*Programmawet*, 27 April 2007). The 'indicators' were announced as a method to enable institutions, who are subject to the reporting obligation, to make more and more profound reports in relation to money laundering funds based on serious and organised fiscal fraud. These indicators were seen as a first step towards objective reporting standards, on the basis of which banks were supposed to be supported in their reporting practices.[13] The use of indicators was also expected to result in a rise in the number of suspicious transactions that reach the FIU. To what extent these objectives have been met, however, is under debate, as a heated discussion was started with regard to the degree of obligation in reporting cases based on these indicators. The Minister of Justice stated in 2007 that institutions are supposed to report a case when one of the indicators is present (*De Standaard*, 3 November 2007), while the professional organisation of financial institutions has taken the stand that these indicators will be used as *indicators* (in the actual sense of the word) of potential money laundering (*De Tijd*, 9 November 2007), implying a higher alertness for these cases, and a need to further investigate the case, but not per se an automatic report to the FIU. This viewpoint is based on the observation that was made by financial institutions, claiming that the indicators are too vague and broad, which would mean that a number of unnecessary reports would be made to the FIU, something that would undermine the system of 'intelligent reporting' (as opposed to automatic reporting).

The State Secretary for coordination of the fight on fraud has pleaded for using the indicators as a *complementary* source (*Trends*, 16 October 2008). This is also the viewpoint of the financial institutions, as will become clear in Chapter 5, which means that the presence of one or more indicators in a case will lead to a higher alertness and further investigation of the client, after which a decision will be made on the need to report the case to the FIU.

Taking these evolutions into account, we can state that apart from the introduction of the indicators, the Belgian legislator has chosen an AML system in which the reporting entities are given room for discretion and appraisal on a case-by-case basis. This also implies that any institution that is willing to take this reporting obligation seriously, has to invest in developing not only an AML policy, but also a framework in which investigations of atypical transactions can take place. The pros and cons of this system will be discussed in the following chapters.

The regulator's view on detecting atypical transactions

A second source on which the Belgian financial institutions need to base their AML arrangements, are the circulars from the regulator for the Belgian financial sector, the CBFA. The Belgian regulator has devoted considerable attention to the battle against money laundering. In its circulars of 2004 and 2005, the CBFA also specifies the way in which banks are supposed to accomplish detection of suspicious transactions (CBFA, 2005).

According to this circular, banks need to install a first and second line of detection of money laundering, in order to achieve an optimal discovery of atypical transactions and clients. The first line consists of the vigilance and watchfulness of employees: employees need to be alert, trained and able to recognise suspicious clients and transactions, based on a number of procedures (see Chapter 4). The second line consists of a monitoring system that allows for continuous monitoring of all transactions carried out within the bank (CBFA, 2004, 2005). After alerts are triggered, these should be investigated by the compliance department as soon as possible (CBFA, 2005), resulting in either an analysis of the alert and a report on the reasons for not assessing the alert as suspicious, or a suspicious transaction report to the FIU (see Chapter 4).

In general, both the legislator and the regulator remain vague on the subject on when exactly to report and which cases need to be reported. Legislation and regulation also demand an investigative effort from the banks (they are, after all, supposed to 'report in good faith'). Next to this observation, it can be stated that the current framework leaves relatively much room for discretion. And it is precisely this discretion that forces banks to investigate cases themselves before reporting them to the FIU: they do not want to '*overreport*' or '*underreport*' (as both may lead to a reputational risk and/or commercial damage) and therefore conclude that a thorough investigation is needed to assess the potential suspicious transactions.

We witness a constant enlargement of the compliance function, with new tasks, duties and responsibilities. In November 2004 (updated in 2005), a code was issued by the regulator of the financial sector, which introduced a number of specific guidelines related to client identification and acceptance policies (CBFA, 2004). One result of these enhanced identification regulations is the compulsory freezing of accounts of clients for whom there is no copy of their identity card available. By the end of 2007, in Belgium 200,000 accounts, amounting to millions of euro, were frozen as a result of this measure (*De Standaard*, 20 November 2007). On the subject of client acceptance the regulator's code specifies that banks' policies should include the assessment and classification of clients according to risk-scales. Furthermore, politically exposed persons can only be accepted after thorough investigation. After the implementation of the Markets in Financial Instruments Directive in 2007 (European Parliament and Council, 2004), a number of obligations deriving from this Directive were added to the job responsibilities of compliance officers. This is just one of the examples of the steady growth of duties that are gathered under compliance. It may be clear that not only is this range of tasks rather intensive for one function, but it also implies the combination of several interests and concerns.

More recently, the Directive 2005/60/EC of the European Parliament and of the Council of 26 October 2005 on the prevention of the use of the financial system for the purpose of money laundering and terrorist financing, was implemented in Belgium. In order to comply with the directive, national provisions had to be adopted by December 2007, but it took the Belgian Chamber of Deputies until 16 July 2009 to vote a bill (and until January 2010 to actually publish it in the Belgian Staatsblad[14]). The change for financial institutions seems relatively limited, although the law tries to clarify the concept of politically exposed persons (article 12, paragraph 3), which could be helpful. Furthermore, it states that banks are now indeed allowed to exchange information between themselves[15] (which was forbidden at the time of this research), and the law no longer obliges banks to document the address of clients during their identification procedures. It also allows professional organisations to access the national register.[16] Another difference is the fact that the government now also takes a different stance by changing article 3 of the AML law, that states that organisations will 'identify all acts of money laundering and terrorism financing' into 'by employing every means to identify actors of money laundering and terrorism financing'.[178] From this we can derive that the legislator has also realised that AML can be judged by the means and the efforts that are invested in it, not necessarily by its results. What the effect of this legal adaptation will be in practice, is to be awaited.

The compliance industry

The overview we have given before regarding the origins and growth of the AML complex, does not represent the only push factor in the development of AML initiatives. As stated in the introduction, this progress of AML implementation is supported by a parallel influence related to a more commercial approach associated with reputation risk management. We have labelled this second force behind the AML evolution as the compliance industry. The compliance industry represents the *entrepreneurial* approach to anti money laundering and compliance. This supply side of the market on compliance is built around a number of services that provide support for AML and compliance officers: software providers (to enable in-depth transaction monitoring), trade information bureaus (for information on potential organisational clients), databases of high-risk individuals (to enable thorough checks of potential individual clients), advisors (such as KPMG or E&Y), but also the provision of training and education for staff or for compliance officers themselves.

The tendencies towards a strengthened control on integrity and ethics of companies result in the willingness of, but also the need for, companies to propagate their compliance, reliability and social responsibility. This willingness did not surface without any pressure; it took several scandals before companies realised the danger non-compliance can imply for their business and the harmful effects these scandals can have with respect to the company's image. The supervision from the US also plays an important role in this respect: without trust from the US supervisor, banks will not be able to work on the US market.

The compliance industry takes advantage of the need for an image of integrity and compliance and stimulates the demand for advice, support and software by advertising compliance as 'adding value to the business'. They stress the advantages of the implementation of compliance systems (such as transaction monitoring and know your customer devices) by stating that this kind of information may also be used in a commercial manner. After all, having a large amount of information on customers enables the banks to offer tailor-made services and 'solutions'. The compliance industry has grown extensively in recent years: estimations show banks (and other companies) have invested large sums of money in this kind of assistance and support (KPMG, 2007).

Conclusion

Today, a large number of (inter)national actors are united in the battle against money laundering, working on preventing, detecting, investigating and reporting potential money laundering cases. It is precisely this all-inclusive approach that characterises anti money laundering. The AML crusade represents a worldwide system in which quite a few public and private organisations are involved, aiming at preventing, detecting, and sanctioning the flow of illegal money towards the legal economy. Earlier, Levi (2002, p. 182) referred to this as a 'global risk management process in which entrepreneurs are primarily responsible for implementing public policy goals and developing a "security quilt"'. Controlling the flows of money has become an immense legislative and entrepreneurial task, uniting several countries, regulators and private organisations (Naylor, 2007).

One of the explanations for the growth of such a global control system may reside in the power motive behind money laundering. When criminal activity results in increasing power accumulation, it may be perceived as particularly threatening, hence the urgent need to prevent it and control its effects.

Policy-makers convince us of the fact that money laundering harms society as a whole, by threatening the economy and the 'healthy' political and economic climate in a country (Kochan, 2006). These 'mirages' as they are sometimes called (van Duyne, 2006), although contested on a regular basis, have served their policy purpose and resulted in an impressive fight against money laundering, permeating not only the public sphere of justice, police services and regulators, but also the world of private corporations: banks, casinos, lawyers, notaries, etc.

What is often forgotten, however, is that money laundering is also functional; it forms a bridge between the legal and the illegal market, not only for drug dealers, as is assumed, but for all sorts of entrepreneurs in criminal activities (Hoogenboom, 2006). This results in a market in which several illegal, informal and formal entrepreneurs function in their own way and with their own economic objectives. And although the focus of policy-makers and legislators remains mainly oriented towards organised criminals infiltrating the legal world, we may need to fear the 'business criminal' more.

Within the AML complex, private institutions are charged with a specific whistle-blowing task: the detection and reporting of transactions that may be linked to money laundering or terrorist financing activities (and are liable for punishment in case of non-compliance). This obligation for private organisations not only implies the shift of responsibility to private entrepreneurs for the implementation of public policy goals (Levi, 2002), but has also resulted in a massive investment in compliance- and AML-related issues. A number of services and instruments have been developed in support of these obligations (for example, the automated monitoring devices for banks, or software, providing lists of 'suspicious' individuals) – which results in the supply part of a market in compliance support – referred to in our research as the 'compliance industry'.

This combination of all these actors within the AML complex proceeded with surprisingly little public disquiet; privacy issues were overruled in pursuit of the ultimate goal: fighting money laundering (Shields, 2005). Although the fight against money laundering seems to have united several institutions in this – what is considered as crucial – objective, we may question the extent to which fighting money laundering actually is the solitary goal of all 'partners' in this AML complex. After all, each type of organisation engages in this fight (voluntarily or not) from its own standpoint, striving for its own purpose. Private organisations who are obliged to fulfil the AML commitments, primarily have the interest of their organisation at heart: preventing any association with criminal activities, protecting the reputation of the company and avoiding regulatory fines or loss of confidence from other banks (Helleiner, 2000). Regulators have a more general interest: keeping the financial system's integrity safeguarded, resulting in a 'healthy' economy (although the events of the past year have shown that this is not exclusively related to the prevention of money laundering). Law enforcement (police, public prosecution and the FIU), as a third associate, mainly aims to fight (predict) crime (possibly combined with the confiscation of assets deriving from this crime) (Gouvin, 2003). As each institution works from a different perspective, each partner in the complex will have his own interests at stake. These different interests need to be taken into account when trying to assess the effectiveness of the system. After all, to say something about the effects of a system, we need to know which goals are pursued by the system.

4 The compliance officer

Functioning between the hammer and the anvil[1]

Introduction

In February of 2008, when the crisis is at full strength, a newspaper article reported on the ever-increasing demand for 'skilled anti-money laundering professionals'. Quoting from the article: 'apart from immediate concerns stemming from the credit crunch, the research finds that battling money laundering (AML) remains a top priority for financial institutions as new regulation continues to be introduced'.[2] The observation that, even in times of credit crisis, anti money laundering (AML) is considered to be one of the main concerns for financial institutions in the US, raises several questions.

As stated earlier, to capture the origins of compliance in Belgium, a survey among compliance officers was conducted in April and May 2007. The survey aspired not only to compile a preliminary profile of the compliance profession in Belgium, but also to get a first view on the visions, perceptions and practices of compliance officers (see Chapter 1 for more details on methodology). Where applicable, the results of this survey on Belgian compliance officers will be compared to their Dutch and French counterparts.

Practice of the AML complex: KYC, CDD, monitoring and reporting

Institutions under the AML legislation, burdened with the obligation to report suspicious transactions, are obliged to follow certain procedures in order to meet the requirements of the legislator. The Basel committee has made recommendations on the practical procedures (BCBS, 2005), and the Belgian legislator has refined these guidelines. Legal requirements have been specified and refined in the Belgian AML law and the Banking Law in 2007,[3] but also in the circulars of the regulator, the CBFA (Banking, Finance and Insurance Commission) (CBFA, 2001a, 2001b, 2005). We have already discussed the 2001 circular of the regulator, which defined the compliance function and listed anti money laundering as one of the tasks of the compliance officer's mandate in the implementation of the integrity policy of the bank.[4] The circular of 2004, updated in 2005, specifies which AML efforts a bank should implement. The first obligation in the 2005 circular relates to the development of a 'know your customer' (KYC) policy, and introduces a number of guidelines for identifying customers and beneficiaries of transactions. For example, this implies filing a copy of each client's identity card and mapping their background, family relations, business involvements, etc.

Furthermore, the circular details the procedures for accepting (new) clients, which also implies classifying clients by their 'risk rate'. Each client needs to be screened for the degree of risk they represent. 'High risk' clients are for example insufficiently identified individuals, or politically exposed persons (PEPs – individuals who may, because of their political status or otherwise, pose a higher risk for the bank). An example of a high-risk transaction is a banking operation carried out by persons who are not identified by the financial institution itself, but by other institutions, which means identification takes place at a distance.

This risk assessment of clients automatically implies asking many questions in order to know the customer and his or her activities. This 'customer due diligence' (CDD) also entails matching clients with the list of PEPs. According to the circular, PEPs can only be accepted after a thorough investigation of the person involved (CBFA, 2005).

Related to this first phase in the implementation of AML guidelines regarding identification of customers and knowing their backgrounds, the monitoring (and subsequent investigation) of transactions is also detailed by the circular. The circular specifies the need for a *first*- and a *second*-line supervision related to suspicious transactions.

The so-called first-line supervision consists of the supervision carried out by employees who actually make contact with the clients through their daily activities. Specific employees, such as personnel working at the counters of banks, should be able to detect atypical transactions on the basis of predetermined criteria. After detection, they are required to report these transactions – in writing – to the compliance officer. The detection of these transactions needs to be based on the 'economic basis and legitimacy' of the transaction (why is this transaction carried out; why would this client make use of our bank for this purpose; does this transaction fit into the profile of our client; the amount of money involved in the transaction, the amount of cash, etc.). Banks are supposed to develop specific procedures for these routines. This watchfulness should be enhanced by providing procedures, training and education, which should enable employees to recognise and detect atypical transactions. Training should be aimed at raising questions when seemingly strange transactions are carried out. After detection of an atypical transaction, employees are supposed to report these transactions to the compliance officer (CBFA, 2005).

The second-line supervision consists of a 'supervisory system', a system which allows for the detection of atypical transactions of all accounts and transactions by customers. Second-line monitoring serves as a second detection mechanism, when the first line is not able or is not in the position to detect a suspicious transaction (for example when transactions are carried out online, by the client himself).

Every bank needs to develop refined, specific and pertinent criteria for the detection of these transactions. In addition, these criteria should be geared to the services and products the bank offers on the one hand, and to the clients they serve on the other hand. The formulated criteria should be connected to the risks related to money laundering or terrorist financing when dealing with transactions that, first, are carried out by high-risk customers or, second, transactions that are atypical or raise suspicion regarding either the amount of money involved or when compared to the normal habits of the client. In order to fulfil this last demand, the system should be able to recognise 'normal' behaviour of clients and – by formulating a profile for his or her 'normal' or routine activities and transactions – detect abnormal transactions by clients, alerting the bank when a client's transaction does not fit his or her profile, or when there is no clear explanation for a transaction that has taken place.

This second-line supervision is more detailed in the circular: it has to meet certain demands. For example, the system should produce written reports on the detected atypical transactions ('alerts'), the reasons why these transactions are reported as atypical and, not unimportantly, it is supposed to be an *automated* system, unless the bank can demonstrate that this is not necessary (CBFA, 2005). This implies the development (or more often the purchase) of a monitoring device, which is often a type of software that allows for both monitoring and analysing transactions. This monitoring device needs to be examined for its pertinence on a regular basis. This monitoring system should be installed and provided with detailed and tailor-made criteria, allowing for a consistent check of all transactions passing through the banks' systems. This implies that each bank should develop its own criteria and triggers for alerts, considering their clients, services and products.

After these two lines of supervision have resulted in several alerts, the circular states that the banks should analyse the alerts arising from both systems, 'as soon as possible'. This is a specific task for the compliance or AML officer. Banks are required to employ the necessary means and implement proper procedures to allow for an analysis of these alerts, as this analysis should result in a decision by the bank whether or not to report the alert to the FIU.

Apart from the obligations of the regulator with regard to the detection and reporting of suspicious transactions, banks are also subject to the obligation to train and educate their staff, which should enable them to detect and recognise potentially atypical transactions. Compliance departments are in consequence responsible for training employees in potential money laundering and terrorist financing methods.

These obligations result in rather detailed sets of measures a bank should take, although the criteria for assessing whether a transaction should be seen as atypical or even suspicious remain rather vague. As we will discuss later, both the KYC and the monitoring obligation imply the need (and in a sense the obligation) for making use of services provided by the compliance industry, supporting the implementation of AML measures. The market for AML monitoring software, for example, is relatively large, consisting of not only software providers that allow for the monitoring tool, such as *SAS* or *Norkom*, but also databases that allow for checking persons' identities with several official lists to detect potential relations to terrorist groups or other high-risk individuals. 'World-Check' is one of the many examples. These services and software will probably be utilised further as the obligations imposed by the regulator keep rising. Furthermore, banks will also need to seek advice from professional advisors, such as KPMG or Ernst & Young to support the implementation of procedures and methods for AML activities.

The compliance function

Perspectives on compliance functions in Continental Europe

In Continental Europe, academic research into the compliance function, let alone from a criminological point of view, is rather scarce. Although consultants such as PricewaterhouseCoopers (2002) or Capgemini (2005) have given the compliance function the necessary attention in their surveys, scholars appear to have little interest in this domain. However, occasionally some studies have paid attention to private functions engaged in the battle against money laundering. We discuss two of these studies: a Dutch study, aiming to profile the compliance officer, and research carried out in France, with a more qualitative approach to the compliance function. These recent studies are not only relevant because they are carried out in Belgium's neighbouring countries, but also because of the insight they provide in the field of compliance officers. These studies therefore allow for a meaningful comparison with the Belgian case.

The Dutch Compliance Survey 2007 was carried out in cooperation between Nivra-Nyenrode and Capgemini (Nivra-Nyenrode *et al.*, 2007) and presents a quantitative study of compliance functions in the Netherlands. A questionnaire was sent to compliance officers working for insurance companies (13 per cent of the respondents), trust funds (6.5 per cent), but mainly banks (60 per cent), resulting in sixty-two responses on backgrounds and visions of compliance officers. This survey can be seen as a first attempt to map the domain of compliance, and to gain an insight into the world of compliance professionals. The Dutch compliance officers' profile is characterised by several features: the majority are male, have a university degree in either law or accountancy, and have worked in compliance for more than three years. Many of them have worked in business units within the bank. The survey posed a number of questions regarding risk assessment, compliance competences and the integration of compliance within the organisation, but it would take us too far afield to discuss these subjects here.

In France, Favarel-Garrigues *et al.* (2006) made use of more qualitative methods by interviewing compliance officers on their activities and opinions. The French compliance function has developed mainly within a self-regulatory framework, from a growing concern by the financial sector about potential reputational and other damages resulting from the association with money laundering or terrorist financing, not per se from a regulatory obligation. The authors established that compliance officers often have a police or judicial background. They are hired by banks for their expertise in conducting criminal investigations, for their contacts with their former colleagues, and for their ability to cooperate with the authorities (Favarel-Garrigues *et al.*, 2008). However, more recently a mixture of professional backgrounds of compliance professionals has appeared. Both former policemen or magistrates as well as the banks' own personnel that have been trained to perform AML tasks are employed, resulting in a mixed profile of both public and private working experience. This process has resulted in the establishing of renewed relations between banks and law enforcement, specifically the police: 'information exchange has become a routine procedure and led to the development of joint intelligence "production"' (Favarel-Garrigues *et al.*, 2008). This works both ways, as it also implies that the banks gain access to police information in return. The authors therefore state that close relations between banks and the police have been considered as 'normal' since the 1990s, and the activities of compliance officers have become entangled with the activities of the police. They conclude by stating that one of the reasons compliance officers actually exist within French banks, is exactly their potential to gain access to law enforcement information, in order to protect the bank from 'penal and other harm issues arising out of laundering' (Favarel-Garrigues *et al.*, 2008). The link with the police services allows for a more fluent exchange of information and access to sources of information that would otherwise be out of the banks' reach.

Belgian compliance officers

General backgrounds

The number of professionals working in a compliance (or compliance-related) function in Belgium is unknown, and opinions on this amount vary from 350 to thousands. Respondents state that the number of people working for AML or compliance within their bank varies between one individual compliance officer and 330 FTEs (Full-time Equivalent) performing compliance (related) tasks. The French study mentioned that there are about a thousand compliance experts active in France (Favarel-Garrigues *et al.*, 2008). Although the Dutch 'Association for Compliance Officers' had 436 members officially registered in June 2008,[5] estimations are that there are about four thousand compliance experts active within the financial sector in the Netherlands.[6]

When looking at the educational level of the respondents in the Belgian survey, we observe that to a large extent, compliance officers have a university degree in either economics or law. Most of them have a professional background in the banking sector. Only one of the respondents had a background in law enforcement. These results differ profoundly when compared to the profile resulting from the French study, where a law enforcement background seemed common. One possible explanation for this discrepancy is that in Belgium, compliance officers are to a much lesser extent employed within a law enforcement paradigm, but mainly in an advisory role to the financial institution and its employees in general. This divergence between an advisory and a control function is a subject of discussion, as a compliance officer fulfils both roles (Dasselaar, 2008).

In relation to this discussion the survey examined which characteristics are desirable for a compliance officer. General characteristics of a good compliance officer, according to the respondents, are related to communication skills and reliability, which seems to underline an advisory role. The most mentioned competences are to be communicative, discretion, immunity to stress and integrity. A compliance officer is considered to be a crucial person when it comes to the integrity of a bank and reflects the AML investments by a bank. Therefore, he/she needs to be a strong individual in order to carry out his or her compliance function in an optimal way. A 'weak' compliance officer may lead to weak compliance implementation, with less openness of employees and management as a result.

Contrary to the results in the neighbouring countries in which the diversity of the compliance officers was emphasised, the Belgian compliance sector seems more homogeneous regarding their education and their backgrounds. This can be due to the fact that the Belgian regulator, as we demonstrated earlier, has determined both an early obligation for installing the function (also connected with AML) and a job description that states which tasks a compliance officer should be able to manage. In the Netherlands, for example, the obligation for financial institutions to install a compliance function was already regulated in 1999[7] (although related to insider trading, not money laundering), but a clear job description is still absent.

Profiling the Belgian compliance officer

It soon became clear that there is no standard profile for a compliance officer. There are nonetheless some similarities as to the background of the respondents. As stated, most of them are either economists or lawyers (or both), and have followed several additional courses or training in anti money laundering. Their age ranges from 28 to 63, with an average of 37 years of age, and the majority (70 per cent) are men.

The majority of the respondents are employed by a large-scale, international bank (56 per cent), while the others work for a small bank (26 per cent) or an average-sized bank (15 per cent). The banks are mainly based in Brussels.

Although their most common title is 'compliance officer', there are also compliance coordinators, heads of compliance, (chief) money laundering reporting officers, internal controllers, head legal and compliance, etc. One of the explanations for this diversity is the fact that about half of the respondents are responsible for more than just the compliance task. One may wonder to what extent the combination of different responsibilities (such as the combination of legal advisor, or a senior position on the board, and the task of compliance officer), impacts upon the autonomy and independence of compliance functions. We actually see that compliance officers who combine the compliance responsibilities with other tasks, also have to report to two separate departments or persons. This could conflict with the independence of the compliance function in an organisation and put them in a difficult position, as it implies that 'part-time' compliance officers report to and are judged by a commercial entity regarding their tasks outside the scope of their compliance responsibilities. These functions entail a juggling of a commercial task and an AML task at the same time, which may lead to conflicts of interest. This observation is in line with the research question we brought forward in the introduction.

Organisation of compliance departments in Belgian banks

While in France the compliance function started to emerge within banks in the late 1990s, in Belgium this picture is not so clear. We could derive from the survey that banks started organising compliance departments before it became an obligation. The large, international banks started to set up compliance departments in the late 1980s or early 1990s (although these were by no means exclusively linked to anti money laundering), while the small-scale banks waited until 1997 to introduce a compliance department in their organisation. Some of the respondents state that their bank started implementing a compliance function in 1993–1995, while other banks waited until 2003–2005 to develop a specific compliance function or department. In the main, the large internationally oriented banks started implementing compliance departments before this became an official obligation (2001). By that time, more than half of all Belgian banks in the sample had a compliance department at their disposal.

The internal organisation of compliance functions is not prescribed by the circular of the CBFA. Banks can decide for themselves which structure suits their institution best. This results in different choices by financial institutions: most of them (73 per cent) opted for a centralised approach[8] to compliance, which means that there is a central compliance department (in the head office, often in Brussels), combined with a national compliance policy (69 per cent). This policy regarding compliance implementation varies: sometimes a degree of regional discretion is permitted, and in other cases, there is a compliance policy, specified for each business unit in the institution.

The compliance departments vary in size, related to the size of the bank, ranging from one single compliance officer to seventy-five people working in compliance. The size has an effect on the hierarchy within the bank, but also on the level of responsibility that rests on one person or several persons. This is also reflected in the way in which they have to account for their compliance tasks: most of them make activity reports or have weekly meetings. Next to this day-to-day reporting most of them make annual reports or are assessed by use of certain quality criteria.

The majority of the compliance officers state that they are provided with sufficient powers and means to practise their compliance function and that their independence is guaranteed within the bank. However, this is the majority. One-third of the respondents hold the opinion that they have insufficient powers and means to be able to perform their duties. These respondents may have a difficult time implementing AML actions in their bank, as a shortage of means may lead to a lower level of training, awareness and inadequate monitoring. This partly confirms the actual stressful relationship between commercial goals and compliance with regulation. On the other hand, the majority of the respondents state that their management *accepts* compliance investments, although not all of them state that management also *supports* compliance investments. This is also illustrated by the response to the question 'a very stringent compliance officer will get into trouble with the management', which was judged as 'recognisable' by one-third of all respondents. The balance between commercial and legislative goals apparently still needs to be found in some cases.

Compliance tasks

The circular of the CBFA regarding compliance prescribes several tasks as main responsibilities of the compliance function (CBFA, 2001a). In order to gain insight into the extent to which compliance tasks are actually related to anti money laundering we asked the compliance officers to what extent they perform these tasks on a daily basis. The result was a very diverse picture of task descriptions, leading us to suggest that the compliance function is a flag that covers different cargos.

Most of the respondents state that transaction monitoring is a daily task, together with the screening of clients and keeping up with legislation and regulation. However, we must emphasise the difference between respondents: some of them state that they never screen clients or stay up to date with legislation. On a less frequent basis, they perform tasks like making guidelines for employees, developing procedures and codes of conduct or providing training to personnel. Control functions are also performed on a frequent basis: controlling staff, investigating or reporting breaches of the internal codes, and reporting incidents to external parties are examples. A compliance function is not only a control function. On the contrary, a main part of the compliance officer's task is to give advice. The advisory role is also emphasised in the regulation. This duality may be difficult to separate as employees may find it hard to ask advice from the same person that needs to check their actions and decisions. This could lead to a conflicting position within the organisation. Still, only a minority of the respondents felt that they functioned mainly as the banks' police officer which could imply that they give priority to their advisory role.

AML in practice

What actually happens when a compliance officer suspects that a money laundering attempt has taken place or when funds that have entered the bank may be linked to terrorist financing? The steps that are taken after suspecting a transaction may shed some light on the functioning of the reporting system but also on the considerations that are taken into account when assessing a suspicious transaction. Most of the respondents state that the first thing they will do is to start their own investigation, complemented with performing a thorough screening of the client. Some respondents state that they will report this to the authorities immediately (without any research) or that they will contact a higher placed compliance officer. Only two of them state they will contact the client after receiving such a signal from an employee. Other possible actions they may consider are blocking the transaction if necessary, and contacting the employee in question or his/her office to get more information on the client and the transaction. One of the respondents stated: 'it depends on the type of transaction, but in order to avoid the risk of tip-off, we'll choose to let the transaction proceed – but report it to the authorities afterwards'.

In deciding whether or not to report a 'suspicious' transaction, several criteria are used. The most important criterion for compliance officers to actually make a report to the FIU is the background of the client: his or her precedents or previous suspicious activities. Second, the amount of money involved in the transaction is also important in assessing the suspicious nature of a transaction. When the transaction has crossed borders – international transactions – this may also be a reason to raise suspicion. Two other criteria that are important triggers for reporting are, on the one hand, the fact that similar cases were reported by the FIU to the public prosecutor's office and, on the other hand, when fellow compliance officers advise them to report it. Of less importance is the relationship with the client, or the chance that reports will be taken seriously by the FIU, although opinions vary on the latter: exactly the same number of respondents state that this actually *is* an important decisive factor. Other examples of standards used in assessing the suspicious nature of a transaction can be the relationship between the nature of the transaction and the profile of the client. This can give significant information: when transactions do not fit into the profile the bank has of a client, this is a reason to start asking questions. The same applies to the economic context of the transaction: are there specific reasons why this transaction should take place in Belgium, or through this particular bank? Some compliance officers also mention criteria such as the client's age and the behaviour of the client during his visit to the bank. One of the respondents stated that reporting a suspicious transaction depends on the level of risk a transaction entails with regard to the bank's reputation. This final observation reveals some of the conflicting interests that are at work during assessing suspicious transactions. It may imply that reporting to the FIU functions as an 'umbrella' for banks: when a report is made, a risk is covered. If there is no report, this is a calculated risk. In this sense, reporting suspicious transactions is a form of risk management. A well-considered risk management, as banks do not take lightly reporting their clients to the FIU: half of the respondents stated that the suspicion had to be 'very serious' before they reported it to the FIU. In combination with the fact that a large part of the respondents estimated their reporting rate (the number of reports they make to the FIU per year) as equal to or lower than other banks, we may assume that the reporting of suspicious transactions will only be carried out after the investigation has shown there are profound reasons for suspicion.

Based on these answers, our first conclusion is that reporting suspicious transactions can be seen as a well-considered strategy. Banks and compliance departments play their role in the AML complex, but in the meantime, they are very
well aware of the risks involved and adopt their own strategies.

After sketching this more practical picture of the compliance departments, we
think it is time to make an inventory of the visions of compliance officers regarding legislation and the perceived impact of their battle against money laundering
in general.

The compliance officer's perception of AML legislation

Many of the respondents state that the application of legislation and regulation
has become too complicated compared to the year 2000. They point out that the
current framework around the AML approach in Belgium has its shortcomings.
One example of these shortcomings is the fact that AML legislation not only
remains vague and open to interpretation, but also lacks focus on the most risky
activities (one of the respondents explained this view by giving the example of
the thorough checks on inland PEPs).

A substantial part of the Belgian survey examined the level of and the need
for information exchange between public and private actors. Although Favarel-
Garrigues *et al.* (2008) observed a close cooperation between compliance
officers and police services in France, the Belgian respondents state that they
think there is an absolute lack of information exchange between the police and
financial institutions. This is in spite of the fact that, in general, the banking
sector would welcome more flexible cooperation. About 80 per cent of all
respondents stated that there is a lack of information exchange between
compliance and police services, and a large majority (90 per cent) stated they
were receptive to a more structural form of cooperation with the police services.
Some of them made clear that this lack of cooperation and information exchange
is due to the attitude of police officers. Police services apparently treat banks as
suspects during money laundering investigations, instead of partners in the fight
against money laundering. Based on these results, relations between public and
private need improvement. The fact that the French study on the contrary showed
close cooperation between public and private actors was explained by the
presence of many former policemen in the compliance departments, which
advances an old boys' network between police and compliance.

Another concern of compliance officers is related to their (in)capacity to
exchange information within the banking sector. The Belgian privacy legislation
does not permit any information exchange on individuals within the banking
sector, not even within the same Group.[9] This impedes their daily activities and
respondents state that banks should be able to exchange more information
between themselves.

In their view, both law enforcement and AML implementation would benefit
from information exchange, for several reasons. First of all, individuals engaged
in previous incidents would be exposed at a much earlier stage. This would

avoid the possibility of contracting a potentially criminal client. This would result in a more efficient system and generate an increased preventive effect. Second, compliance officers state that this information exchange will lead to the identification of groups of offenders, cooperating in money laundering schemes – which is not possible now. Today, the bigger picture of all transactions is lacking.

Third, information exchange would prevent 'bank shopping' (offenders approaching one bank after another), as banks would be able to warn each other about clients who perform dubious transactions. This would, to put it more bluntly, result in the ability to blacklist those clients who pose a serious threat to the bank and beyond. Finally, one of the compliance officers stated that, in order to perform their compliance tasks, more information exchange is an absolute necessity: 'information is crucial during investigations and in fighting money laundering and terrorist financing activities. Banks are not police services, and lack law-enforcement data.'

How is the problem of information exchange between banks tackled today? Information is exchanged between banks, but on a non-structured and informal basis, through telephone calls or in meetings, but also via e-mail or by making use of an incident database. Half of the respondents state that upon receiving information from another bank, they will also provide that bank with their data. Most respondents state that they know their compliance colleagues quite well, and they know who to contact if needed. These results are identical to the French study: the compliance sector is a small world, a niche in which people know each other quite well (Favarel-Garrigues *et al.*, 2008).

Bottlenecks in AML and compliance

Finally, Belgian respondents pointed out a lack of feedback within the AML complex is a source of discontent. Neither compliance officers nor financial institutions have a clear view on the outcomes of the reports they make to the FIU. The FIU provides a minimum of feedback to compliance departments, consisting of a list of filed cases every semester, but based on these lists, it is very difficult to determine whether reporting mechanisms are working well or, on the contrary, are below standards. Moreover, without any information from the FIU, banks may find it difficult to decide how to act regarding their relationship with the client. Should the client relationship be broken off or continued? More transparency and communication within the AML chain, allowing for an assessment of their work and for more extensive cooperation between public and private actors, would make compliance and AML activities more efficient, and more importantly, more effective.

Other suggestions the respondents made with regard to improving the functioning of the reporting system on money laundering include permitting access to the national register, signalling suspicious individuals to the banks by the authorities, developing and updating a national politically exposed person's (PEPs) list and a database of the banks, containing individuals of high risk.

Financial institutions may improve their AML investments by introducing employees' compliance with AML regulations as a part of their merit ratings. Other suggestions were exchanging information on methods, policies and procedures used within the banking sector and subsequently benchmarking the best practices on AML.

That reputational risk is actually of great importance in the whole approach to AML by banks, could be derived from the responses to a question on penalties for non-compliant banks. In Belgium, non-compliance in the sense of non-reporting potential money laundering transactions can be punished by the regulator, but also by penal law. The fear of regulatory or penal sanctions is present in the discourse of compliance officers, although it may be that the reputational harm that results from these sanctions outweighs the sanctions themselves.

When asked which punishments are suitable for financial institutions who get involved with money laundering, the answers were rather repressive, though nuanced in proportion to whether the bank was actively or passively involved. Respondents in general stated that severe sanctions should be imposed: fines, penal sanctions, seizing proceeds of money laundering, industrial discipline, blacklisting the financial institution, revoking the licence, etc. Others are more solution-oriented, stating that banks should be forced to undergo an independent audit in order to prevent future faults. One of the respondents stated that reputational harm, for a bank, is the most severe sanction, a private bank depends on clients' trust for its living. 'Reputational damage or loss is a more severe punishment than any administrative sanction.' Some of the respondents therefore refer to 'shaming' sanctions, such as publishing the facts in the press and on websites regularly consulted by the financial sector. Communicating the events to the market is seen as one of the most effective punishments of all.

These attitudes suggest that a shift of mentality has taken place in the financial sector, in which association with money laundering – or terrorist financing – has become condemnable. It also highlights the importance of reputation and reputation protection and the crucial role compliance departments need to play in this respect. We argue that the perceived risk of the costs of being caught plays a crucial role in this respect. Wikström (2006) argues that this can be an 'equally strong or even stronger feared consequence'. The perceived risk of the costs are related to the risk of a public display as an offender, resulting in reputational harm, loss of confidence and loss of clients.

Is AML a private sector task?

Do compliance officers think that they are performing an improper task, that actually is up to the authorities? One of the compliance officers stated that, in Belgium, all the responsibility for AML is unloaded onto the banks. Most of his colleagues agree: 77 per cent think the government saddles the banking sector with governmental tasks. As banks are supposed to investigate any suspicion before reporting these to the FIU, the investments by banks in the AML implementation are rather high. Other respondents state, however, that AML monitoring can only be carried out by banks, as an investigation by the bank is necessary in order to assess the level of suspiciousness. Some of the respondents stress the importance of this possibility to exercise discretion, in order to tailor their decisions to specific situations and circumstances.

Introducing reporting criteria

In relation to this demand for discretion, we need to remark on a change in Belgian AML legislation that took place during this study. In 2007, the legislator decided to introduce a number of indicators the banks should use in trying to assess whether a transaction is linked to organised and serious fiscal fraud. The introduction of these indicators is a political compromise: in the summer of 2007 there was a debate resulting from the 'dematerialisation'[10] of unregistered savings certificates, securities and bonds on 1 January 2008. As many of these savings are not fiscally known, banks accepting these funds could be guilty of cooperating with money laundering in the meaning of article 505 of the penal code which relates to fencing (handling of stolen goods and money laundering).

To prevent this and protect bank employees, a law was accepted that had consequences on two levels.[11] First, article 505 was changed in the sense that only handling the proceeds of 'organised and serious fiscal fraud' in which complex mechanisms of international dimensions are used (as opposed to 'common fiscal fraud') falls within the reach of article 505. Together with this amendment of art 505 of the penal code, a new article was introduced to the AML law of 1993: article 14 quinquies, establishing thirteen indicators for serious and organised fiscal fraud.[12] Banks (and all other reporting institutions) are obliged to use these indicators in assessing the suspicious nature of transactions. However, several weeks after this article 14 quinquies was introduced, a discussion started in Belgium on the compulsory nature of these indicators. The financial sector, the regulator and the FIU first stated that these indicators should be used as *signals* for possible money laundering cases. However, the government gave a different interpretation to this article, stating that the moment *one* indicator is present in a case, banks are obliged to report the case to the FIU. The banking sector did not agree with this interpretation, stating that the indicators were too vague and may be present in many non-suspicious cases. They gave the example of international transactions (indicator nr. 9) or the absence of documentation to justify the bonds or savings (indicator nr. 10). After the official governmental interpretation, the FIU was forced to adopt the same position.

The Belgian government justified the introduction of these specific reporting guidelines by referring to the reporting system of the Netherlands in which the number of reports is much higher than in the Belgian system. However, they apparently failed to notice that the Dutch legislator, after an evaluation of the reporting system, actually decided to abandon the system of objective indicators on money laundering reporting to a large extent. An evaluation of the Dutch system showed that a high number of reports does not automatically result in a higher effectiveness of the system (Regeling indicatoren ongebruikelijke transacties, 2005). It is therefore at least surprising to observe the introduction of measures that were already found to be ineffective in another country.

Anticipating the introduction of these indicators in the Belgian AML system, we asked the compliance officers in our survey for their opinion on using specific guidelines for reporting suspicious transactions. Concerning the introduction of indicators, thirty compliance officers stated that more specific indicators for reporting suspicious transactions would be welcome, while fourteen respondents stated that on the contrary, more discretion was needed in deciding whether to report or not. Those wishing for specific directions for reporting justified their response by stating that this would lead to a more transparent system, identifiable cases of money laundering, more uniformity in reporting suspicions throughout the banking sector, or the limitation of grey areas on suspicious transaction reporting. Some stated that this would lead to more objective decision-making, and a better assessment of risks, as 'now the regulator judges arbitrarily whether we have taken appropriate action or not'. The lack of information provision by the FIU is another justification for wanting more detailed instructions. Assessing whether a transaction is suspicious or not can be difficult, and help and feedback is welcomed in this respect. After all: 'the bank has no police investigative powers, and this is not the role a bank should play'. It seems that the ability to use specific guidelines lightens the responsibility of banks by prescribing when to report or not, which implies that banks are more able to cover and calculate their risks. This is a good example of the impact of the AML system on banks and their decision-making process; as a result of a strict follow-up and ever-expanding rules, banks want to be able to limit their risks by making a sound judgement of cases and by assessing their reporting duty and risks. Now it seems as though they feel the sword of Damocles hanging over their heads every minute. This may lead to a counterproductive interpretation of the reporting system. Nonetheless, when asked directly, almost all respondents state that compliance does not necessarily equate to 'cover your ass'.

The opponents of the introduction of specific indicators for reporting, however, stress the fact that introducing specific instructions can only lead to more formality and may result in automatic reporting without any substantive consideration of the case.

> More specific indicators lead to a rise in reports of clients that may be acting atypically, but are not laundering money. Actual money launderers will know the indicators better than anyone and will make sure they will not apply to them.
>
> (cpl 2b)

They call the indicators 'pointless' and state that they will have no impact whatsoever on the level of actual money laundering. This is an example of the window-dressing characteristics of the system. Having a high number of suspicious transaction reports does not automatically mean the prevention or detection of a large number of money launderers. Introducing measures just to increase the number of reports may only result in a widening of the gap between public and private actors within the AML complex, as the usefulness of the system is increasingly questioned by the private institutions.

Furthermore, compliance officers state that a thorough analysis of cases will always remain necessary. This should be left to the compliance departments, as the knowledge and experience as a result of years of reporting by the compliance sector should be used for interpreting potentially suspicious transactions. This experience is more valuable in assessing transactions than 'any typology or badly defined rule'. 'The compliance officer is best placed to carry out a first investigation and assess "authenticity" of the transaction. Experience shows that criteria are not helpful in this respect. One needs a certain "feeling", which is not supported by criteria' (cpl 9). Indicators are likely to be too general, and will need to be refined for each business line, as money laundering risks can differ according to the business clients are working in. The current process is risk-based, which implies a need for discretion, insight and experience, but also the possibility to make certain decisions. Only half of the respondents thought that the introduction of indicators would result in more *useful* reports to the FIU.

Some compliance officers remark that the introduction of indicators will remove an uncertain factor for commercial employees on the one hand, but will also result in a heavier burden on the commercial structures within the bank. One of the respondents stated that in fact, when such burdens are placed upon the banking sector, the authorities should also provide the sector with the means to enable implementation of these measures.

The introduction of these indicators may be an indication – as our respondents stated above – that the government is still not convinced of the trustworthiness of the banks. But how can the AML chain function when there should be a cooperation, but there is no partnership?

Compliance officers and their opinion on compliance and AML

Investment in compliance can serve several purposes. Not only may it prevent victimisation of the bank, it can also provide a competitive advantage. More than half of the respondents stated that there are ways the sector can cope with dubious practices by other banks. A bank that structurally ignores the rules and regulations on money laundering (for example by accepting clients that other banks refuse), can be handled differently by the banking sector. For example, banks may warn the sector about this specific bank, or will break off any relationship with the bank in question. A minority stated that they would report this bank to the regulator, and seven respondents stated that they would consider leaking this information to the press. These statements not only emphasise the self-cleaning capacity of the banking sector, but also confirm the hypothesis that compliance investments can serve as a competitive tool. However, as we shall discuss later, compliance and AML investments may also result in a weakening of the competitive position.

Compliance as a contribution to the business

Related to our hypothesis on compliance officers as being an ambiguous function within the bank – a non-commercial function within a commercial context – we tried to assess to what extent compliance officers either support the AML goals of AML legislation or whether they comply with this legislation for other reasons. We asked the respondents for their ideas on the positive and negative impacts that compliance may have on the functioning of a financial institution.

One of the most important positive consequences of compliance functions is the protection that compliance offers against reputation risks. Prevention of negative newspaper reports or other reputation damages (such as lawsuits or regulatory fines) are of major importance in assessing the value of compliance departments. Compliance has added greatly to the awareness of these risks by both management and employees and can now be seen as an important way to manage and minimise the risks of a financial institution: 'Today, without compliance, a bank can no longer function.'

The emphasis on risk management and loss prevention also emerges from the weight that is attached to the preservation of integrity; a profound integrity policy will teach banks to focus on the healthy and therefore profitable clients, clients that pose no risks for the bank. As a result, the compliance department contributes to the strategy of the bank as a whole. Furthermore, as one compliance officer remarks, 'organisations that have their risk management settled, will be remunerative and have a positive effect on the outside world'. This image or appearance of a trustworthy and honourable institution is for many respondents an important *raison d'être* for compliance. The image of integrity, which should not only be apparent on the outside, but also perceptible on the inside of the bank, is also important for the banking sector at large. Compliance, as a contribution to reliability and integrity, is therefore a 'good advertisement'.

Other positive elements of the compliance function are the proactive involvement of compliance sections in developing new products, services or marketing activities of banks, but also the guiding and advisory role the compliance departments take up in financial institutions. Compliance has taught financial institutions to find a reconciliation between legislation and entrepreneurship. The merit of the compliance function precisely lies in the ability to transform regulation into new business opportunities, according to one of the respondents.

Furthermore, it is thanks to the efforts of compliance departments that employees are aware of the risks and are taught to handle these risks by respecting the internal and external rules and regulations. The emphasis on compliance in recent years has also resulted in the staff being now well informed, educated and trained in operational control and anti money laundering. In other words, professionalism within financial institutions is enhanced through the introduction of compliance in banks. Only a minority of the respondents mentioned the prevention of cooperation or conspiring with criminal activities as an important consequence of compliance investments.

Compliance as a hindrance to the business

On the other hand, the compliance officers also state that compliance functions can have negative consequences. Although two respondents were convinced of the fact that compliance only has positive outcomes, the majority mentioned a number of drawbacks. For example, compliance '*can slow down the business*', or scare clients off. Entrepreneurial and commercial activities can be hindered as a result of too many rules, formality or bureaucracy and may result in conflicts between compliance and sales functions. The jungle of rules and obligations that has emerged in the last decades makes compliance, according to several respondents, an essentially bureaucratic process, but also a process that may harm the development of commercial activities. It implies a heavy administrative burden and slows down commercial processes and decisions because of the time investment, excessive monitoring and disproportionate reporting for the sake of accountability. All of this has resulted in a certain 'compliance weariness' within banks.

These factors not only hinder short-term profit maximisation, but also in the medium term the implementation of compliance and AML measures leads to reduced profits. After all, AML compliance also entails lower sales figures and reduced turnover, a consequence of having to refuse customers – also the bona fide customers. One respondent nonetheless made the observation that a commercial decision without compliance interference may cost the bank more in the long term.

One of the compliance officers commented on the competitive role of compliance investments, which may have some *adverse* effects: the use of unequal norms or differences in procedural demands between banks can have a negative impact on the position of a bank with a strict compliance policy. Clients will shop around for the least strict bank, where less questions are asked and less checks are carried out, which results in a faster service. These banks will have a competitive advantage in relation to the stricter banks. The only way to tackle this form of unfair competition is to enforce regulations in a serious way. However, this may also have some side effects: the banks' fear of being accused of non-cooperation with AML legislation is high: some of the compliance officers state that the risk of being fined or losing their banking licence has a significant impact.

Compliance efforts may, on the other hand, also have a *positive* outcome: some state that banks can only survive in the market when they have put several compliance procedures in place (which impacts on the competitive position in a positive manner – compliance as good advertisement). Investment in compliance seems to work in both ways: it may serve as an impetus but also as an obstacle for competition. This image is reinforced by the observation that the banking sector makes sure that banks who are known for not complying with regulation or legislation are dealt with one way or the other by the sector.

Making use of the compliance industry

A small part of our survey was dedicated to the services provided by the compliance industry: software, training and advice on AML and compliance. We asked the respondents whether they make use of these services and, if so, which kind of software they prefer.

The result was a very diverse repertory of monitoring software, applied for several goals. The compliance officers report using software for screening black-lists of clients and suppliers (name-matching software, of which World-Check was mentioned most frequently; FircoSoft is also often used), but also transaction monitoring software is used extensively. Examples are Norkom, SAS, Complinet and many others. In most cases, a combination of both kinds of software has been purchased by the bank. Fifteen respondents note that their bank has implemented 'in-house developed software', aimed at monitoring transactions. These banks are often smaller banks, as they are not able to make use of programs supplied by a parent company (in contrast with the large banks, which have software at their disposal through the parent company). But also medium-sized banks may choose to develop their own software, to have a tailor-made program, suitable for their activities. A small minority (four respondents) state that they do not make use of any monitoring software.

In general, the respondents state that they are satisfied with the software they have at their disposal, although some state they would like to have a name-matching program. Another dimension of the compliance industry is the provision of training and education for compliance and AML professionals. Respondents are positive about the supply of training on AML, although one-third state that the supply of training possibilities is insufficient.

The final question related to the services of the compliance industry relates to the employment of expert advice on compliance and AML. These services are actually used: 57 per cent of all respondents state that they hire external advisors (such as KPMG or Deloitte and Touche) occasionally, or on a regular basis. 43 per cent state they have never made use of this service.

These results make clear that the compliance industry actually is a reality in the implementation of AML measures in financial institutions. Most banks make extensive use of the services provided by the compliance industry, which gives us not only an idea of the investments related to the AML system, but also shows how many interests (and thereby profits) are involved. However, the presence of software does not automatically imply a watertight system, moreover, it may serve as an alibi, showing the bank is actually investing in AML and complying with regulation, while it is the effectiveness of the system that needs to be questioned.

Conclusion: the compliance officer between the hammer and the anvil?

The comparison between the French and the Belgian survey was to a large extent fruitful, as the questions were relatively comparable. A short overview of the main differences and similarities that we found in both surveys illustrates how different professional backgrounds can bring about divergent dynamics in the same line of work.

Table 4.1 Comparison compliance function France–Belgium

	France	*Belgium*
Professional background	Law enforcement and banking sector	Mainly banking sector
Educational background	Diverse	University degree in law or economics
Policy on AML	Centralised policy	Centralised policies, or policy by business line
Cooperation with law enforcement	Close cooperation	Lack of cooperation
Information exchange law enforcement	Possible and mutual	Limited and one way street
Compliance sector	Close contacts	Close contacts

We think it is obvious that the emphasis on compliance, AML, customer due diligence and risk assessment has resulted in an increased alertness and expertise within private organisations. Compliance officers often have a university degree, and are trained and skilled in AML issues. The compliance function has become a new and increasing profession, although in Belgium the certification of the compliance function is still under discussion. Notwithstanding the professionalisation of this professional group, an official body or association representing and bringing together compliance officers is still lacking, in contrast with the Netherlands and France, where such associations were established a few years ago.

Based on this compliance and AML expertise, employees are also likely to be more aware of potential dangers regarding the toleration of money laundering, than they were in the 1990s. This implies that the level of protection for the formal economy, at least with regard to entrance to the formal economy provided by the financial institutions – the most regulated sector – has risen. Entering the formal financial system has been made more difficult as a consequence of the efforts of the private sector. Individuals can no longer enter a bank with a suitcase full of cash with no questions being asked.

As half of our respondents stated that compliance remains a battle between commercial interests on the one hand, and rule observance on the other hand, we conclude that the compliance function has an inherent contradictory characteristic. Although the respondents state that compliance as a whole is not limited to a 'cover your ass' policy, the thesis 'the good reputation of the bank still comes first' was unanimously answered with 'yes'. This seems to imply that compliance mainly aims at preventing risks, but particularly reputational and regulatory risks (the risk of getting fined or excluded from operating in the sector), and not per se money laundering risks.

When we asked the compliance officers to list the most important goals of compliance (in their view), the two goals, unanimously endorsed by all respondents, were to prevent the bank from getting involved in criminal activities and the protection of the bank against reputational damage. The three goals that followed were 1) to comply with current rules and legislation (98 per cent); 2) to support the battle against money laundering (94 per cent); and 3) to know the clients' backgrounds (84 per cent). Although it remains important, we can deduct from this that fighting money laundering is not the primary goal of the AML efforts by banks. In this respect, we may ask ourselves to which extent the authorities' policy of fighting money laundering is a goal in itself overlapping but not fully covering the mindset of the financial sector. It is very difficult to assess the extent to which the AML philosophy has pervaded the organisation, and which reasons underlie the implementation of AML measures. The survey results also suggest that compliance officers think that in order to be able to carry out their obligations thoroughly they should be allowed more access to several kinds of information. They state that the obligations imposed by the government to investigate transactions and clients also requires something in return. Now the system leads to a one-way street, demanding investments and a serious input from the private organisations who get very little in return.

Most banks state that without government regulation, the efforts of the banking sector on the prevention of money laundering would not be as high as they are today. According to the majority of compliance respondents, self-regulation by the banking sector would not lead to the same effects. This is in some senses surprising, as most respondents state that investments in anti money laundering serve a primary goal – reputation protection. This raises the question: why would this goal no longer apply when no enforcement is carried out in this respect? Or would reputation no longer be at stake when supervision is no longer present? Or is reputation concerning *money laundering* rather the product of the creation, while in normal circumstances the public would rate the bank's reputation in terms of solvency and efficiency?

5 The anti money laundering complex

A public–private approach of anti money laundering[1]

Introduction

One way of studying the impact of AML legislation on the (formal and informal) economy is by making estimates of its size and subsequent changes to its size. Several researchers have attempted to measure the extent and size of the informal economy – based on, for example, the proceeds of crime or based on gross domestic product (Unger, 2006). However, these calculations remain rather vague and sometimes inconsistent. We therefore consider them as 'attempts' (van Duyne, 2006), as conclusive statistics are lacking: we do not know how much money the informal economy represents, nor do we know what amounts of money cross the borders between illegal-informal-formal economies. This makes measuring the effects of legislation very difficult; we lack both a pre-measurement and a measurement of impact (see Chapter 8 for more details on measuring effectiveness).

By studying the attitudes, relations and interactions of actors engaged in the implementation of AML legislation, we aim to deduce some conclusions with regard to their effectiveness and efficiency. This chapter therefore presents the results of the interviewing phase (2007–2009) with compliance officers of financial institutions (responsible for implementing AML measures), police members, regulators and the financial intelligence unit. Within this phase, a total of thirty-two respondents[2] were asked for their opinions on the feasibility of the battle against money laundering, their practices, challenges and problems, and their views on, and interactions with, the other associates in the AML battle.

First, we will consider how AML legislation is experienced by banks and what consequences AML activities may have for compliance departments. We will do this by studying the ways in which banks position themselves in the AML complex. Second, we will consider the functioning of the complex and flows of information (or lack thereof) within the complex. We will reflect on the extent of the AML duty on commercial organisations and their own interest in implementing AML procedures. The focal point of this chapter, however, is the section in which mutual relations within the AML complex are discussed. In this section, we explain the experiences, opinions and mutual views of the participants in the complex.

Banks and their position in the AML complex

The reporting system in Belgium

The 'risk-based approach' to money laundering, on which 'intelligent reporting' is based, involves a number of problems for the reporting institutions: first of all, they have the difficulty of deciding – based on a limited amount of information – which cases to investigate. Second, they need to decide which of the investigated cases should be reported to the FIU. Adding to these problematic decisions is the fact that banks run the risk of being sanctioned for non-reporting (by the regulator, or by criminal law). The threat of this sanction even increases when banks are internationally active – especially when US regulation is involved. Not only are regulations stricter in the US, but also the sanctions from the US regulator – or ultimately exclusion from the US market or withdrawal of the US licence – can have far-reaching consequences for a financial institution, as history has shown (Shields, 2005).

> The risk is bigger in US regulation. The consequences can also be greater. One specific procedure is the 'look-back', in which the bank is forced to look back at all transactions for a number of years. We process millions of transactions each day, and when they ask to re-examine everything for five years, then you need an army.
>
> (cpl 8)[3]

The solution to this problem would seem to be to report as many 'potentially suspicious cases' as possible, to be on the safe side.

> You're only completely 'cleared' of liability when you've reported the case. But even then, if you investigate and decide not to report ... it's a matter of interpretation. You're safer when you report because normally the bank and its employees will be covered.
>
> (cpl 12a)

However, excessive reporting also involves some dangers. After all, a bank's clients may reproach the bank for unnecessary reporting, leading to potential lawsuits or at least the loss of the client.

> One time a bank was sued for reporting a client and that bank was with its back to the wall. Because you are not allowed to tell the client that you have reported and on the other hand you are summoned by a client and you want to say: I have made a report in good faith, but you are not allowed to say that you have made a report. An impossible position.
>
> (cpl 1)

Second, as we will discuss later, reporting may also expose the bank and its employees to other dangers. This difficult position for the compliance department causes a feeling of being torn between several interests that may surface at the same time. This is why compliance departments and banks look for some input during their decision-making, input from the authorities who – according to the respondents – have obliged them to adopt the position of whistle-blower, which should make deciding on the reliability and benevolence of a client less complicated. As we will see later, this input or feedback from the authorities is – much to the frustration of the banks – rather limited. This makes deciding on what should happen with the client relationship very difficult. As a result of the lack of feedback, banks are left with their own appraisal of the situation and have to decide on either ending or continuing the client relationship. This could result in respectively a commercial loss (and a possible complaint by the client), or, in the latter case, a reprimand by the authorities.

> But after you have reported, we will make an appraisal: will we continue the client relationship or not. Sometimes we explicitly decide to continue, because a client can be monitored intensively when you let him proceed his transactions. If you discontinue the client relationship, a client can go to another bank, or will be alarmed. But still, now and then we are reproached: you have reported to the FIU but why did you not stop the client relationship?
>
> (cpl 12b)

Automatic reporting versus 'intelligent' reporting

Compliance officers have a number of critiques with regard to the feasibility of the current Belgian legal framework. As we will see, these critiques are dual: the lack of concrete rules is perceived both as a hindrance and as room for manoeuvre.

On the one hand, the large majority states that the guidelines are too vague, which results in the fact that the responsibility is placed with the reporting institutions: they have to decide which cases could be potential money laundering ones. It also takes a lot of time, as the lack of concrete rules more or less obliges banks to investigate cases rather thoroughly – in order to decide whether something is 'black' or 'white', a lot of information on the case needs to be gathered and analysed. 'The only aspect is ... that regulation is not clear enough, it leaves too much room for bypassing. We really do not know concretely: this we should report, this we should not report' (cpl 14).

On the other hand, none of the compliance officers openly said they were in favour of automatic reporting to the FIU; they appreciate the room for discretion and are aware of the fact that this also allows them to prevent bona fide clients from being reported for a strange transaction. After all, every report to the FIU may result in the blocking of the clients' accounts, which could have serious consequences for their business.

Taking this into account, the system that was implemented in the US (in which automatic reporting – the duty to report every case above a certain sum of money, for example – takes place) is appealing to some because responsibility for analysing and reporting stays at the level of the government.

> It could be very easy; you design a programme, scan autographs and let it run every night and the FIU will be flooded with 1,500 reports each day. Then we'll hear what they have to say. And when all banks do this, there will be 10,000 reports each day.
>
> (cpl 11a)

On the other hand, the Belgian system is regarded as more useful and functional. First of all, the Belgian FIU 'would never be able to process systematic reporting by the banks. It would be the best way to sabotage them' (cpl 2b). Second, compliance officers consider blindly reporting customers or transactions to the authorities as useless, 'intellectually frustrating' (cpl 6a), which will reduce the quality of the system. Furthermore, it would also imply that banks lose a lot of information on their clients:

> in the current system we need to investigate clients, which implies that we know the client better and we have to decide whether to keep the client or not. In a system of automatic reporting, this knowledge will disappear. It will all disappear (...) maintaining our client-database would become extremely difficult.
>
> (cpl 6b)

Automatically reporting (without previous investigation by the bank) also implies commercial dangers. After all, 'banks are supposed to do business in the first instance' (cpl 6b). Although the current system may cause dilemmas,

> either you report as much as possible in aid of the battle against money laundering, or you report specific cases – therefore too little – and the clients will be pleased but the public prosecutor can tackle you. It's a continuous field of tension for all reporting institutions.
>
> (cpl 1)

The overall impression is that this system is preferred to a process of automatic reporting. Many compliance officers state that they have built an expertise in AML matters and are best placed for carrying out the AML task. After all, even in the case of automatic reporting, compliance officers will still need to investigate cases to prevent harm to their institution: criminal clients can also lead to commercial losses and therefore need to be detected. Furthermore, if an automatic reporting system is introduced, it could be very likely that files that have nothing to do with serious fiscal fraud or money laundering fall into the hands of the authorities. This could be the case for regular fiscal fraud cases. Whether this is still a function for the bank, is up for discussion.

Feasibility of AML legislation for banks

Because of the fact that Belgian AML legislation leaves certain room for interpretation, this forces the banks to investigate cases and clients rather thoroughly. This subjectivity also implies that a significant responsibility rests on the banks in relation to preventing and detecting money laundering. The banks are obliged to install certain measures (training for employees to detect money laundering; transaction monitoring systems that allow for a continuous check on all transactions and set off an alert in case of suspicious activity; Know Your Customer – or identification – and acceptance policies, etc. (Shields, 2005; Levi and Reuter, 2006; Verhage, 2009c)). Needless to say, compliance departments are characterised by a heavy workload: 'The problem is, add ten people to the AML cell and they can all work full-time. Everything we do here, everything that approaches us, is priority and we need to put priorities before priorities' (cpl 12a).

The extent to which banks are able to meet these demands is not only dependent on the willingness of the financial institution. Some of the compliance officers pointed out that there are also practical issues that need to be taken into consideration. 'In an institution like ours, we have several million clients only in Belgium, and over 1,000 branch offices, these offices have thousands of clients, they cannot know all these clients personally. That is impossible' (cpl 9). 'Compliance implies checking, observing all legislation and regulation and examining whether it is executed by everyone within the company. That is impossible, you cannot do that' (cpl 17).

The level of AML compliance also depends on the type of bank involved.

> The level of complexity is also dependent on the clientele: the advantage is that we are a savings bank, aiming for families, with rather simple products, we don't have any dealing rooms ... and on the level of financial instruments we don't give advice but merely provide information.
>
> (cpl 17)

Some compliance officers point out that even when AML is seen as a high priority within a bank and a professional compliance department is trying to implement an AML philosophy, it is not that easy to expect the employees who are working at the desk to always be vigilant and alert.

> When they see a client enter the bank, the first thing they think will not be: ah here a criminal enters the bank, or a money launderer, or a human trafficker ... I don't know whether you've ever been behind a counter, but when fifteen clients are standing in the queue you don't start asking 'sir, what are the origins of these funds'. Furthermore, the people at the counter are often younger colleagues who just started working, they of course don't have the knowledge of that client of colleagues who have worked here for twenty years.
>
> (cpl 9)

On a more general level, there are a number of objections with regard to the AML legislation by compliance employees. These objections mainly relate to the feeling of being a 'whistle-blower', specifically coming from an institution that thrives on its image of trust and trustworthiness towards its clientele.

> We have to carry out the job of the police, the public prosecutor, but we don't have their powers – fortunately – but for me there's a problem with regard to the client relationship based on trust. How can a client be able to trust us when we have to report him in so many circumstances?
>
> (cpl 15)

Some of them emphasise the intrusiveness of the system, affecting privacy and potentially harming the relationship between a bank and its clients.

> … the legislator has implemented a system with reports, behind a client's back, who is by definition not informed. This is a true Stasi situation, going against all healthy principles of law. Unless in this case, when it is carried out with the consent of the government and the public, because of the huge dangerous consequences it may have for the country – organised crime, serious crime.
>
> (cpl 7)

Feedback within the AML complex

Information provision as a one-way street

To a certain extent, the associates within the AML complex need to cooperate and exchange information. Evidently, compliance officers are obliged to provide information to all associates: the FIU (reporting), the police (during investigations) and the regulator (during audits). Information provision is crucial in both the reporting and the investigation phase. However, this information stream only flows in one direction: from the reporting institutions (i.e. the compliance officers) to the authorities. Much to the frustration of the compliance officers, information the other way is very limited, and officers find themselves stuck.

According to the compliance officers, feedback from the regulator or the FIU on reporting activities of banks is completely lacking. Apart from quarterly feedback on dismissed cases and incidental information on convictions (often many years after the initial report was made), formal feedback is absent. Because of the fact that they are bound by a duty of professional confidentiality, the FIU states that it are not in the position to give much information on cases or clients. This results in the FIU functioning as a black box: compliance officers make reports, but do not have a clue what happens with their report after they have sent it. This not only complicates the decision on what to do with a client once he or she has been reported by compliance, or trying to assess whether the reporting duty is carried out in compliance with the expectations of the authorities, it also impedes future reporting.

After all, when compliance departments have no idea of the outcome of their reports, this makes building AML expertise very difficult as they cannot learn from previous cases or reports.

> To refine your system, more feedback would be useful. If only a small percentage of your reports are transmitted to the public prosecutor, you may ask yourself whether you are doing a good job. If ten out of ten are 'bingo', you need to ask yourself whether you should report more cases.
>
> (cpl 16)

Furthermore, the lack of feedback and, more broadly, the lack of provision of official information and typologies, forces compliance officers to rely on the limited official information that is available on money laundering activities in Belgium. The majority of compliance officers state that they base themselves on the annual report of the FIU, in which a number of typologies are also published. However, this information is not very diverse, and not always concentrated on Belgian or smaller-scale banks.

> The only thing we get is an annual report, which also includes typologies. But that is of little use for us, because many of those typologies include international transfers, while we, as a local bank, have hardly any transfers outside Europe. How are we supposed to make an assessment?
>
> (cpl 14)

This annual report is also used for self-assessments by compliance departments to check how they compare to the total of reports. 'I keep track of our reports and the annual report of the FIU. Then I see that, based on these statistics, our reports ought to be of good quality' (cpl 2c).

Compliance officers consider that the lack of transparency has a negative effect on the effectiveness of the AML chain. One of the examples was referred to by a number of respondents and relates to information questions from the FIU. When the FIU asks for information on a client, it will not explain why it has requested this information. However, the compliance officer will be alerted and will try to find out why this client is investigated by the FIU. After all, it is in the interest of the bank to exclude criminal clients from its clientele.

> When the FIU asks us for information on a client, they give us no information on the reasons why they ask for this information. 'It is a question in general.' But we cannot ignore this, because it may lead to a serious file. And if we do not investigate this, we will hear: you have an indication from the FIU and did nothing with it!
>
> (cpl 11b)

This lack of information provision can have other counterproductive effects. In order to cover themselves against potential sanctions, banks may decide to play it safe and report more cases than necessary (defensive reporting). 'Sometimes you hear banks state: it's so vague, we simply report anything' (cpl 14). But this is not the most distressing result. More problematic is the fact that – as the FIU's typologies are used as the main basis for reporting policies – this might hinder the detection of new types of money laundering and result in simply finding the same type of money launderers that were found in earlier years. As the FIU's annual report is based on the reports made by banks and other reporting institutions in previous years, this leads to the AML system continuously repeating itself and confirming earlier 'suspicious activities'. The AML system is a self-fulfilling prophecy: when you look for a specific type of activity, you will find a specific type of activity.

> We ought to be investigating continuously how money launderers work. Now we base our actions on indicators that we read in annual reports of the FIU, common sense, the regulator, seminars ... but these are cases that were discovered. Criminals find new ways. And if you publish indicators in the Staatsblad,[4] then you know that people will pay attention to them and try to avoid them.
>
> (cpl 2b)

The same lack of information provision applies to the content of 'the thirteen indicators'. We described in Chapter 4 how, in 2007, thirteen indicators were introduced in the AML law, for detection of serious and organised fiscal fraud.[5] These indicators are supposed to enhance the reporting of these types of cases.[6] In the survey results, it became clear that compliance officers were rather sceptical. The interviews confirm this picture. Furthermore, they criticise the fact that there is no explanation accompanying these indicators and the FIU does not explain itself further: 'we have asked the FIU, who has written the indicators, to give their definition. But they say: ah no, we have written them on the basis of your reports' (cpl 15).

An urgent plea for feedback

The frustrations regarding the lack of information exchange would not be very significant if the position of the compliance officer (and in general, the bank) were balanced more easily on the tightrope. However, it now seems as though the sword of Damocles continuously hangs over their heads: if they report too few cases, this will result in problems with the authorities, while too many unnecessary reports leads to dissatisfied clients. Accordingly the compliance officers (and specifically those of small banks who have fewer contacts in the sector and less access to the FIU or the regulator) feel left to their own devices. This forces some of them to seek refuge with the large banks who have more means at their disposal and often more international experience in AML, but most importantly, large databases on money laundering cases.

What is atypical? What is a sector that is susceptible for money laundering? Now we have no information on this, everyone needs to figure it out for themselves. So what do we do: we go to the large banks for help, they have more experience, large databases, they will know better than us. And they give us that information. But is that the way to do it?

(cpl 14)

This observation makes it clear that banks are emphasising the need for information, both on reporting in general (typologies) and on their reporting behaviour.

When do we have to report? There has to be a suspicion. But what is a suspicion? It is very subjective. Depending on how a file is presented, a decision may vary between black to white, and that is what is so frustrating: it is not an exact science. And in that respect feedback from the FIU or the public prosecution would be very helpful.

(cpl 6a)

When compliance officers get in touch with the authorities such as the FIU with questions on specific cases or reporting policy in general, the majority say that they are referred to the legislation in question.

The FIU will never tell you: that should be reported or that case should not be reported. They say: it's up to you to make the decision. Very little information is given. They refer to their annual report. The regulator will ask questions during a check, and ask why, but the regulator will always put up their umbrella, they will not help you any further. They will not give you concrete criteria: do it like this ... because ... on that issue, the authorities are of very little help. We try to exchange information between ourselves, but the authorities only provide information through their annual reports.

(cpl 17)

It should not be excessive, but the legislator needs to realise that he has passed on one of his responsibilities to the banks, namely the detection of money launderers. Then we need to have minimal assistance and means.

(cpl 6c)

We must note however, that the level of information provision by the FIU also seems to depend on the scale of the bank. This might be due to the fact that large banks have more regular contacts with the FIU and probably have had more time to build up connections; as a result, large banks are often more satisfied about their contact and information exchange with the FIU compared to smaller banks. Here we must also note the importance of personal relationships: knowing the investigators who are working for the FIU can also be helpful.

We have informal contacts with the FIU and we can ask questions. We don't have precise feedback, apart from the official questions they ask us. But when we invite them, we also ask 'would you like to have more information on...'

(cpl 4)

It has changed. In former years, we would contact the FIU to ask: do you know this client. And they would sometimes answer: yes, probably. But now they say: make a report.

(cpl 7)

All things considered, it may be no surprise that banks develop reporting strategies and policies and base these strategies on how to best protect the interests of the bank. After all, the AML complex is composed of a continuous shirking of responsibilities onto other associates in the complex. Compared to the situation within the banks, where desk employees are answerable to the application of AML rules, we see that responsibility within the whole of the AML complex is also shifted towards the base of the complex.

By providing a limited amount of information, the authorities force the reporting institutions in charge of making reporting decisions to do so based on partial and incomplete information. This results in a system in which everyone puts up his or her umbrella, trying to push accountability towards the others.

It is possible that an inspector from the regulator comes here and says: I would certainly have reported that file. While we say: we will not report, because it fits into the profile of the client. While a third party, in all subjectivity, says: why did you not report this? For us it is incomprehensible that not everyone understands that we have an obligation to perform to the best of one's ability, not to a specific result.

(cpl 6a)

They ask the banks to be gendarmes, and therefore an extension to the Ministry of Finance. But we still do not have the instruments: we have to rely on what the client asks us. And we can ask for documents, but not for everything. We cannot ask for copies of bills or fiscal declarations. Banks would no longer be able to function. There is limited information and it would be helpful to have official information.

(cpl 4)

AML as a task for commercially oriented institutions

Governmental or corporate responsibility?

To what extent is AML implementation a government task? Is this something we can expect from private organisations? Compliance officers state that compliance and AML can be seen as a type of outsourcing by the government. Many of them emphasise that this outsourcing implies that not only the practical execution of the AML system is left to the bank, but that also the responsibility for anti money laundering rests with the financial institution. According to the compliance officers, the government has simply stated: this is now your responsibility. 'In this system, the legislator has passed the responsibility to the society – the banks' (cpl 6a), while most of the police respondents simply take it for granted that the private sector carries out these tasks. Several compliance officers, however, are not convinced of the fact that AML is naturally a task for the private sector and question the range of the requirements that need to be met by the banks. 'We are evolving towards undertaking debt collections for the government' (cpl 7). This quote makes it clear that banks also have doubts about their function within the AML chain and ask themselves how far this should go. Some of the respondents point out that future developments might lead to an even more intrusive monitoring role for banks. Currently, banks are obliged to report only 'serious and organised fiscal fraud' to the FIU. 'Regular' fiscal fraud is excluded from the reporting obligation. However, in 2007, a new bill was proposed, aiming to make fiscal fraud or tax evasion one of the specified crimes under the AML legislation.[7] This led to some reaction in the financial world, as this would imply that banks will be obliged to report any customer they suspect of committing fiscal fraud, which, in Belgium, could mean that 'there will be huge problems for our clients, they will no longer want to come to us' (cpl 6a). This could cause many clients great concern and they would be much less inclined to do business with that specific bank. 'It would be against business. The socialists want the economy to function, but when they block it like this, it doesn't work either' (cpl 6a). And, even so: 'How will we check that? It could have enormous consequences. The AML law should not be abused by adding all kinds of problems that will ultimately overrule the initial issue' (cpl 6b).

These concerns that banks will be mobilised as tax officers indicate the worries banks have in being used for tasks far beyond the range of organised crime control.

Reasons for banks to invest in compliance

In spite of these concerns, banks have shown their willingness to invest in anti money laundering (Harvey, 2007), which leads to the question: what are the incentives for banks to make these investments? On the one hand we observed the reservations of banks regarding the effects of their input in the AML system and the problems and dilemmas they encounter during their reporting activities. On the other hand, it is also clear that banks are making enormous investments in anti money laundering, both at the level of personnel and at the level of technology (mainly software). Considering both of these findings, one could wonder why banks are willing to invest this amount of time and effort in implementing AML legislation and thus investigating clients and cases. We therefore asked the compliance officers what reasons and motives there are for banks to engage in the AML complex. Are the interests for the bank motivated purely by 'loss prevention' and are they – according to economic theory – therefore solely focused on company interests, overruling criminal law objectives (Hoogenboom, 1988b)?

Compliance departments reacted diversely in relation to this question. The first reaction of a few respondents to the question 'what is the goal of compliance?' is 'to fight crime'. This more idealistic point of view, however, only represents a minority of the compliance officers interviewed.

> We try to avoid thinking that we do all of this to avoid penalties or sanctions and keep out of range. We try to think that we do this because it has a value, that's idealism. Maybe that is true. If you would allow dangerous crime to take over your economy then it becomes impossible to deal with society in a healthy way.
>
> (cpl 8)

Some respondents adopted a more general approach and referred to the integrity of the economic system. According to them, it is also in the interest of the bank to fight crime, because financial institutions can only function optimally in a healthy economic climate. 'They take over your economy. What would it be like to be a bank office at the corner of a street in Palermo? Not so simple!' (cpl 8).

Other compliance officers emphasised the need for banks to be profitable in the first place, while supporting legislation took second place. 'Compared to other legislation, AML is special, because for a bank it is purely self-interest to protect yourself from the outside world, secondly it should have a preventive result and thirdly it is an enormous whistle-blower's arrangement' (cpl 3). Some of the compliance officers also referred to the sanctions that are given by the regulator in case of non-compliance. 'I say: if you think compliance is costly, then try it without compliance. Compliance needs to cover two risks: the risk with regard to the regulator and the reputational risk' (cpl 15). Surprisingly, banks most fear the effect on their reputation with regard to other banks. Not many respondents worried about the effect of money laundering scandals on their clients. 'When it's an isolated incident, it's different. But you also need to consider professionalism, the image towards other banks and what image you want to radiate. Do you consider the integrity of banking as important or not' (cpl 16). In this sense, compliance investments serve to enhance the competitive position of a bank, supporting the reliability and professionalism of a bank in relation to other financial institutions.

Taking all the answers together, protection of reputation remains the most mentioned motive for investments in relation to AML. We must note here that, as in any group of respondents, the diversity of compliance officers should be taken into account. Each compliance officer has a personal view on AML and personal motives for carrying out his or her job. In studying the different motives that compliance officers suggested for the fight against money laundering, we can discern several characteristics that may be a prelude to a typology (Micucci,

1998) of compliance officers, reflecting different styles of 'policing the bank': 'the crime fighter', 'the reputation guardian', 'patron of the economy', etc. This is not the place to enter at length into this typology, but the differences in viewpoints are remarkable.

But do money laundering cases lead to reputational damage? It is difficult to translate reputational damage into financial terms. Several compliance officers referred to the ABN AMRO case,[8] in which fines of $80 million were imposed, and that the financial costs of this sanction do not end with paying the fine, but also imply huge investments in compliance personnel and software. Furthermore, the additional reputational damage is said to be much more important than the financial damage. 'We would not like to see our logo worldwide in the press because we have assisted in handling criminal money' (cpl 1). It may also be the case that reputational damage is dependent on both the extent of support given by the bank and the crime that a bank is suspected of. To be caught having supported the financing of terrorism is unlike any other type of crime, and one to which the public reacts excessively. Within the financial sector, every bank is perfectly aware of the level of law abidance by other financial institutions.

> It depends on which level. In Brussels, there used to be an exchange office, a stock broking firm that only performed exchanges. In the financial world they were known for their money laundering activities. And when they got arrested, nobody was surprised. In the world of finance, it is known who is strict and who is not.
>
> (cpl 16)

Earlier research has shown that the level of compliance is not linked to reputation per se. On the contrary, the fines imposed on non-compliant banks seemed to have very little impact on customer perceptions or the image of the bank (Harvey and Lau, 2009). A small-scale analysis of Belgian newspapers during the past fifteen years showed us that very little attention is paid to banks' association with money laundering cases, and if attention is paid, banks are mainly perceived as victims of money laundering rather than as perpetrators. But even when we take this into account, there is still another reputational impact: although the first interpretation of 'reputation' may suggest that this is aimed at protection of reputation vis-à-vis clients, many compliance officers specify that the most important impact lies in 'interbank' reputation protection.

The AML benchmark – finding the centre of the playing field

Another interbank phenomenon that was described in the interviews relates to the level of AML investment. The supply of services, advice, software, training, etc. that is available for AML compliance and other compliance-related issues, is very extensive. Banks have to decide how much they are willing to invest in AML regarding means, people and effort. The workload of compliance departments today also demonstrates the fact that resources are limited.

It's a matter of finding the balance between the means we invest and what we should do as a bank. In the end a bank should also be profitable at the end of the financial year, have equity capital, make profits, that is also part of the deal. Which implies that banks will invest in compliance and AML, but also say: we want or can spend this amount of means.

(cpl 2b)

Because of the fact that banks lack clear guidelines from the regulator or the FIU on the extent of AML investments, they need to look for other criteria. After all, compliance is also costly, specifically because there is no direct return on investment. 'That is added value, which is vague and difficult to quantify and not so easy to justify the investments' (cpl 8).

How do banks decide on the degree of AML investment and how far do they need to go in their investigations? What are the criteria they use in assessing their level of AML compliance? According to the majority of compliance officers, banks look to each other for the assessment of the level of AML investment. This is not a surprise, given the value that is attached to interbank relations.

The domain of AML prescribes that you keep within the pack, it's not interesting to break away from the pack. That may be a minimalistic approach, but who breaks away, pays over the odds on investments – often without obvious added value – that is the drama.

(cpl 8)

The benchmark is what happens in the market. We always attend the compliance forum and there you also hear how others function, which allows you to check if you're doing a good job or not.

(cpl 7)

This makes it clear that banks exchange information on compliance matters, and try to look for a central position: if they make their AML procedures too strict in comparison with other banks, this could scare clients away, but if they are too lenient, they are at risk of a regulatory sanction. 'The system is based on an intelligent duty to report. And every bank wants to be the most intelligent' (cpl 6a). This, in accordance with the remarks made regarding the image banks want to present to other banks, supports the idea of compliance investment as a means of competition.

Information on the level and content of AML investments and procedures is exchanged between banks, within large or smaller groups, on compliance gatherings and in more structural consultation, for example between banks in the same group. Most of the respondents emphasised the need for this information exchange. This need is even stronger as a result of the lack of feedback by the authorities in the complex. After all, interbank information exchange allows for some insight into the functioning of the compliance department in comparison with other banks.

I think that all banks look at each other to see how it's done, how do they interpret this. Many banks think I don't want to be number one but not the last one neither. The middle group moves in a certain direction, which balances one another out.

(cpl 16)

As such, information exchange is helpful for gaining expertise and building knowledge.

Banks are also alert to the need to limit costs, as clients will eventually be charged for these costs. Some compliance officers warn against potential contrary effects:

Then we enter an Adam Smithian analysis: I raise my pricing for risky clients because I have to protect myself from potential risk. If you are very good at assessing the risk of your clients, you have a competitive advantage in relation to your competitors in the market, who cannot assess the risk precisely and therefore need to overprice their fares. I'm purely reasoning Kafkaesque now; it is very absurd, but actually, this is the direction in which we are strolling now.

(cpl 8)

Another way of determining this benchmark is by means of information from the regulator. 'We also ask the regulator how we are positioned within the sector. We check with other banks of the same size how they do it and when these parties confirm our practice, it is ok' (cpl 14). Then again, not all compliance officers have this kind of positive experience with information provision by the regulator: 'I've also asked: how do we compare to other banks? Ah, we don't know. So they will not examine the money laundering reports' (cpl 2a).

The market remains the major benchmark for AML investments, although information from the regulator is important:

There are a number of stakeholders, such as regulators who say: it needs to be stricter, legislation should be stricter and then we state: we also should take account of the fact that a number of money launders find the loopholes. To find the balance is difficult. But that balance will not be found in legislation, the balance is found in the fact that banks keep looking at each other.

(cpl 3)

There are limits to the degree of information exchange. First of all, some of the smaller banks say that they do not know how strict the large banks' AML procedures or policies are. Second, in spite of everything, each bank and each compliance department is responsible for managing its own risks. Even though compliance officers state that AML is not an issue on which there is a direct competitive aspect, every bank chooses its own path and tries to prevent its own losses. 'At the end of the day it's about your own company. And no one will come and save me' (cpl 9). Another restraint in AML cooperation is the fact that it is practically impossible to design a system that suits all banks at the same time: there are different clients, different business lines, different risks to manage, etc. 'There are many different organisations, it's not possible to attune this to each other' (cpl 9). We can therefore conclude that there is an exchange of information between banks regarding the level of AML, but the information that is shared is limited (which could be due to the importance of AML with regard to its impact on the competitive position) and concrete cooperation is difficult.

Mutual relations within the AML complex

Mutual relations within the AML complex are important with regard to the proper functioning of the AML chain and may add to (or downgrade) effectiveness. We therefore asked all respondents – compliance officers, regulators and law enforcement representatives – for their opinions on the interactions between the associates in the AML complex. It soon became clear that some of the respondents still have (reciprocally held) prejudices towards the other parties. The relationship between law enforcement and compliance departments, for example, is not an easy one, partly due to incidents in the past. Compliance officers are, in their daily AML activities, frequently confronted with the regulator, the FIU and the police, which is why these actors are discussed here.

The compliance function: gatekeeper to the AML chain, actor in the AML complex

Eight years after the introduction of the compliance function, after a period of evolution and growth, both the compliance officers themselves and the authorities state that a professional sector has emerged in which banks have invested money, time and effort. Not only has the function of the compliance officer progressed, the attitudes of banks and bank employees have also evolved towards a higher awareness of the risk of non-compliance. Banks now realise that a compliance function is needed. 'In 1996 "compliance" meant: make sure that there are no huge transactions of drug money, but over the last ten years this has grown considerably' (cpl 7). This, however, does not imply that all banks adopt a cooperative or even proactive attitude. In a minority of small financial institutions, the compliance function still needs attention. A very small number of compliance officers are still in the process of struggling for the creation and/or the scope of their position within the bank. 'It is new, from 2001, and needs to grow, continuously evolving, which means that we are up to our necks in work. That is normal for a new function that is very focused within a highly regulated environment' (cpl 2a). Although none of the respondents applied this to their own position, they noted other compliance officers who were having difficulties:

> I can imagine that in some banks it is different; that compliance is just advisory or stands less firm and has to carry out what the board of directors

prescribes. Or that someone writes a policy and that the board of directors says: withdraw that document and write this or that.

(cpl 14)

For some compliance officers this is the case: out of fear for keeping their jobs they will represent certain things differently than in reality.

(cpl 14)

In relation to specific cases or clients, compliance officers sometimes still seem to be confronted with reluctant directors or colleagues, as a result of conflicts between commercial goals and compliance objectives. The difference in attitude towards compliance issues between commercially oriented employees on the one hand and compliance departments on the other hand mainly surfaces in discussions about specific cases. It can be difficult to explain to colleagues why a client relationship should be terminated, while this client is very profitable for the bank.

One of the challenges or dilemmas is to reconcile the commercial aspects and compliance aspects. It is a matter of short, medium or long term policy. Commercial employees mainly think on a short term, while we – as compliance – think on the medium or long term.

(cpl 6c)

Compliance departments see themselves as those who draw the lines and define the boundaries for commercial activities.

People are never satisfied because there are always little rules that are not respected or we ask too much information from the clients, service is not quick enough … etc. This is also the case with the branches who say to us: you always need to authorise everything or more documents and that takes time. Our job is to say what the laws are and how far they can go, while respecting the laws and doing business.

(cpl 4)

On a more general level, however (a non-case specific level), most banks are convinced of the usefulness of compliance, specifically when it comes to protecting the bank's interests. Generally speaking, we can say that banks recognise the importance of the formal creation of a compliance function, responsible for AML implementation. This view is supported by several authorities within the AML complex (the regulator, the FIU and the police):

I would describe it as a very professional sector. It has become one of the core activities of a bank.

(FIU)

I have the impression that banks are imbued with the necessity of the law, and that they report when they have to. They know that if they do not report and we can prove that they should have, it will have consequences for the bank.

(pol 1a)

The regulator

The regulator carries out inspections with regard to the functioning of the compliance department. The inspections by the regulator seem to be mainly aimed at procedures and processes, and are less focused on an in-depth review of the AML system. 'They do ask: do you have a system, how does it work, are there scenarios ... but they have not really concretely...' (cpl 2b). Nonetheless, all banks state that the regulator knows what they are doing and how. Inspections or audits are carried out on a structural basis, and many banks express a need for more feedback on the quality and functioning of their compliance departments. The level and depth of monitoring by the regulator also varies according to the type of financial institution and the associated risk. The regulator has adopted a 'risk based approach' in its evaluations.

The regulator's opinion on how compliance departments currently work is rather positive. After an adjustment period in 2004, everything now seems to be functioning well: there were compliance charters put in place, and banks were well aware of the necessity of compliance. This is also illustrated, according to the regulator, by the fact that Belgian institutions are rarely mentioned with regard to money laundering, in, for example, the US. 'I have the impression that we are rather careful' (REG1). Furthermore, it could well be the case that the largest impact of AML is not so much in detection, but in its preventive activities (such as identity checks, and so on): 'I personally wonder whether it is not the preventive effect that is more important than the cases they [the banks] actually detect' (REG1).

A number of banks say that there is structural and constructive contact with the regulator, while others state that cooperation is limited to audits and the recommendations that follow from these audits. The majority of the compliance officers would welcome more specific information on how they assess the quality of compliance practices by the bank, and support in case of problems. Others wish to have more training or education on compliance matters, as the regulator now only takes up a monitoring role, not an educative role. Compliance departments do express the hope that the regulator will treat them as a discussion partner in the future, for example when new regulation is imminent.

While banks are looking for more contacts, so is the regulator. The regulator emphasises that it is open to more structural consultation with the compliance sector, but that it lacks a contact person for the whole sector. At the moment, it states that it has no overview of how many people are working on compliance and how compliance is organised within the bank. As such, a compliance association would be very helpful to structure consultation between compliance and the authorities, and the regulator is hopeful that periodic – and closer – contact will be the result.

The FIU

With regard to the FIU, we must first note that there is a level of appreciation by compliance officers as to the way it positions itself in the AML chain. Although sometimes referred to as 'an ivory tower', it is precisely this position in the AML chain that enables the FIU to play an independent role, which is reassuring for compliance departments. The FIU performs a filtering function, acting as a barrier between the financial institution and the public prosecutor. This implies that it is 'safer' for banks to report because files do not fall directly into the hands of the police or public prosecutor (and hence, the press). Some compliance officers remark that the reporting system would not function if they were obliged to report directly to the police or public prosecutor. The FIU itself underlines the good relations with the banks in money laundering matters: when information is needed, banks are very willing to provide this. This information flow has been stimulated by the recent introduction of an online reporting system. Financial institutions are responsible for the majority of the reports that the FIU receives, and also qualitatively (as regards the content of the reports) banks represent the best reporting group (CTIF-CFI, 2008).

Although banks are in favour of the filter function of the FIU, there are some critical remarks. Examples of matters broached for improvement are the time the FIU takes to investigate cases and the level of information provision and feedback. Some compliance officers experience very long processing times.

> My experience is that the FIU transmits a file rather quickly to the public prosecutor in the case of files in which other banks have reported or when the client involved is known at the FIU. But sometimes we get a phone call or a fax about a report that we have made a year ago, which has been sent to the prosecutor a few weeks ago. Apparently a number of files take a long time to arrive.
>
> (cpl 1)

There are some explanations for this delay, such as for example, the workload of the FIU:

> the inspectors of the FIU have a mass of files and when there is no indication that a file is urgent, it will end up on the bottom of the pile. And they will be processed at the same pace, which can take a few months.
>
> (pol 1)

Furthermore, when international information gathering is needed and other FIUs need to be contacted, this may also take a long time.

The slow working processes of the FIU are also mentioned by the public prosecutor's office, as in many of the FIU files that reach the public prosecutor's office, there has already been a financial investigation making the FIU report redundant. Furthermore, the police services state that the preventive AML system does not necessarily result in criminal charges, as it is sometimes easier to start from the instant crime than it is to start from money laundering and look for a connection to a crime. 'For the police, this is more successful in terms of results, and the criminal justice method will be therefore be carried out more often' (pol 4).

Relating to feedback to the compliance departments, a considerable concern for compliance departments, the FIU itself points out that its duty of confidentiality does not allow for more information exchange and that that the secrecy of investigation also forbids this. 'It would give a wrong signal if we would say to the banks: we have reported that person. Because an indication does not equal evidence' (FIU). Concerning feedback on the quality of cases, it also signals problems:

> It would give them no information: whether we transmit files to the public prosecutor's office has nothing to do with the quality of the report by the bank, it has everything to do with the results of our own investigation.
>
> (FIU)

This is confirmed by the police services: 'this could lead to blacklists and the principle of "once a criminal, always a criminal", which is not a good development. We don't want to end up in a police state' (pol 1). But we must note here that, while the lack of feedback can be explained by referring to confidentiality, the lack of information provision cannot. When we see this within the framework of the current philosophy within the Belgian police – as one of the police services noted – this method of working is not very productive. After all, the fact that banks need to establish their reporting policy on – basically – their own reports, can be considered more as a type of reactive policing; instead of using the available data and information to gain a better, more profound insight into the phenomenon, based on an analysis of a combination of sources (intelligence-led policing), this same information is recycled.

Although the police and the FIU work closely together, information management by the FIU still needs some work and could be refined. One of the police respondents gave the following example:

> annual reports of the FIU more or less remain in the same framework. When we make suggestions they interpret this as criticism, while other possibilities would give richer information. With the sources they have now, they could be able to retrieve more information.
>
> (pol 4)

Further criticism by the police is mainly aimed at the position of the FIU in the AML system, stating that FIUs are expensive organisations ('with no police skills on investigations whatsoever' (pol 1)) that have grown out of proportion ('creating their own economy' (pol 2)) and hinder a quick flow of files through the system, completely surpassing the goal of the AML chain:

This while the philosophy of the system is based on continuous flow of these reports: you cannot demand from the banks that they report within a certain time span, if you know that from the time you push 'send', a time span develops of not just days, but years. If you want to relate this to preventing abuse of the financial system, there should be a time limit. You cannot oblige the banks to train people, to develop infrastructure, to comply with all kinds of legislation under penalty of whatever ... and then fall into a system in which we have fourteen months to deal with this report. The seriousness and logic is completely missing.

(pol 2)

These issues raise important questions with regard to the effectiveness of the current AML chain. When both police and compliance departments have these kind of reservations towards the operation of the AML chain, this calls for a more in-depth study of the problems related to the execution of AML legislation and the position of the FIU in all this.

The public prosecutor

Direct contact between the public prosecutor's office and compliance departments is very limited, as these contacts often pass through either the FIU or the police. Nevertheless, a number of compliance officers remarked on the manner in which investigations are carried out. A comment that was frequently made, for example, concerns the fact that during investigations by the public prosecutor's office, the suspect is told (in most cases by the police) which bank has made the report. This is not an isolated incident, but was quoted repeatedly by different banks. 'The client came to us and said: you have reported me, I was invited to the public prosecutor's office and before me, on the table, I saw faxes with your bank's letter heading' (cpl 14). Clearly these practices are not very helpful in developing good relations within the AML complex. Not only does this have an effect on the relationship between the bank and the client, it may also result in dangerous situations for bank employees.

I know there are banks where – luckily we have not experienced this until now – the employee had to act as a witness. Those kind of things are not good for a point of sale ... sometimes they are also threatened by clients 'you have refused this transaction' or 'you have reported us to the FIU'.

(cpl 4)

Certain banks have therefore pleaded for the possibility of anonymous reporting, to protect their employees, but also to prevent jeopardising the AML system within their bank. After all, once an employee has been threatened or intimidated after reporting a suspicion, the will to report other cases will disappear. 'If an employee gets into trouble or is hurt because of a report, no employee will ever report a case anymore. And in such circumstances I would not be able to oblige them to report any more either' (cpl 15). And as the financial world is a small world, this news will spread, which could affect the willingness of desk employees within the financial sector. 'In one of the banks where the point of sales was assaulted and the day after, 90 per cent of the offices knew about this' (cpl 4).

The police services, who have practical experience of the functioning of the public prosecutor's office, state that there is a lack of personnel working in the financial crime departments of the public prosecutor. Some illustrate this by referring to the fact that the court in Brussels only accepts three financial files each month. According to the police service, another reason why files are dismissed at the public prosecutor level is the delay in the system: 'a number of magistrates, when the file is too old and there are no Belgian perpetrators, in which the money just passed through Belgium, will dismiss the case' (pol 1).

The police services

Compliance's perception of the police

The most problematic relationship within the AML complex is that between the police services and compliance departments. In some cases relationships with the police are strained, as a result of prior cooperation (or the lack thereof) and difficulties in specific cases. On top of a number of negative experiences, this situation is even more complicated because of traditional prejudices that still exist between both worlds. One of the examples of bad experiences with police investigations is related to the problems described above on informing the client about the 'whistle-blower'. Other points of criticism are mainly related to the attitude of police services, for example during investigations. Compliance officers often feel judged by the police and state that they are treated more like a suspect than as a partner in (anti) money laundering.

> You get the feeling as if you're being a target. The basic assumption is that we're accomplices and that we do everything to enable the launderer. That is just too crazy. And if you see which investments and efforts are made here, and then you still have to justify yourself...
>
> (cpl 12b)

The fact that, even after years of investment in compliance and AML, they are still not treated as partners in the battle against money laundering, but more as the usual suspects, is very frustrating and can lead to a resigned attitude. 'How many banks worldwide are paying for the battle against money laundering? You would be flabbergasted. Then why don't they consider us as equal partners? Because in anti money laundering, there is no competition' (cpl 12a).

The delicate relationship between compliance on the one hand and the police on the other, is illustrated by the compliance respondents who state that they are sometimes doubtful about whether or not to report a case. As stated before, each choice (making a report or not) may have negative consequences for the bank.

Some of the compliance officers feel as if they should be constantly watchful and that both the regulator and the police are stuck in their negative perception of banks in general. This results in heavy workloads as more cases than necessary need to be investigated, to enhance compliance:

> 'We investigate too many cases. But it is very delicate to exclude certain categories of transactions, because if years later it becomes clear that these categories covered a type of crime, the government will return to the bank and say: didn't you see that? (...) And by means of a government and police or judicial services who try to prove their usefulness with regard to society, by throwing it to the media or whatever. 'We have dealt with a bank.' Afterwards, it could well be the case that the bank wins the procedure, but you will never hear that from the media.
>
> (cpl 8)

This tendency of law enforcement officials to present themselves as crime fighters against banks is cited by many compliance officers: 'Just to show you: we are not regarded as an equal partner, we are regarded as accomplices or ... we're responsible for everything that goes wrong. "C'est la banque!"' (cpl 12a).

Next to the perceived negative attitude of police services, the compliance officers' impression of police capability to investigate fraud or money laundering cases is rather pessimistic: the police have too little expertise for complex financial investigations.

> Swift, international payments, sheets on the opening of accounts, history of an account, documents of specific transactions ... often you see that they look flabbergasted, that they do not know the subject. So I hereby plead for specialised departments in the federal police.
>
> (cpl 9)

Many compliance officers still feel that police and compliance still live in completely different worlds, which may result in communication problems: police have little insight into the tasks of compliance officers, while compliance officers on the other hand, sometimes perceive police activity as patronising and even naive.

> I'm going to give you an example. We were invited by the police services for a meeting on terrorist financing. They say to us: you need to check all your non-profit organisations because they are used for terrorist financing. So we look at each other: we have hundreds of thousands of non-profit organisations in our database ... they say that we need to look at certain small amounts of money that are deposited which are transferred abroad. But a youth football team, also a non-profit organisation, also receives small sums of money and may pay for their tournament abroad. How can you check all this?
>
> (cpl 11a)

Obviously, these mutual perceptions are a hindrance to developing constructive working relationships between police and compliance departments. The prevalence of negative perceptions and attitudes towards other associates in the complex – sometimes based on impressions that were developed years and years ago – cannot be adding to the effectiveness or efficiency of the AML chain. It could, for example, result in banks developing strategies to prevent potential sanctions by the regulator or the police, while losing track of the 'real' objectives of the AML implementation. 'We only get hit on the head. And what you do is cover yourself against everything and try to have an audit trail so you can state: this is what we did' (cpl 12a).

Police perceptions of compliance

From a police point of view, however, we hear a different story. Although some police officers do mention the possibility of banks as perpetrators ('cooperation becomes very difficult when someone is implicated as accomplice' (pol 4)), we noticed a relatively high level of appreciation towards compliance and AML activities. The negative attitude towards banks, as described by compliance officers, was not made explicit during conversations with police respondents. On the contrary, in general, the police were relatively positive about the AML efforts by banks, and stated that the attitude of banks has changed tremendously in the past ten years. The police also noted that banks are carrying out their reporting duties very conscientiously, in contrast with other organisations under the AML law.

The overall impression after the interviews is that police services lack a clear idea of what compliance officers actually do and represent, regarding both their expertise on (anti-) money laundering, and the efforts that are made in controlling money laundering. The police are therefore asking for more insight into compliance tasks and their knowledge of the phenomenon of money laundering, to learn from each other's knowledge and tools. 'It's the private sector and specifically banks, institutions that have more means to develop software and other tools ... whereas the police is a little behind concerning equipment' (pol 4). The police are willing to have a more active cooperation with compliance departments, and some have – contrary to the constitution of the current framework – even asked compliance departments to report suspicious activity to them. It seems that the police are asking to receive information on reports earlier than is currently the case. Some compliance officers have pointed out that although the police have requested more information exchange between banks and themselves, they are not inclined to do this, not only because this type of information exchange is not allowed, but also for other reasons:

> the federal police have asked for more interaction, but we cannot do that, for reasons of privacy, but also because of the fact that the Belgium system functions through the FIU. So we make reports to the FIU and not to the police. (...) We notice a sort of competition between the FIU and the police.
>
> (cpl 1)

Other compliance officers welcomed closer cooperation, as it could help protect the bank's interest:

> I really think they do not know which efforts are made to guard that risk as much as possible. Because for me the principal part of our job is to safeguard our bank's name and integrity. We are working very hard with the means available. And we should have many more means, also from the outside world; liaison officers, for example: you might create a relationship based on mutual trust with one or two persons, with whom you can exchange information on a formal basis.
>
> (cpl 11a)

In cases in which there is ad hoc cooperation, the police state that in large banks, compliance departments are well structured and expertly handle anti money laundering. In small banks, cases may sometimes result in problems:

> we once had a case in which we needed to freeze the safe on the day of a police operation. And two days later, we come there with the suspect and the safe is not put under seal, and the bank manager says 'but I know everyone who comes here'.
>
> (pol 1)

Apart from ad hoc cooperation, there are some structural contacts between police and compliance officers, in which information is exchanged. These interactions are dependent on personal contacts between police and banks, sometimes based on years of cooperation in money laundering cases. Within these relationships, some of the compliance officers stated that the police are willing to provide information on an informal basis. 'We sometimes also exchange information with the police, practical information, but of course that is confidential and only by telephone' (cpl 2a). Conversely, others refuse this kind of cooperation and state that there are no contacts with the police services prior to a report to the FIU.

We must note here that our results differ from results among French compliance officers. In one of the very few studies in this area, close cooperation was observed between compliance officers and police services in France (Favarel-Garrigues *et al.*, 2008). The fact that the French study came to contrary conclusions can, in our opinion, be explained by the fact that in France the majority of compliance officers are former police officers, whereas in Belgium compliance officers are mostly economists or lawyers. The Belgian compliance officers are therefore unable to rely on their 'old boys' network'.

Partners or associates?

We can discern a diversity of perceptions on and appreciations of each contributor to the AML battle. Mutual relations within the complex are sometimes difficult because of problematic experiences in the past (such as police-compliance cooperation) or because of lack of transparency (such as the ivory tower mentality of the FIU). Important to note, however, is that some of the difficulties are also caused by a lack of open mindedness with regard to 'other' sectors (public versus private) or a lack of willingness to adopt another viewpoint and try to put themselves in the position of the other parties.

We can divide the remarks that were made into two levels: a level of principle and a practical level. On the level of principle, predominantly the problems regarding feedback, provision of information and the position of the FIU are discussed. These are issues that are partly due to the legislation surrounding AML, although should the FIU have more personnel and more means at its disposal, it would probably be able to provide more (non-case related) information.

On a practical level, relations are more problematic, as these are built on years of frustration and mutual misunderstandings. Most of the contacts within the AML complex take place between compliance and police officers. Compliance departments think in relatively pejorative terms about policing and their know-how, while they experience a deprecating attitude from the police. Banks, as institutions that are burdened with the paradoxical duty to report their own clients, while not having law enforcement as their core business, feel as if they are more sabotaged than supported by other associates in the AML complex. This is particularly galling because in fact, anti money laundering is not something that is needed to protect their purely financial interests. After all, banks are not victimised by money laundering, the government is. The result of detecting money laundering is profitable for governments, who have shifted this duty to the banks. And banks are very aware of these economic forces behind anti money laundering:

> At the time of the introduction of new guidelines, the government predicted a sum of €35 million of proceeds as a result from the higher amount of reports. This makes you wonder: what does the legislator want, what is the goal of an AML cell? Is it about money laundering or something else?
>
> (cpl 6b)

Perhaps it is time that these joint negative perceptions are discussed openly. More transparency between all associates within the AML complex could help transform the current associates into partners and stimulate effectiveness.

Perceptions of the effectiveness of AML efforts by banks

As the views of law enforcement agencies on effectiveness were discussed in the previous section, here we focus on the compliance officers' perceptions of the effects of their own work. A number of compliance officers cast doubts about the actual effectiveness of this system. They wondered whether the AML systems essentially fulfil the goals that were presupposed at the time of the introduction of this system.

In the first place, this is to suppress serious gangsterism. And I think it has an effect, at least in the financial sector: people cannot go anywhere with their money. Drugs, human trafficking, illegal weapons, we will fight this with the greatest enthusiasm. But when we see which types of transactions we also have to investigate ... that has almost nothing to do with those crimes.

(cpl 7)

Besides pointing out the fact that the financial sector was and still is the most targeted sector in terms of AML efforts and demands, some of the compliance officers are aware of their limited ability to detect the sophisticated criminal structures which are in part the goal of the AML legislation.

Of course, banks are capable of seeing things. But you cannot expect a bank to find every money launderer in his database. Because the ones you find are the bad launderers, the bunglers or the amateurs ... The typical cases, everyone spots them. A homeless guy who comes into the office and hands you a sum of money ... everyone has noticed that: 'this is an atypical transaction'. But when it's more sophisticated, it's not so easy.

(cpl 9)

This also emphasises the relativity of the efforts and investments by the financial institutions. While millions of euro are invested in AML activities by banks, there is a chance that the criminal groups that are actually targeted by the AML complex remain largely out of sight. One of the compliance officers stated: 'How many drug dealers have we had as a client? It could happen, and we are very careful, but this much effort for which result?' (cpl 15).

The doubts with regard to the effectiveness of AML within the financial sector do not only relate to the type of crime that is targeted, but also to the (in) ability of the financial sector to exclude money launderers.

As a compliance officer, you might say: at least you protect yourself from the outside world. But when you take all the banks of Belgium and measure the impact, you might conclude that money laundering has shifted to real estate or to offshore countries. Then you have to ask yourself how effective this is. It will only be effective if you forbid all banks to bank.

(cpl 3)

Conclusion

Through the introduction of AML legislation and by making private corporations responsible for the detection and reporting of crime, governments have contributed to the 'multilateralisation' of policing (Bayley and Shearing, 2001). Compliance officers have been forced to take up a role in policing the enterprise and the client, which – contrary to private security – not only suits the purposes of the corporation, but focuses on meeting the wishes of the authorities. Financial and other institutions under the AML law were gradually urged into a framework on anti money laundering, by making governmental problems into corporate problems. After all, when banks do not comply with legislation or regulation, they can be sanctioned by the regulator, their colleague banks and, finally, by their customers. Today, this has resulted in a very uneasy position for compliance officers, in which uncertainty and a continuous awareness of risk prevails. Immobility or at least loss of effectiveness can be the result.

Although this was not initially the objective of the research, we cannot avoid the question of effectiveness. However, none of the respondents were clear about this point, because they have no insight into the results. There are, apart from the views of the respondents, some conclusions we can draw with regard to the functioning of the system that, by its very nature, may affect effectiveness.

Within the AML complex, relations between different parties are constructed in such a way that responsibilities and liabilities are shifted mainly towards the base of the complex. While the government states that the financial sector is the key to the problem, the financial sector points to its compliance officers, and they, on their part, refer to the desk employees. The perception of who is in control and which party is most powerful in convincing others of their ideas, shapes the complex and hence its effectiveness. This deduction can also be made from the statements of compliance officers. They say that, with very little support from the authorities with regard to not only the provision of information that ought to feed into AML tactics and money laundering identification, but also regarding their appraisal of how banks actually fulfil their obligations, looking at relations within the complex, an outsider starts to wonder whether this complex is actually striving to fight crime. A system in which the base of the chain – responsible for the input of the system – is not supplied with information, forcing them to rely on their own information sources, on informal information exchange with other banks, or on annual accounts from their own reports, functions as a self-fulfilling prophecy as institutions are obliged to continuously confirm their own analyses. This might lead to banks using either the wrong criteria for reporting ('defensive reporting'), or those criteria that are most suitable within their commercial setting. All things considered, we cannot then be surprised that banks develop reporting strategies and policies, and base these strategies on how to most favourably protect the interests of the bank. In these contexts, 'blaming the bank' is rather easy.

A number of problematic relationships occur within the AML complex. One of the examples is the position of the FIU towards all other associates. Its role as a black box has pros and cons, but is interpreted by some as a way of providing for its own reason for existence. The FIU becomes a mystic part of the AML chain: you know the input, but not the outcome, nor what happens in between. Another example is the interaction between police and compliance employees, dominated by misunderstandings, negative experiences in the past, and relatively unconstructive attitudes towards each other. Compliance officers also find themselves divided between a law-enforcement role on the one hand and a commercial responsibility on the other. The combination of these conflicting interests and attitudes can make the functioning of a system rather complex.

However, we should not judge the AML system by its cover. Fighting crime is not the only outcome of the complex; the prevention of criminal elements entering the financial system is also a significant concern. The preventative effect of the system is probably obvious, but the problem is that there is no way to prove it (Hoogenboom, 2006). We do not know how many 'criminal entrepreneurs' have turned away from the official financial system and turned towards other channels. Clearly, it may be that there are numerous other methods to launder money, and the number of methods will probably only increase as 'formal' methods become more and more limited. We can only guess that there are certain displacement effects of the AML policy, but we have no insight as to the impact of this policy on the scope of the informal economy. With regard to activity within the informal economy, however, there are some suggestions. Van de Bunt, for example, describes how Hawala banking can be used for the transfer of illicit funds, which may increase as a result of stricter formal economy rules (van de Bunt, 2008). One of the police respondents, for example, signalled the rising popularity of travelling with suitcases of money. Others state that offshore and tax havens constitute important 'nodes' for these kinds of illicit transfers (Brown and Cloke, 2007). The possibilities are numerous. What we do know is that the number of suspicious transaction reports made by banks in Belgium keeps rising steadily (CTIF-CFI, 2008), which might suggest that at least not all criminals have turned their back on the banks.

In conclusion, we should add that the power relations between the actors may result in a system that purely functions as CCTV without the roll of film: it provides a feeling of safety, reassures the public that 'something is being done', while behind the cameras, when we look more closely, we don't know if anybody is watching or whether the camera is aimed at the right places. We do not know what the effects of the system are, or whether the feeling of safety is legitimate.

6 The beauty of grey

The investigation of suspicious transactions[1]

Operational AML is actually real police work. The report to the FIU implies that we discover the unusual, that we are insecure and worried about client behaviour.

(cpl 8)

Introduction

In this chapter, we will focus on an important task within AML and compliance: the detection and subsequent investigation of suspicious transactions. We will discuss the perspective of the compliance officer by focusing on the manner in which 1) transactions or clients are filtered by the system and 2) the investigation of a selection of these cases is carried out. Of course, we are aware of the fact that this kind of information is often confidential and difficult to discuss overtly. Our aim is therefore to make a construction of the system and the processes that are used, by filling in the blanks and reconstructing issues and strategies that are not made explicit during the conversations.

We will describe the phases that a client or transaction passes before the financial institution decides to report a case to the authorities and/or end the client relationship. As many cases remain 'grey' – difficult to assess – as a result of lack of information or lack of insight in the case in itself, we conclude by raising a few questions on the challenges a compliance officer has to cope with.

We have made clear earlier that both the legislator and the regulator remain vague on the subject on when exactly to report and which cases need to be reported. Legislation and regulation also demand an investigative effort from the banks ('report in good faith'). Next to this observation, it can be stated that the current framework leaves relatively much room for discretion. And precisely this discretion forces banks to investigate cases themselves before reporting them to the FIU: they do not want to 'overreport' or 'underreport' (as both may lead to a reputational risk and/or commercial damage) and therefore conclude that a thorough investigation is needed to assess the potential suspicious transactions.

Empirical results: how do you know whether it's 'white' or 'black'?

First line: client identification, acceptance and due diligence – filtering out the 'black'

Financial institutions make use of several strategies to detect atypical activities of either clients or accounts. All the banks that took part in this research project actually have installed a first and a second line for the detection of atypical activity. Compliance officers state that detecting atypical activity is not as easy as it may seem. 'Belgian legislation makes it difficult for us (...) we are supposed to report any atypical activity, but what is atypical? You have to sort that out for yourself' (cpl 1). In general, this quote accentuates the difficulties that compliance officers encounter when they try to develop procedures for AML arrangements. The lack of clarity in legislation and guidelines is emphasised by the fact that the majority of respondents refer to relying on an 'instinct' or 'intuition' in decisions on whether something is suspicious or not.

They emphasise the importance of the first-line detection and prevention of potential money laundering cases. After all, next to reporting, also procedures developed for preventing criminal elements to be accepted by the bank as a client, play an important role in preventing and detecting money laundering. These procedures take place within the first line of the AML practice in financial institutions and entail the client identification, KYC (know your customer) and client acceptance policies.

AML, as some state, starts at the beginning of the client relationship. An AML policy is not only constituted by the investigation and subsequent reporting of suspicious transactions, but actually consists of multiple procedures that are intertwined with the daily activities of every employee. Most of them have followed training on this subject, while software and other procedures are put in place to support these first steps in the AML policy. It is important to note that – even when we only take the first line into consideration – anti money laundering has a huge impact on company systems and internal working procedures.

> It's very important that staff is well trained (...) They are able to see that someone has already deposited the same amount of cash for many times within the last two or three weeks. I would not be able to see this for myself.
> (cpl 13)

The first line is fully based on the cooperation and alertness of employees who are working at the front office and actually meet the clients in person. The front offices are expected to carry out a first check on the clients, to map their background and activities and to ask the right questions when needed. 'They have face to face contact with the client and can signal anything that may seem suspicious, abnormal or that raises questions' (cpl 2a). In this same rationale, they are supposed to ask clients about the origin of the funds they want to deposit, which needs to be substantiated by documents.

> We have been pushing employees to ask for documentary evidence for the origins of cash deposits, which has encountered resistance. Now we notice that branch offices, when we ask for more information, often know what the background is and very often have copied the statement of account of the Fortis bank (especially today).
>
> (cpl 17)

When employees have suspicions, they ought to report these to the compliance department, who will undertake action and, if needed, investigate the client.

Client identification

Client identification is carried out whenever a new client wants to open an account at the bank. Identification is also a continuous process (in most banks an overnight control of all clients is carried out), and can also be carried out in retroaction, such as in 2005, when several Belgian banks were forced to block accounts for those clients who did not provide a copy of their identity card. In 2007, still 200,000 accounts remained blocked (*De Standaard*, 20 November 2007).

In many cases the identity card or passport of the client will simply be photocopied to obtain identity details of the client (name, address, place of birth, date of birth), while in case of corporations (among other documents), a copy of the most recent articles of association or the details of the general board need to be handed over to the bank. By making use of these sources of information, banks are able to identify clients and make a first assessment of the level of suspicion that is needed. All names of (new) clients are also monitored through a comparison with existing lists of persons convicted, suspected of or related to, for example, terrorism or other crimes, or people who have political mandates (PEPs). These blacklists are made available and updated by a number of organisations (such as the EU or OFAC) but there are also a number of private enterprises that provide databases of names and persons on sanction or embargo lists, such as World-Check. These name-matching tools are rather costly, but serve an important objective: preventing the bank from starting (or continuing) a client relationship with people who may pose a high risk to the bank.

> Earlier this year, one of the software providers found during an investigation that the bank of Osama bin Laden was only seven steps away. Well, then you can stop discussing the cost of World-Check, as you've had a positive return on investment for the next ten years.
>
> (cpl 12a)

Still, when it comes to identification and the role of front office employees in this matter, a number of reservations are made by compliance officers. How will an employee know whether the client is telling the truth or whether the documents he provides are real or fake? 'When it concerns a new client, the passport has been copied and they do not see that it is fake, can you blame them? It's an interpretation at a given moment' (cpl 16). The question is: how far should they go and how deep are they supposed to dig?

Know your customer

Know your customer or KYC entails asking the client a number of questions that need to be answered in order to get to know the client, his or her activities, background and family relations, financial status, assets, etc. (Shields, 2005), in order to gain a comprehensive picture (a 'profile') of the client and his or her needs. Starting from a risk-based approach, this should enable banks to have some insight into the client – which is not only needed in relation to AML (banks need to know what is 'normal behaviour' for a client in order to detect 'abnormal' activity) but is also very useful from a commercial perspective. After all, knowing who your client is, what he/she does, what their family situation is and so on, also allows for the provision of a tailor-made service. To know whether your client is married, has children, or not, may determine which services you can offer the client and whether you can approach them to sell insurance policies or mortgages.

> Before we open an account we need to know who we're dealing with: compliance and commerce go hand in hand at that moment. If you don't know if anyone is married or not, how do you know whether you should start talking about prenuptial saving? These things are important for commercial cross-selling; you need to be able to offer the right services.
>
> (cpl 10)

The extent of KYC may differ in relation to the size and activities of the bank: for many banks it is simply impossible to know all their clients personally (large banks may have several million clients and over a thousand offices), while in other banks this is perfectly realistic. In practice, this implies that banks that know their clients personally may have a better view on the circles in which a client moves, his activities, his family, etc., because of the personal contact and the gossip or other information from informal networks that are present in small villages. The focal point of the KYC procedures is to build a profile of each customer by outlining an overall picture of the client's normal activities and connections on the one hand. On the other hand, this profile provides the opportunity to at least get an idea of the degree of the client's trustworthiness, which will determine whether the bank is willing to take its chance with this client.

> We always check whether there is a link with Belgium. When a potential client is not living in Belgium, not working in Belgium, has no income from

Belgium, does not rent any property here, has no company in Belgium, but is born in Rumania and is living in France ... what then is connecting him to us? Is there a justification why they should open an account with us?

(cpl 13)

In this respect, knowing a client's activity also implies being able to estimate whether the amount of cash he offers at the desk fits into his daily routine or not.

We evaluate: when someone comes in with €10,000 in cash and that person owns a total capital of €15,000, and it's a garage owner who deals in second-hand cars ... or a client with a portfolio of €10 million who deposits €10,000, it's a totally different case.

(cpl 16)

Client-acceptance policy

Another mechanism that functions as a filter regarding customers of financial institutions is the client acceptance policy. Financial institutions can decide to reject specific clients. As in the case of a mortgage application, where a client may be refused because of the fact that he or she represents a disproportionate financial risk or may not be able to repay their loans, banks are allowed to reject any client that poses a (non-financial) reputational risk for them. This can also been seen in the view of corporate ethics, which implies not doing business with certain types of corporations. Some banks are rather clear on this issue and follow a strict and limited client acceptance policy, to rule out a number of risks. Still, we must note that this policy varies between banks. One of the respondents gave the following example:

We state: we don't want to come into contact with blood diamonds. Not because we are not allowed to deal with diamond importers. But because we are not able to perform a proper compliance function in those branches: we will not know where those diamonds come from or where the money comes from and therefore are not able to execute our compliance function.

(cpl 10)

This observation also suggests that every decision whether or not to accept a client, funds, or stocks influences the degree of alertness that is needed (after client acceptance) within an institution. After all, a number of risks can be eliminated by simply refusing to engage in commercial relationships with certain clients – the danger and risks are simply averted. One example: 'We have sent out a clear signal to the commercial network: we don't want to serve as a cash deposit for money that was received under the counter. You will find no clients in our bank that solely consist of cash money' (cpl 16). Other banks may decide to allow certain types of clients, but try to closely observe them, to be able to take prompt action whenever something suspicious occurs.

Risk level

After the stages of identification, knowing the customer's background and accept-ance of the client, the financial institution has an overview of the client at its dis-posal. This general image of the client will be used to assess the risk the client represents. In general, every client that is accepted for a client relationship with a financial institution will be allocated a risk level (or 'AML rating'). 'AML has a tre-mendous impact on your corporate systems, it has far-reaching impact: sales manag-ers for example, are obliged to give an AML rating for every client' (cpl 3). Depending on this risk level, the client will be monitored. High-risk clients (when accepted, such as politically exposed persons or PEPs) will be monitored more inten-sively and according to other parameters than 'medium' or 'normal' risk clients. These risk levels are also used to make a prioritisation in the cases that need to be investigated. Risk levels are assigned on the basis of several parameters, such as geographical risk, sector or types of activity of the client, types of products the client is willing to trade, antecedents of the client or his/her network, etc. When a client poses a higher risk, the compliance or AML unit will perform a check on them, to see whether there are any connections to other cases that are known within the bank. Compliance will have to give positive or negative advice on whether or not to con-tinue the client relationship and in the case of a continuing relationship whether the customer due diligence will be enhanced or toned down – based on the risk level.

First line: conclusion

This first line not only helps to detect atypical activity, it also allows for the pre-vention of starting client relationships with clients that may have dubious objec-tives. The first-line model also implies that the responsibility for detection and prevention within the first line is transferred to the lower ranks of the organisa-tion. People working at the front offices have to carry out these tasks. Com-pliance officers admit that this is a very difficult task, specifically for employees who do not have 'compliance' as their only concern, but have to be alert while performing their daily tasks, working with commercial objectives. 'Will the client tell you everything? A real fiddler or money launderer who has a perfect appearance, wearing a suit, driving a nice car … the story may seem plausible' (cpl 16). It might be very difficult for employees to recognise a potential money launderer or money laundering transactions. The chances are that they will expect and look for the ideal typical image of 'the criminal': either a bad guy who looks 'criminal' or a very nervous person, who is afraid to get caught.

> The way to unmask them is at the opening of the account. Someone who has something to hide and has to answer a lot of questions, will become nervous and will not answer; when someone who means well has to answer a lot of questions, he will interpret this as a personal interest in himself as a human being.
>
> (cpl 10)

However, although there well may be such money launderers, this is not the majority and there is a possibility that only the stereotypical cases will be filtered out.

Second-line control

The second line of control is the subsequent filter that should enable the detection of potential money laundering transactions. This filter takes place at the level of the compliance department. This second line implies that a monitoring system should be installed in the bank, constantly checking and investigating all clients' transactions, trying to find atypical transactions, strange patterns, or dubious beneficiaries. The circular of the CBFA (Banking, Finance and Insurance Commission) obliges financial institutions to make use of an automated system, unless banks can make a reasonable case for being able to do this manually (CBFA, 2004).

Monitoring software

All compliance officers in this research state that they make use of (some kind of) software to perform the monitoring of transactions: '400,000 transactions on a daily basis, you cannot succeed in convincing them that you do this manually' (cpl 17). Some of the respondents only have a few years of experience with this automated monitoring system, as they carried out the monitoring manually until recently. Other banks have a complementary system, next to the monitoring software, through which certain transactions (for example large international transactions) will be investigated independent of the results of the monitoring.

The monitoring software determines whether transactions are atypical on the basis of parameters converted into scenarios (if ... then scenarios) that are built in the system. The input for this software – the 'rules' that determine when a transaction is atypical – is on the one hand delivered by the software provider (of which there are many: SAS, Norkom, Erase are some examples), and on the other hand by the bank – as a result of AML expertise within the bank. 'We have made use of the expertise of the company and our own expertise (which cases do we look at, what are recurring cases, what are the triggers) and we have translated that into a number of scenarios' (cpl 7).

The information provided by the FIU and the Financial Action Task Force (FATF) (the typologies) is also used to build scenarios and parameters. This also implies that large, international banks, which can rely on the expertise of many years' standing, may have an advantage regarding know-how of and insight into the money laundering issue and are therefore more able to supply information for the software. There is quasi no input from the FIU or the regulator, on these scenarios, apart from the yearly report or ad hoc feedback, for example during an audit by the regulator. This implies that there is an imbalance between banks regarding the amount of information that can be applied in the software. The scenarios that are applied in the monitoring software are based on several parameters and methods. One of the methods is to compare transactions and features of a client, to 'normal' transactions for that client. Atypical transactions, a large amount of cash transactions, variations in behaviour and other variables are put side by side, taking into account recurrent variations that may be, for example, seasonally related (such as considerable expenses in December, holiday allowances or new year bonuses). These variations may lead to a 'hit' the first time they occur, but they will be saved in the program, which implies that next time a holiday allowance is received by the client, this will not lead to an alert. Comparisons are made over time (for example transactions in May 2007 will be compared to transactions dating from May 2006) in order to detect sudden changes in transaction patterns. 'The most important aspect is: we need to assess what is atypical. In order to do that, you need to know what is typical. Everything that is not ... is de facto suspicious' (cpl 9).

Alerts

The result of these scenarios is a number of alerts that need to be investigated. Each morning, an AML or compliance officer starts his day by checking these alerts and deciding which ones need to be investigated more thoroughly. The number of alerts varies according to the size of the bank, the clientele and the services the bank provides. Based on these differences, the number of alerts can vary between twenty to hundreds of alerts on a daily basis. An important issue regarding these monitoring systems is fine-tuning these programs in such a way that a 'controllable' number of alerts is the result. It therefore also depends on how well the software is fine-tuned and which parameters are processed. By adjusting the parameters, the 'acceptable' number of alerts can be obtained. 'Acceptable' in this respect means the amount of alerts or hits that can realistically be checked by compliance employees. After all, although alerts are often false – some state that 999 out of 1,000 alerts are false – all alerts still need to be checked and someone has to decide whether it is necessary to pay more attention to one or more – which implies an investigation – or to ascertain that an alert was false – which results in 'whitelisting' the client. In the majority of cases, this decision is made on the basis of a risk-based approach: clients or transactions that pose the highest risk will be investigated.

> The number of alerts is higher than you can manage. We follow a logical approach: we look at the client related to the alert, the risk level he represents but also the weighing that the tool gives to a certain alert of a certain amount of money. There are different criteria to prioritise which alert we will investigate.
>
> (cpl 2b)

Not all compliance officers are convinced of the usefulness of these systems.

> The problem is that we have to build scenarios and we get a lot of alerts and we have to check all of them to see if these are legitimate alerts. And people

who really want to launder money, still can: they know that kind of software, they know how ... We need to have this software ... but really ... it's ok to have it, but as for the time it consumes...

(cpl 13)

Furthermore, simply having a software program at your disposal does not automatically mean that you are 'safe' or that your reputation is protected: 'It's a magnificent system, but it is also dangerous. Everything is in there, but if you haven't seen it, you still get blamed for it' (cpl 12b). The degree of usefulness also depends on the way in which the system is fine-tuned and whether the alerts that are generated are of high or low quality.

I can say to our IT department: make sure that the system gives us twenty alerts per day. You can do that! You can put your parameters so high that nothing will come out. And at the end of the day we can say: we have processed 100 per cent of our rules. Good job! But what kind of risk are you taking?

(cpl 12a)

In Belgium, the regulator carries out checks on these systems, although the interviews seem to insinuate that these checks are mainly procedural controls, not indepth tests of the system that was put in place or of the way it is fine-tuned.

Other sources of information that may lead to investigations

Before discussing the investigation process, we need to clarify that the first (alertness by employees) and second (monitoring transactions) line do not give the only input to the investigative process. There are also other sources of information that may give some hints as to which cases or clients need to be looked into more closely: the questions or information requests by the FIU, the appeals from the magistrates, the media, warnings from other financial institutions, etc., may all provide reasons to investigate a client more intensively. Although the banks are usually not informed about the reasons for requests of information by the authorities, an official request of course suggests that something might be seriously wrong.

Deciding on black, grey and white: the investigation process

After all these sources of data (first and second line, informal information and formal requests) have resulted in a number of alerts, the compliance department has decided which cases will be investigated and which will be 'whitelisted', the real investigation process starts. Compliance and AML officers are supposed to investigate those cases that could be most harmful (reputation-wise) or most threatening (in terms of risk, scale or type of crime). How do they carry out these investigations and on the basis of which sources of information?

Sources of information

The different types of input result in a number of alerts that are generated and sent to the AML/compliance officer. These alerts need to be checked. The first actions that are undertaken are: 1) checking the alert (what has caused it: which client and which rule has generated the 'hit'); 2) gathering information on the case through searches on the Internet, and by using databases that provide information on individuals and corporations; and 3) contacting the front office and asking them for more information on this client and the transaction (possibly by asking them to contact the client and make enquiries about the client's activities). These three phases can be summarised as 'information management', through which the compliance department tries to gather as much information as possible on the client, his or her network (e.g. business partners, family or other social networks), activities and history.

> In fact, we try to put together the information of the branch office, the information we have here based on the overviews of the accounts and the information found on the Internet, we see if this adds up and, if necessary, we look for complementary information.
>
> (cpl 5)

All available information may be useful during an investigation. After all, the compliance department should be able to assess whether a client is actually laundering money or whether the suspicion is undeserved. Still, as compliance officers are not granted access to 'official' sources (such as the register of births, deaths and marriages or police information), they are obliged to be somewhat creative regarding the ways in which they collect information. However, although they lack access to the official sources, the financial institutions' own databases also provide for a richness of data on specific clients, their family situation, assets, business partners, economic activity, financial status and financial network (the 'usual' transactions). This information is crucial during AML research, as it is this data that will allow for a first assessment of the transaction, which leads to either an explanation for the activity or makes clear that there is no explanation at all, in which case further investigation is required.

The absence of official data also implies that compliance departments resort to open sources for their data gathering. Open sources, primarily Internet sources (Google), are of main importance for AML investigations. Virtually all compliance departments have access to information databases such as Graydon, Euro DB, Dunn and Bradstreet, business information bureaus that gather all kinds of information on businesses, management structures, board of directors, annual accounts, and so forth. Business information bureaus in general combine several databases on corporations and corporate activity and analyse the available data. Based on this information, such bureaus are able to give a rather detailed picture on customers' or suppliers' financial situation, reliability and solvency. Another type of database that is often mentioned is World-Check, a database combining information on persons and companies for the screening of customers, partners, transactions and employees. According to World-Check, its database covers: 'money launderers, fraudsters, terrorists and sanctioned entities, plus individuals and businesses from over a dozen other categories. It also covers politically exposed persons (PEPs), their family members and potentially high-risk associates worldwide'.[2]

A third source of information is the client him/herself. In many cases, the compliance department will contact the branch office with a view to gathering information on the client. After all, the branch office may know the client personally and will be able to provide more detailed information. When questions remain, the branch office will be asked to contact the client (without telling them that he or she is under investigation on account of money laundering) and get him or her to come up with explanations, more information and possibly documentation that corroborates his or her story.

> Most of the time it takes a few days before we have gathered all the necessary information and are able to pass a judgement. We will not ask the client directly for information that will pass through the branch office. We have to proceed with caution, and that may take a file to drag along for a while.
>
> (cpl 2b)

Front offices are confronted with a difficult task: they have to ask clients questions, questions that sometimes may interfere with personal information, while not being able to explain the reasons why these questions are asked. 'As an employee you have to be creative to find excuses: we have a problem in the procedure, or a document is missing. They are not allowed to tell the client anything, not even when their accounts are blocked' (cpl 6b). Front offices do not only obtain information from the client himself, but can also make use of more informal information channels. Rumours that were overheard by front offices or employees, for example, may also be a relevant source of information, as well as media attention.

Alternative sources of information that can be used by the compliance department are informal contacts with police services or the FIU on the one hand, and informal information exchange with other compliance officers on the other hand. Although the first type of information gathering is relatively exceptional and highly dependent on the size of the bank and personal contacts that were developed between compliance department and law enforcement authorities, the latter is a more widespread phenomenon. This is illustrated by the fact that this is generally accepted by the sector and everyone is willing to talk about this, though emphasising and regretting the informal nature of these contacts.

> One time we had someone at the desk with a lot of money, cash deposits. The branch office calls us because they felt uncomfortable. It soon was clear

that the same client had collected cash from another bank. I immediately contacted the compliance officer from the other bank who said: yes, they have collected that here. And why do clients act like this, because the client does not want the other bank to know that his savings are now going to our bank. The compliance departments, amongst themselves, are perfectly aware of this. Then you cannot believe that people are willing to go outside carrying €200,000.

(cpl 1)

Both types of information exchange, however, seem to remain limited to ad hoc communication, primarily based on personal contacts.

Investigation

After the phase of information gathering, an analysis of this information needs to be made. In some cases, the software that provides the monitoring system is also applicable during investigation. Some software, for example, has the ability to map clusters of transactions, detect networks (clients with similar clusters), outline the beneficiaries of transactions, and so on. This allows for a broad investigation, taking several transactions, persons or corporations into account.

The length of the investigation may vary from one day up until several weeks or even months, all depending on the amount of information that is available. Internal information is used as the primary source, while open source information (a professional search on Google, for example) will be used only as secondary data, for reasons of reliability of the information.

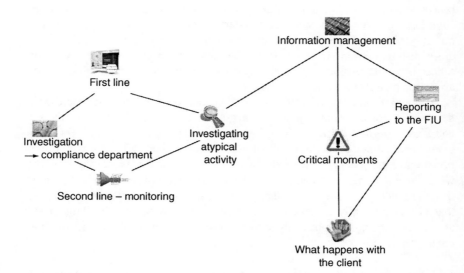

Figure 6.1 AML investigation procedure.

We receive an alert and we have to investigate, to reconcile the information we have on this client with the transaction. If this cannot be reconciled, it becomes an atypical transaction and we have to apply a suspicion of money laundering. First, we will see whether we have all the necessary information on the client, then we will look for informal identification: what do we know of this client, about his activities, the origins of the funds, why is he transferring money abroad, etc. We will approach the branch offices, the commercial employees, what do they see of this client and what could justify this transaction. We will also look at the accounts, the products, we will check statements of account, see if there is some continuity – is this transaction abnormal? We will check the Internet: is this person known in newspapers, does he have a good or bad reputation ...

(cpl 5)

Some compliance officers state that their investigations are rather thorough, others state that they do not have the time nor the means to invest months in one case. As a result, the latter will decide to report cases to the FIU in an earlier phase, compared to those compliance departments that are able to invest a lot of time and effort. The number of staff, the type of software and the amount of money that banks are willing to spend on compliance therefore determines the level of AML investment by the compliance department. Still, apart from the priority that is given to AML and compliance, at the end of the day, a large part of AML remains, irreverently put, guesswork. All of the respondents emphasise that the decision that is made is always based on a personal interpretation of the information that is gathered. 'You're making a puzzle of the client to have an idea of the client and to see whether the transaction that was carried out, fits the profile of the client' (cpl 12a). Several compliance officers refer to using their common sense, or even intuition, when deciding on a case.

When asked for criteria or common denominators in AML files, the respondents give some examples. 'Atypical' turns into 'suspicious' for a number of reasons. Although it is difficult to distil concrete criteria from the several conversations with compliance officers, there are some corresponding principles. First of all, the level of suspicion may depend on the risk level that was allocated to the client. The higher the risk level, the more a compliance officer will be inclined to report the case to the FIU. Second, but this is also related to this risk level, the sector in which a client is active and the countries involved in the transactions may also impact the decision to report or not. Some of the examples that compliance officers give are cases in which transactions cannot be explained in the financial context of a client, when many rapid international transactions are carried out or when persons are linked to 'known perpetrators'. Criteria that may give an indication of the level of 'suspiciousness' are, for example: the age of the client, the economic activity, profession, sector (for example, prostitution, second-hand car dealers, etc.), the amount of money involved, the countries that are involved (for example, African countries, Pakistan, India).

AML files

During and after the investigation, the compliance department makes a report on the investigative actions that were taken, which searches were carried out, what the results of these activities were and which decisions were taken during the investigation.

> The relevant documents, possible pieces of evidence that the client has provided, things we find in external sources, will be printed and put in the file, just like the reflection of the report to the FIU. This is information that is in our database also.
>
> (cpl 2c)

This report is not only useful for internal purposes, it is also a necessary part of the compliance task. After all, in case of a judicial investigation, the compliance department must be able to show which stages were completed during the investigation and why specific decisions were made. The file therefore also serves as a justification and protection to potential complaints afterwards.

> Because, when the federal police knocks on my door and they want to have a go at me, they will say: where is that file. They will accompany me to the cabinet, take the file out of it and I'm not allowed to take anything out of it.
>
> (cpl 12a)

This also implies that not all of the information that was gathered during the investigation will be put in the official file: informal contacts or information exchange will not be written down.

Reporting to the FIU

Once all information sources are analysed and put together and a file has been drawn up, a decision on whether to report or not needs to be made by the compliance department. The procedure for this differs from bank to bank: in large banks, where specific AML officers are employed, the files that arouse (a lot of) suspicion will be discussed in a committee, specifically assembled for this task, on a weekly basis. In other cases, the decision whether or not to report a case to the FIU is taken by the compliance department, whether or not in consultation with the management. In the majority of cases, however, the compliance officer does not decide this by himself, but the decision to report is made in consultation with colleagues.

> Especially when you're in doubt, what should I do with this case, we always have the principle of looking at this with two persons. We will definitely not trifle with reporting. We have the feeling that we report relatively many cases. You don't know, there is no benchmark, you get no information about it, there are FIU statistics but these cover the whole year.
>
> (cpl 17)

In smaller banks, this decision will be made on a more ad hoc basis through consultation and deliberation with (commercial) colleagues. In other cases, the input from the business units is very small to non-existent. To summarize, each bank has developed its own procedures for this.

Follow-up

Instead of reporting directly to the FIU, some compliance officers also choose to follow a case before reporting the client to the FIU. Following up a case/client, based on more strict parameters and criteria (such as for other higher risk clients) may also provide the necessary information:

> it is also possible that we follow certain clients for a while, their transactions, to see what happens in that account. On that basis we can decide whether we'll make a report or not, or we'll keep an eye on him.
>
> (cpl 2c)

This routine is confirmed by other compliance officers, some of whom state that these clients will be entered into a risk database. Being in a risk database, or on a watch list, as a client implies that

> when any branch office wants to execute a transaction for this client, or the client himself or herself wants to make a transaction, we will be informed and we need to give them the go-ahead to execute the transaction.
>
> (cpl 12b)

Which criteria determine whether a report will be made to the FIU? This question is difficult to answer, and most respondents emphasised the diversity of cases and the case-by-case approach that is needed in this field.

> Normally we will take up our responsibility and say: anything that we have not reported can and will be used against us. Will we therefore report more cases? No, we will consider the quality of the case and look at the facts. On the basis of those facts we will report it, or not.
>
> (cpl 11a)

Standards for reporting vary and some banks will go very far in their research before reporting a case to the FIU. What also became clear was the risk assessment that is carried out: in the decision to report the case to the FIU, the reputational hazard also plays an important role. When a case, once discovered, can result in a scandal with important reputational consequences, this will also be a reason to report the case to the FIU. After all, the interest of the bank remains self-protection and damage control.

Number of reports

The yearly report of the FIU in Belgium states that in 2007 (the year preceding the interviews), 4,200 reports were made by banks to the FIU. Banks state that they are processing twenty to hundreds of alerts per day. Both of these observations combined implies that there are probably many 'false' alerts on the one hand, but also indicates the use of a reporting strategy within the banks on the other hand.

Banks are looking for a balance in this respect; some compliance officers say that they keep an eye on the 'average' number of reports that are made by banks (through the yearly report of the FIU). Reporting too much will result in a large number of false alarms and raise questions with clients, but reporting too little implies that the regulator and the FIU will be alarmed and that too many cases can pass through without being noticed. Banks therefore look for a 'modal' position in reporting, allowing them to report precisely enough cases, not too many, nor too little.

> If I understand the FIU correctly, they want us to report immediately in case of any doubts. We are not supposed to perform a due diligence. That, however, is not how we work. Before we make a report, it is a very serious case. But, if we want to, we can make over a thousand reports a day. If we do that, we will laugh and they won't.
>
> (cpl 15)

This does not imply that compliance officers are 'counting cases' and stop reporting after their limit has been reached, but it does suggest that remaining close to an assumed average is the most comfortable one. One of the explanations for this attitude is the lack of official feedback (in the case of the FIU this is due to an enhanced confidentiality), which results in the search for other benchmarks, of which the number of reports by other banks is just one example.

Reasons for hesitance in reporting

There are several reasons why banks may hesitate to report a client, which also explains why banks are investing that much time and effort in investigating cases and clients. After all, not only non-reporting of cases may lead to reputational damage. Reporting a client can also imply a reputational risk for the bank, apart from the fact whether the report was made in good faith or not.

> The FIU says: when you have a suspicion, when you're not sure, you make a report, as they are the filter in the whole process. All the same, in some cases we establish that after we have reported a client, the FIU freezes the account and reports the case to the public prosecutor ... who decides to drop the case after a few months. Then one of the problems is: the client often knows who has reported him: either he has an account with only one bank,

which makes it clear, or there's a leak in the investigation. And at that moment, it becomes our problem. The government has stated: we have done our job, while the client says: you have wrongfully reported me. The client then knows. And that is one of the bottlenecks of the system, because then it is our problem.

(cpl 2b)

This means that banks also become vulnerable when cases are reported, as their reputation may be harmed.

Lawyers for example are difficult clients because they know the law very well and they know how far they can go and how far we can go. It amuses them to challenge us a bit. And sometimes we risk having problems regarding reputation because the client may complain and go to the ombudsman.

(cpl 4)

This vulnerability, however, is not only linked to reputation, also in other aspects can reporting result in liability and vulnerability: several banks indicate that their employees have been threatened by (former) clients who knew that they were reported by the bank in question.

There have been threats. Clients or former client who came to branch offices and said: I know your address and I will come by. That has happened, and creates a lot of fear, because this news travels fast.

(cpl 6b)

A number of times our bank employees have actually been threatened. The day after he was released, the suspect goes to the branch office and make threats like: I will find you, I will destroy your children...

(cpl 9)

These threats have been mentioned by several compliance officers, and is a very problematic phenomenon. After all, when employees are afraid and intimidated, the willingness to report will decline. It is difficult to assess how many of these examples there are, but in theory one case suffices to frighten employees. The world of financial institutions is a relatively small one, in which this kind of news travels fast.

In view of these phenomena described above, banks have an even higher interest in making a realistic assessment of the seriousness of the case and the criminal intentions of the client. In order to avoid further risk, the bank will not be inclined to report too many cases. A consideration of the pros and cons, with caution, is needed. In this respect the lack of information may well be an extra impediment and make the decision whether a case is criminal case or not even more difficult.

Not only is there a doubt about the origins of the funds and about the facts, there's also doubt about the interpretation and definition of these facts. It's not our job to define crimes, but even so we have to do that due diligence.

(cpl 15)

The relative lack of input from the FIU, regulator and legislation makes it difficult for banks to decide when the report – that they do not want to send unless it is of vital necessity – should be made or not. Therefore, it is important to look for that benchmark – as described in the preceding section – that indicates how many reports on average are made by banks each year, in order to position themselves in the medium range. In my view, this can be explained as a reporting strategy, developed as a result of the current straitjacket in which banks (and other reporting institutions) are forced.

What may be the outcome for the client?

What became clear during the interviews was that the reporting of a case to the FIU does not have a direct connection with the question whether a client relationship will be ended. Both decisions can be made separately. This is partly the result of the absolute absence of feedback by the FIU. Banks are not informed about the outcome of their reports to the FIU, which implies that they have to decide for themselves what to do with the client they have just reported. This is another reason why compliance departments are 'forced' to investigate a case rather thoroughly: they need to be able to assess the level of risk the client represents, in order to judge the necessity of ending the relationship.

This means that it can be perfectly possible that a client is reported, but still retains his or her accounts with the bank. Terminating a client relationship can be a major business dilemma, depending on the type of client and the assets he or she represents.

Respondents state that from time to time, this may lead to discussions between commercial and compliance employees.

When it concerns a very remunerative customer that has to leave, business will try to convince us to adjust our advice. The higher in the organisation, the sooner one will say: reject. Persons who have direct contact with the client, will always want to defend them and I understand that, that they don't want to lose the client immediately. For us this is easier: out.

(cpl 9)

Ending the client relationship

In some cases, when the case is very clearly linked to criminal activities ('when it's black') the client relationship will be discontinued. The reputational risk in these cases is very clear.

We will not report everything, of course, and we also go a few steps further in the investigation to decide on the consequences for the client. Will we keep them or will we end the client relationship. This only happens in cases ... when we really ... When it's black. There's white, black, and the beauty of grey. And in cases of the beauty of grey, we really need to be watchful. We're only a bank, not a police service.

(cpl 12b)

In other cases, the reputational risk is not that clear. As we discussed above, there are many cases in which reputational damage may be the result anyhow, no matter which choice is made: it works both ways. When there is no report and the client relationship is continued, but the authorities state that there should have been a report, this may lead to a judicial claim. On the other hand, when a report is made, resulting in the blocking of the accounts of the client, but the file is dismissed by the authorities, this may also lead to a claim – from the client. In practice, this may result in the compliance department choosing the lesser of two evils. 'The reputational risk is certainly the sword of Damocles' (cpl 13).

Ending the client relationship in case of dubious activities depends on the policy of the bank. Some banks refuse all clients that may have some connotation with ambiguous affairs, while others make a calculation of the risk that this client poses versus the income the client represents. This is highly dependent on the type of bank and the policies in this field. Another dimension in these types of decision-making is the connection with the US, which also results in different attitudes and risk assessments. US regulation is more strict, and a sanction by the US regulator may have serious consequences for banks. This is an important factor in the cost-benefit calculation. Other banks say that they will only terminate the client relationship when the case is patently obvious.

We have become very careful in this respect. I now take the stance that it has to be black. 100 per cent certain black. This implies that we have been confirmed that it actually is black, though we cannot use this confirmation. But it's black. Then the next step is to see whether we actually can get rid of the client.

(cpl 12b)

Continuing the client relationship, but ...

In those cases, when the bank decides that there is not enough information to end the client relationship, this relationship will be continued, even though a report has been sent to the FIU. This does not imply that the client can simply go his own way. The client will be followed up to make sure that when he carries out any future 'suspicious' activities, this will be detected as soon as possible.

When it's black, we will end the relationship. But the grey is not so obvious. We will not let them go loose, we will take one step further and put them in a risk database (...) this is a type of permanent control.

(cpl 12b)

This decision can also be seen in the view of reputation protection.

Although this was not stated that clearly, and the attitude towards this varies largely on the type of bank in question, the main philosophy was that the client relationship will not be ended unless something was clearly very wrong with the client. In several interviews the compliance officers said: yes, we 'once' ended an account, or 'in some cases we end the account', but the overall impression was that this will be the last resort for a bank, mainly because of evident financial interests. In cases where a client has a mortgage or credit, the bank will have to take the loss on these accounts. In some cases, the account is not that profitable (specifically when it concerns a client who mainly transfers money around the world through several accounts, or in the case of 'dormant accounts') and the interest of the bank is not that large. These kinds of relationships can be stopped without any loss of income, which means that there is no commercial dilemma.

Problems and challenges for compliance officers: the grey area of risk assessment

Grey cases

The most important challenge for compliance officers is when cases – after thorough investigation – remain a grey area. The obvious cases (the stereotypical ones) are easy: they will be reported and the client relationship will be ended. When cases remain a grey area, in which there is no certainty about the criminal intentions of the client, the decision is much more difficult, specifically because each decision (either way) may result in reputational harm. The lack of input and information from the authorities plays an important role in this respect. The compliance department, and at large the bank, is more or less left to one's own devices. The compliance officer who is working with limited information and very little certainty, needs to assess the level of risk in a case. As such, he may find himself stuck between preventing harm to the financial institution, protecting his own liability as well as commercial interests and may not be able to predict the outcome of either reporting or not reporting, as both may be harmful.

> We have to be able to prove that we have done our job. But how will a judge react in case of a problem? You may never know. Maybe, for a judge, simply the fact that the money comes from Luxembourg, is sufficient to be suspicious. But that's for the judge to decide, and we will not know this for another few years, when something goes wrong.
>
> (cpl 15)

In short, a compliance officer may feel straitjacketed.

Fortis alerts

Second, the credit crunch has highlighted the absurdity of the system, loading all responsibility for reporting onto the private sector. Some of the interviews were carried out in September and October 2008, in the middle of financially turbulent times. This gave a new outlook on the AML issue, as the problems related to (among others) the Fortis bank, have led to new kinds of AML obstacles. As one of the indicators for potential money launderers is the occurrence of many and/ or high value cash deposits, the credit crisis has led to a number of alerts as a result of this indicator. After all, as a result of the turbulent bank climate, many panicking clients were withdrawing their money from their accounts at Fortis or Dexia, and depositing these funds in the accounts of more 'reliable' banks. A number of 'cash alerts' was the result. How are compliance departments supposed to cope with these alerts and what does this mean for the investigation of other, potentially criminal, cash deposits? How can they tell the difference between them, especially when they have no authority to keep the evidence of withdrawal with them which implies that the client can go to every bank with the same Fortis voucher (including those who have less noble intentions)? Does this mean that the credit crunch leads to massive opportunities for money laundering? 'We mainly have families as clients, someone that transfers more than a few €100,000, is exceptional. Apart from the last few weeks [*smiles*]. But normally, that is exceptional' (cpl 17).

Information and feedback

A third challenge is the lack of information. On the one hand, little information is provided by the authorities; on the other hand, compliance departments are not granted access to official data. All compliance officers complain about the absence of feedback from the authorities, both after a specific case and regarding the input for their systems and scenarios. Hence compliance departments are forced to use second-hand or general information, such as the annual report of the FIU. This, however, is based on the reports of the reporting institutions. This means that the compliance departments actually base their systems on the results of their own reports (or of sister institutes) and thereby confirm their own typologies and scenarios. Or, to put it more bluntly, the AML system as a self-fulfilling prophecy.

> There are no definitions. What a 'shell company' is, is not defined. Or what is an offshore area, or a financial haven. There are absolutely no definitions. We have asked the FIU, as they have prepared these indicators, but they say: we have written the indicators on the basis of your reports. So ... we are actually doing the job of the judicial police?
>
> (cpl 15)

This may result in the fact that compliance departments keep focusing on the investigation of the 'usual suspects': stereotypical cases based on previously identified stereotypes. This worrying observation is not only for the Belgian case; Levi also noted this several years ago with regard to the US reporting of suspicious transactions (Levi, 2002). If this remains the case, an opportunity for building expert knowledge on money laundering methods has been missed.

The burden on front office employees

Another problem that was raised by several compliance departments relates to the protection of employees in both a physical and a more general sense. The employees are burdened with the responsibility for detecting, knowing and reporting suspicious activities, and can also be held responsible in cases of non-detection. This implies the shift of the burden of the AML legislation towards lower ranks of the financial institution, more specifically to those working at the desks, physically meeting the clients. Apart from the responsibility that compliance officers carry with regard to AML, these employees also carry the weight of AML. The AML system as it is designed today creates a need for self-protection and results in shirking one's responsibility to others, either in the same organisation or in other institutions. Second, the reports on the threats from clients that employees already have received also need more attention. Some respondents signalled the need for protection and anonymous reporting in AML cases. After all, when employees are vigilant and report clients in case of suspicious activity, their name can be in the criminal file. In some cases, this has led to problematic situations: when the client is granted access to his court file, he also is able to identify who has reported him, which is not only the compliance officer, but sometimes also the desk employee. Some compliance officers also signal that police officers may sometimes use names of compliance staff or the name of the bank during interrogations, in order to pressurise the suspect. As a result, there have been accounts of threats of front office employees by suspects who were released. These are important issues, as these kinds of incidents may have a huge impact on the willingness to report. It is therefore in the interest of the authorities to make sure that the chances of such leaks in information are minimised.

Risk management

Finally, the risk that accompanies AML activities or more concretely the risk of being accused of money laundering as a financial institution, combined with the (administrative) sanction, reputational damage and potential commercial loss, is the focal point of the compliance officers' usual discourse. Every compliance officer knows that money laundering can never be ruled out completely. AML is a matter of risk management, trying to prevent the largest risks while hoping to see the smaller risks also. The most important task is therefore to show the regulator and the judiciary that the compliance job was well done, irrespective of the fact whether a money launderer was caught or not. Many of the procedures are designed for this goal: to be able to cover yourself against possible allegations of assistance in money laundering. One of the examples is the monitoring software, that can be fine-tuned until the right number of alerts is the result. This self-protection reflex is not strange, seen from the point of view of a commercial financial institution. It does not mean that banks are not trying to prevent money laundering, on the contrary. It does, however, make something clear about the atmosphere surrounding the battle against money laundering, and the question is whether it is an effective starting point.

The only thing you can do is write a sound policy, communicate it and try to prevent as much as possible, monitor, but you can never be 100 per cent certain that you will not be sanctioned for laundering money, that is impossible. You can only try to prevent it to the largest extent possible, make reports of high quality and prove the court that we are actually doing our job. That's the risk of working in a compliance function.

(cpl 12b)

Conclusion: walking the tightrope across a maze of risks

Risk calculation

The compliance departments are balancing risks and interests on different levels. The trick is to find precisely the appropriate level of risk, in combination with the controllability of AML efforts: the right number of alerts, an accurate number of reports and a correct way of dealing with clients, irrespective of the reporting. The uncertainty for compliance officers is: how much is enough and what is needed to be 'covered'? We can identify the use of an explicit risk discourse during the conversations with compliance officers. During their tasks, there is a continuous search for security, and constant efforts to channel those dangers that may ultimately lead to losses (Ericson and Haggerty, 2002). On the other hand, there is a tendency to focus, not on obtaining something good (preventing money laundering, catching criminals), but on preventing something bad (reputation damage, sanctions, financial loss). This implies that financial institutions and their compliance officers in their own risk-oriented environment mainly work from a negative or defensive impulse (Beck, 1992), weighing all costs and benefits, instead of adapting a more assertive attitude, which could possibly lead to more results with regard to crime prevention. In addition, the current AML system promotes this defensive attitude by placing reporting institutions in a very difficult and ambiguous position.

Holding on to discretion

Although the lack of certainty in reporting cases leads to certain feelings of discomfort, this does not imply that compliance officers are pleading for a system of objective reporting; given the current circumstances this would not resolve their problems on how what to do with a client's account or how to deal with a client after reporting. Objective or automatic reporting would also imply that they would have no insight whatsoever in their own clientele, something that has already proven to be very useful and valuable. Furthermore, they state that the compliance sector has developed an expertise on AML and is best suited to carry out the investigations, simply because it has access to internal information that allows it to create a clear picture of the client's transaction behaviour. The room for discretion that is now granted to compliance officers therefore also carries possibilities and potential. On the other hand, it also implies a larger vulnerability for the banking sector, as they state themselves: 'We are balancing on a very tight rope' (cpl 12b). It is very difficult to assess whether they have done a good job or not as a result of a lack of information. Feedback from the FIU or the other authorities would be – to say the least – a very useful instrument in this respect. We must note that this is not a Belgian problem: other authors have referred to the lack of feedback by the authorities, hindering information exchange and, more importantly, development of AML expertise (Levi and Reuter, 2006; Harvey, 2007). In a recent study, the Netherlands Court of Audit also established the lack of feedback by the FIU, although this is obliged by law. One of the recommendations of this report was precisely related to the provision of feedback by the FIU to the banks to enable the latter to make more profound risk analyses (Algemene Rekenkamer, 2008).

Benchmark

Another issue on a more general level is the benchmark for the level of AML compliance and investments. Some compliance officers have stated that banks try to place themselves in the middle range of compliance level and investment, trying not to be at the top, nor at the bottom. But where is 'the middle'? Who decides on the benchmarks? The benchmark may vary according to the investments that financial institutions are willing to make in AML compliance, which is often related to the level of activity of the regulator and the FIU or after a scandal has occurred. Levi notes that the same observation can be made on an international level, leading to the creation of an 'unlevel playing field' (Levi, 2002). In one of the banks, for example, impressive investments were made in compliance departments and programmes after the regulator (in this case the US regulator) had sanctioned the bank for non-compliance on AML issues. These sanctions have an important impact, not only on the bank in question, but also on the sector at large. After all, these massive investments by one of the banks raise the benchmark for the whole sector. One of the most decisive factors for the level of the benchmark is therefore the activity of the regulator and the subsequent response by the bank. Another influence in this respect is reputational damage in relation to a specific case, which also may lead to higher AML investments and elevates the benchmark.

Another benchmark does not relate to the level of AML compliance in a general sense, but is associated with the intensity of the monitoring and checking within the bank: the criteria and parameters that are used during monitoring. The interviews make clear that there is a difference in the level of information that banks have at their disposal: international banks are able to use information and expertise that was built up on an international level, due to a larger variety of cases, which implies that they have an advantage in relation to local banks. This implies that there are differences in knowledge and strength of parameters, which may lead to an imbalance between banks with regard to know-how and expertise. This is something that needs to be taken into account when thinking about levelling the playing field on AML.

Pygmalion

The role of private organisations within the battle against money laundering is crucial: without reports from the reporting institutions there is no input in the AML chain. The authorities have expressly chosen for a responsibilisation of the private sector, which is not a new phenomenon (Garland, 2001). The deresponsabilition of governmental actors with regard to this type of crime, however, is much more extensive in comparison with other crimes: the AML approach has got to the very heart of the financial institution. AML does not only result in the implementation of changes in procedures, but also requires a shift of mentality within the financial institution, from all its components. However, simply shifting the reporting task towards the private sector does not imply that the authorities are completely released from their duty in preventing money laundering. After all, as the preventive approach of money laundering depends a large amount on the input of private organisations (who do not have crime prevention as their core business), the authorities have the task of making sure that these reporting institutions are actually able to carry out their assignment. Considering the fact that banks have been obliged to carry out these tasks – after all, they were not volunteering – you would at least expect the authorities to give some kind of input on reporting dilemmas and problems as well as a proper feedback on the STRs (Suspicious Transaction Reports). Other authors have also noticed this lack of feedback by the authorities with regard to other national systems (see van Duyne and de Miranda, 1999, for the Netherlands). Now it seems that financial institutions are left to their own devices, which results in an AML system with a high level of absurdity: burdened with the duty to report suspicious transactions, financial institutions search for criteria and typologies that allow them to recognise atypicalities. For this they resort to the yearly reports of the FIU, which are based on the reports that they themselves have made the year before. In doing so, they actually corroborate their own assessment of 'suspicious'. In Chapter 8, in discussing effectiveness, we will refer to the story of Pygmalion in reference to the AML system: a system so blinded by the image it has created and by its own reflection, that it is no longer able to critically question itself. The interviews merely reinforce this impression: the Pygmalion effect of the reporting system (Rosenthal, 1995) – in the meaning of the self-fulfilling prophecy of the system – is striking. Stereotypical images of money launderers, based on limited information from the partners in the AML complex result in catching exactly those criminals that we expected to catch while others slip through the mazes of the system.

The compliance officers or AML investigators can certainly not be blamed solely for this: they must manage with whatever sources they have available. Maybe the expectations of the authorities should be weighed against the means that they provide on the one hand, and the sanctions they prescribe on the other hand. The limited amount of information and feedback in the first phases of the AML chain contrasts sharply with the activity of regulators and other authorities, with regard to the sanctioning by regulators of those corporations that do not fulfil the expectations. The question then remains whether the authorities' expectations really are that high, or that authorities and policy-makers are aware of the self-fulfilling prophecy of the AML system. This would imply that they realise that the limited information that they provide for the reporting agencies in the AML complex will result in the same output, over and over again.

7 Supply and demand

Anti money laundering by the compliance industry[1]

Introduction

Compliance and AML-related tasks are supported by a number of tools, such as monitoring software, compliance procedures, or specific training for compliance officers that should enable them to recognise potential money laundering cases. These tools are provided by an entrepreneurial market built around the institutions that are required to fulfil these AML obligations, supplying services and instruments that may make the AML task less burdensome. As stated in the introduction, we have witnessed the development of a market on compliance and AML support, a booming industry making high profits as a result of indispensable tools for AML (Levi and Reuter, 2006).

In this chapter, we want to take a closer look at the market providing 'compliance services', which we will refer to as the 'compliance industry'. Taking the services that this industry offers into account, we ask ourselves a number of questions. The first question we will try to answer is how to explain the existence of this rather broad industry, or in other words: what are its *raisons d'être*? Second, we aim to map this industry, looking at the corporations that make part of the compliance industry, which services they are offering and what type of sources they use. And finally, we want to explore how this industry fits in the battle against money laundering; which role are they playing?

Triggers for the development of a compliance industry

Demand

In this research, the term 'compliance industry' represents all corporations that take up a role in developing tools or services that may support AML activities by banks. These tools or services may be related to software for transaction monitoring, advice on how to implement AML procedures, or training for compliance officers and employees, to name a few. The compliance industry is a fast-growing market of suppliers of services and products that are supposed to enhance and simplify AML compliance by financial institutions. There are several explanations for the growth of this industry.

First of all, the demand for these types of tools and support from a professional industry fits into a larger framework of risk orientation and reduction. Enterprises within the compliance industry offer financial institutions a feeling of being in control of anti money laundering, by supporting organisations in their risk management. This is why Ericson and Haggerty have named these occupations 'risk professions': 'A risk profession is an occupational group that claims exclusive abstract knowledge concerning how to address particular risks and a unique ability to provide expert services of risk management' (Ericson and Haggerty, 2002, p. 102). Although they did not explicitly apply this terminology to anti money laundering, the compliance industry fits this description. By claiming an 'exclusive knowledge' on how to control money laundering risks, they make their clients (i.e. financial institutions) dependent on them. After all, if financial institutions should choose not to rely on the compliance industry, they may be more vulnerable as a result of being less informed, or less able to protect themselves.

As we pointed out earlier, financial institutions assess the risk of being victimised by money laundering as rather high (higher than the actual risk) (PricewaterhouseCoopers, 2007) while reports by members of the compliance industry keep emphasising that these risks are actually very critical. Ernst & Young, for example, identified 'regulation and compliance' as the number 2 risk for global businesses in 2009, even in the middle of the credit crunch (Ernst & Young, 2009). Banks are aware of these risks and also feel as if the measures that they take will not be sufficient to catch every money launderer (Gill and Taylor, 2004).

As we will see later, this attitude is copied by the authorities who oblige financial institutions to make use of these tools in their AML activities. The compliance industry has capitalised on the emphasis on the prevention of money laundering and the threat image that was created by authorities (van Duyne, 2006) to take up an important role in the battle against money laundering.

How both of these attitudes have led to the establishment of an AML complex that is relying rather heavily on the compliance industry, will be illustrated in the following sections. In this development the role of the authorities and the obligations they have imposed on the financial sector have been very important and have shaped both the compliance industry and its services.

The creation of a compliance function

The creation of this new professional group has in itself resulted in a new demand for services. After all, compliance officers need to be trained to be able to perform their AML tasks. As a result of the introduction of these 'financial deputy sheriffs' (Levi, 1997), simultaneously a demand for support, education and training for this new profession grew. The compliance industry has reacted to this increasing demand by developing training and seminars, aimed at the professionalisation of AML activities and at an increased knowledge of compliance officers on money laundering techniques and other compliance-related issues (such as privacy legislation, fiscal fraud and insider trading). Although in

Belgium an association of this profession is still in its infancy, we see a trend towards association and certification in the surrounding countries. We pointed out earlier that in the Netherlands in 1999, the 'Compliance Institute'[2] was founded, aiming to offer knowledge, training and expertise (and certification of expertise) to compliance officers. Moreover, the Institute provides a forum for compliance officers. In Belgium, there are attempts to organise such an association, but in the meantime this role is partly played by Febelfin, the professional organisation for the financial sector. As the profession develops, so does the demand for more expertise and transfer of knowledge towards compliance officers. We will discuss the contents of these trainings later in this chapter.

First- and second-line detection

A second result of legislation in Belgium is a more technical obligation in relation to the approach of AML. As explained in Chapters 3 and 4, there is a first- and second-line supervision which is imposed by the regulator (CBFA, 2001a). These obligations result in two new opportunities for the compliance industry. With regard to the first phase, the alertness of employees regarding potential money laundering transactions, the regulator expects that employees are trained to recognise these transactions. The AML legislation adds to this expectation that financial institutions are expected to 'familiarise their employees with the stipulations of the law'. This implies that 'the employees involved take part in specific training programmes to recognise the transactions and facts that may relate to money laundering and financing of terrorism' (article 9 now article 17). This implies training and education of these employees, which opens up the market for the compliance industry. We do in fact see some corporations that offer these type of services to financial institutions, although many of the larger financial institutions choose to organise these trainings in-house. Smaller financial institutions, however, may choose to hire external training institutions that provide this service.

The second phase of the two-phased approach to the implementation of AML measures in financial institutions consists of the monitoring phase: compliance officers and compliance departments are supposed to monitor all transactions that pass through the financial institution for potential money laundering or terrorist financing transactions. As stated above, in most cases this involves the implementation of monitoring software, as large banks fail to show that they are able to perform a manual monitoring of the thousands of transactions that pass through their systems on a daily basis. As such, the regulator has imposed the use of software for monitoring these transactions. It may be clear that these software packages represent a large part of the compliance industry's package. Financial institutions all recognise the need for the use of these packages, and have shown themselves to be willing to invest in these software 'solutions'. We will discuss the range of software packages that is offered in the following sections, but must note here that it concerns a broad domain within the compliance industry – there are many software providers, small and large companies, that are offering this type of monitoring device.

Lack of official information sources

As we made clear in Chapter 3, the Belgian legislator has not decided on 'objective' reporting criteria (for example, to report every transaction above a specific threshold – such as anything over €10,000), but decided to introduce 'subjective' reporting criteria. Apart from the standard identification procedures and the know your customer obligations that need to be fulfilled for every client (asking for a copy of the identity card, asking the client a series of questions in order to know his background and economic activity), this implies that financial institutions need to be vigilant with regard to 'any' suspicious activity. This should enable banks to recognise transactions that may be linked to money laundering. These subjective criteria are discussed in the AML law of 1993. Article 12 states: 'When organisations know or suspect that a transaction is connected to laundering money or terrorism financing, they will notify the FIU before carrying out the transaction'.[3] As a result of the relatively vague guidelines for suspicious transaction reporting, financial institutions have started to look for other sources of information. They take these initiatives because they want to make a good assessment of the transactions that are considered to be 'suspicious'. For this, banks can turn to commercial information, provided by companies. They do this because official resources are not always up to date or lack an international approach. Examples are databases that contain information on companies or persons, or lists of people that are considered as 'PEPs' (politically exposed persons). These databases often combine a number of official sources with an expertise in anti money laundering and as such are able to offer important additional information to compliance officers during their investigations of transactions. Examples of these databases are World-Check (covering all PEPs, but also 'known high-risk individuals and businesses' (www.world-check.com), such as convicted fraudsters or money launderers. We will discuss the contents of these databases in the following sections.

Reputation protection

Even though the AML legislation has had an enormous impact on financial institutions, it is not the only motive for financial institutions to make use of the services of the compliance industry. After all, in the financial services industry, reputation protection plays an important role. We suggest that the concern for prevention of reputational damage, in combination with regulatory and legal pressure, has reinforced the anxiety of banks with regard to money laundering and terrorism financing. After all, as legislation has made complicity in money laundering a criminal offence, this has also become a liability and a reputational risk for financial institutions. Moreover, since 9/11, no bank wants to be connected to terrorism financing. Over the last few decades, a number of scandals have occurred (we refer to the KBLux case, Citigroup, but also Madoff) in which financial institutions have been the subject of regulatory and media attention with regard to fraudulent behaviour. Although it may seem as if 'any publicity is good publicity', for financial institutions – as we have witnessed in relation to the recent credit crunch – trust and faith of clients in their services is crucial. Financial institutions therefore are rather susceptible to these types of scandals, resulting in the search for methods through which they can protect themselves from reputational and financial harm. This trend – the fact that corporations put rule abidance and fighting crime higher on the management agenda – could be noticed since the year 2000 (Zimiles, 2004) and will probably increase in the recent circumstances.

One of the responses to this trend is the engagement in the battle against money laundering and terrorism financing. Still, some authors question the extent to which association with money laundering actually leads to reputational damage – and there is debate as to what extent financial institutions actually engage in AML for reasons of reputation-building (Harvey and Lau, 2009). One could in fact question what the specific impact of being associated with money laundering will be on customers' perception of a bank. Nonetheless, the credit crunch has shown how fragile a bank's reputation is, and how much trust – in general – means for the larger public. The public awareness can be considered to have increased during the first months of 2009. Furthermore, history has shown that there may in fact be an influence of these types of scandals with regard to shareholders. The Riggs case of 2005 – Riggs is a US bank that was sanctioned for failing to report suspicious transactions by Pinochet[4] – shows that there actually is an impact on reputation, not with regard to customers but with regard to shareholders. After the allegations became known, shareholders sued the directors of Riggs for bad management of the bank, and were paid $2.7 million in a settlement.[5]

Regulatory sanctioning

Another factor, related to reputation, that plays an important role in this respect is the sanction that can be imposed by the regulator in case of non-compliance with AML legislation. Harvey and Lau argue that this might be a more important 'stick' in comparison with the effect on the bank's reputation (Harvey and Lau, 2008). Regulatory sanctions can have a serious impact on banks, depending on the degree and scope of the sanction that is imposed. The famous ABN AMRO case of 2005 has shown how large the scope of such a sanction can be. ABN AMRO was imposed a sanction of $80 million for

> systemic defects in internal controls to ensure compliance with U.S. anti money laundering laws and regulations, which resulted in failures to identify, analyze, and report suspicious activity; and on findings that ABN AMRO participated in transactions that violated US sanctions laws.
> (Financial Crimes Enforcement Network, 19 December 2005)

Although this sanction is put into perspective by the fact that ABN AMRO stated that this sanction would have no effect whatsoever on the expected net profit for the second half of the year 2005 (which was about €1,882 million), the remedial measures that needed to be taken by ABN should not be underestimated (ABN AMRO, 2005). After paying the fine, the bank was obliged to show that it intended to prevent these types of cases in the future. It did this by hiring external advisors on compliance, adding a large number (300) of employees to the compliance staff, combined with the implementation of AML measures, procedures and monitoring systems. These remedial actions can have a large impact on a financial institutions and should therefore not be underestimated. Banks are therefore inclined to prevent this kind of impact on their functioning by investing in AML prevention measures.

> There have been very major issues in the US regarding AML that have been followed by heavy sanctions. We're talking about millions. But this is actually just one part of the sanction. The other part is that you have to put in place a 'remediation plan'. Banks who have been hit by that have put in place very, very strong controls just to serve this purpose of remediation action.
>
> (ci2)

Taking this into account, there is a chance that fear of not reporting, instead of fear of crime money, will drive compliance (van Duyne and Levi, 2005). Some authors however question the impact of these sanctions, and state that financial institutions continue to conduct business with untrustworthy states and individuals. In their view, banks choose to 'fuel the illicit part of the financial marketplace' because 'the financial benefits outweigh the sanctions' (Baldwin, 2006).

Benchmark

The final reason for investing in compliance by making use of services provided by the compliance industry relates to the 'compliance benchmark'. Once several banks are making considerable investments in compliance and AML (for some because of regulatory action, for others because they are willing to invest in these issues or because the bank proposes a compliance culture – for example in the case of banks that are also active in the US), the other banks have no choice but to follow. After all, by investing in compliance, banks raise the compliance benchmark for all banks. Regulators, the FIU and, to a lesser extent, consumers will expect banks to live up to this benchmark; compliance becomes 'normal'. Commercial enterprises also have a role in the level of this benchmark. One way of having an impact is by publishing surveys; accountants, such as the 'big four', regularly carry out compliance surveys, in which they asses perceptions and visions of integrity and rule abidance in corporations. Advice on compliance and AML is for these corporations a task such as forensic audits or accounting. By publishing these overviews, these companies also point out to financial institutions that a well-founded integrity policy may also have entrepreneurial advantages, such as more insight into company processes and control mechanisms, knowing customers and therefore assessing which services can be sold, and so on. Compliance and AML in this perspective can also serve as a method of competition: banks with well-developed compliance systems may also be able to serve their clients optimally. By using compliance as a marketing product, other banks may also be seduced into taking these initiatives. After all, in order to be successful, a levelled playing field is necessary. It can be expected that the bank sector will promote compliance throughout the entire financial sector. The question of course remains how viable this is with regard to smaller banks.

Services provided by the compliance industry

We have discussed a number of reasons why banks are willing (or compelled) to hire services from the compliance industry. AML legislation or regulation may influence the type of services that are hired (simply because they are becoming mandatory for financial institutions). Second, the lack of information that is provided by the authorities also pushes banks towards the compliance industry. Financial institutions are looking for ways to cover their regulatory and reputational risks (working as a driving force behind AML investments) as well as they can, which implies that if they do not receive information through law enforcement channels (police, judicial services, regulator or the FIU), they will have to resort to other sources of information in order to assess their money laundering risks.

Compliance officers on the one hand and representatives of the compliance industry on the other hand were interviewed to get a clear idea of the volume of this industry and the extent to which banks are purchasing services of this market on compliance. As stated in Chapter 1, we interviewed a total of twenty-three compliance officers[6] and six members of the compliance industry (accountants, software providers and training institutions[7]). Apart from the interviews, in this chapter we will also make use of the results of the survey that was carried out (see Chapter 1). We will discuss opinions of compliance officers by referring to their function, while viewpoints of corporations that represent the compliance industry will be announced as 'members' or 'corporations' of the compliance industry.

A general view of the compliance industry

We have already had a short glimpse on the services that can be provided by the compliance industry, by referring to monitoring software and training for compliance officers and bank employees. However, there are numerous types of services available for anyone who is looking for ways to enhance AML compliance.

The compliance industry is constituted of companies that offer advice, ICT support, software development, training or other types of education. Some of these corporations are able to offer the whole array, while others focus on several core tasks (which is often the case for software developers). Second, we see a mixture of niche players who offer exclusively AML services (examples are

CCL Compliance Consultants,[8] Brunia Compliance Consultancy,[9] Eurogroup consultancy,[10] Uniskill[11]), and other companies who integrate AML into their overall supply of software and actually aim at a much broader clientele than only financial institutions (such as KPMG, E&Y, Deloitte, Norkom, Mantas or SAS). The latter have made AML a specialisation area in which they can make use of the knowledge that they have built in other activities. AML services have been offered by KPMG and PWC from the moment that the regulator became active in this field (2001). And although numbers vary and mainly stem from commercial sources – estimations for AML investments by banks range from €9 million in the Benelux countries in 2002 to £19 million in the UK in 2003 (Datamonitor, 2003), and expectations are that these investments will increase in the near future (KPMG, 2007) – we may say the market in AML is impressive – and growing. Corporations from the compliance industry advertise their compliance and AML services by focusing on the risks that financial institutions may run when they are insufficiently compliant and by stressing the importance of fighting AML and terrorism financing. One aspect of this is by emphasising the amount of money that is laundered globally, or by pointing at others banks that were sanctioned for their role in terrorism financing. 'Financial institutions, eager to avoid legal and public censure, are willing to do whatever it takes' (Moorman, 2005). Surprisingly, banks also support these advertisements, by making statements on the use of AML services.[12]

Supply: software

As mentioned in the introduction, a survey was sent to compliance officers. One of the questions assessed the use of monitoring software by the bank. The answers showed that a very diverse repertory of monitoring software is applied by financial institutions, for several goals.

First of all, banks use software for screening clients, suppliers and business partners. The names of these persons are compared to blacklists of PEPs, known fraudsters or untrustworthy people ('namematching'). These lists are theoretically also provided by (international) authorities (see for example the OFAC lists of sanctioned countries or 'Specially Designated Nationals',[13] or the list of the UN[14] regarding 'the individuals belonging to or associated with the Taliban'), but can also be provided by software companies, that offer a combination of all known names and corporations.[15] The extent to which privacy regulation in Belgium allows these lists probably depends on the information source that is used. It is allowed to make use of the 'official' lists, such as the OFAC list, and World-Check claims to make use of public information sources only. But still there should be some concern with regard to legal certainty of the people who might be on those lists. This applies even more in cases where these lists are used for commercial purposes. One example relates to Patricia Vinck and Nabil Sayadi, a Belgian couple who have fought their appearance on these lists for years. Years ago, Sayadi had started a foundation that was related to the Global Relief Foundation, an organisation linked to terrorist activities and suspected of financing al-Qaeda's activities. Although the allegations of their link to al-Qaeda have been proven false after years of investigation, their names appeared on the official terrorist lists in 2003 and this has not changed since, in spite of several court hearings that have ruled in their favour and ordered the removal of their names (*De Standaard*, 7 January 2006). In 2009, after years of insisting, the Belgian government published a press order that stated that their names were deleted from the UN sanctions list (Foreign affairs, 20 July 2009[16]). This means that Vinck and Sayadi have been on these terrorism lists since 2003, which, in practice, implied the freezing of their accounts, and placed severe limits on their freedom of movement. This example shows that the effect of these lists should not be underestimated and we wonder whether commercially exploiting this kind of information is a good development.

Banks, on the other hand, will be inclined to make use of these combined lists, to have a maximum view on potential money launderers or terrorists. After all, this provides them with a sense of security as all sources are used. Second, there are other applications which are used for reporting transactions. These tools monitor (cash) transactions, transfers to 'sensitive' countries or internal transactions (transaction monitoring tools). Some software packages have about a hundred 'out of the box scenarios' that are ready to go once they are installed (ci6).

These scenarios are based on an 'if-then-logic', and monitor transactions on several levels (such as household, customer, account and transaction) (ci6). In constituting these scenarios, software providers base themselves on the existing legislation and regulation and go a few steps further in the ruling requirements to make sure that clients will be compliant in the future as well. Apart from this official information, they cooperate with banks who have a lot of expertise in these scenarios. One of the respondents told us about a forum (consisting of compliance officers of several banks and the software company) that was set up precisely for this kind of information exchange.

Risk-monitoring software is aimed at identifying unusual or suspicious transactions ('operational analytics'), but some of them also offer modules to establish compliance and AML procedures and policies, to map the entire compliance process, while others complement their monitoring systems with data management, data flow instruments that should allow for the investigation and follow-up of alerts.

The respondents were also asked to indicate which type of software they use. World-Check seems to be one of the tools that is most often implemented, followed by Norkom and Erase. A large number of banks have developed their own software. This is mainly the case for smaller banks who do not have software that is provided by their parent company – as is the case for larger banks – at their disposal, or for larger banks who state that they need systems that are made to measure their specific organisation. Four respondents said that they did not make use of any software.

The costs of purchasing these software systems is not to be underestimated, specifically as many banks state that often a combination of several software applications is needed (for example World-Check for the blacklists and SAS for data management and monitoring). 'Software needs to take into account the official blacklists. But if you look at the official FATF list, the content of this list is very limited. If you only use this list as a compliance officer, you're not doing a good job' (ci3). Several AML software providers therefore have developed alliances with providers such as World-Check, to be able to deliver all these services in one package. The problems with these lists is that what is considered as a 'PEP' is not always very clear, nor how far an institution should go to investigate potential links with PEPs:

> What should be considered as a PEP; under legislation it goes pretty far. That's a very big challenge for financial institutions. And how far do you go in your analysis? These are basically data warehouse issues. And it's different for a retail bank with millions of accounts versus an investment bank, with 1,200 clients, or for a private bank where you're supposed to know your customer quite well.
>
> (ci2)

KPMG has calculated the costs of AML compliance in its 2007 report and confirms that costs in this area are high and keep rising (58 per cent in the last three years) (KPMG, 2007), and transaction monitoring represents the single greatest area for investments in AML and costs are expected to keep increasing (KPMG, 2007). This is fully endorsed by compliance officers:

> The investment that we need to do to buy the software, to run it, to feed it, to get alerts out of it, these are severe investments. So it's not only paying compliance staff, it's also investing in systems, procedures, trainings, and so on. Those costs are also direct or indirect results of AML. For AML alone, for a bank of our size, this will add up to more than €1 million, a six-figure number.
>
> (cpl 2a)

The compliance industry is aware of the high costs for the banks:

> It costs about €50–100,000 to make a system perfect, and when you have to buy all the software, you'll pay tenfold. There still is a lot of work!
>
> (ci3)

> It would be too bad that it will become too high a cost for smaller banks. That is where software can help, to find a balance and to make sure that not only the large banks survive.
>
> (ci6)

Software providers also add to these costs by continuously offering new solutions from time to time. This implies that costs keep rising: banks need to pay for an annual subscription, costs for maintaining the blacklists, updating the systems. This is while the members of the compliance industry that work in advisory or consultancy services are rather sceptical about the use of software: 'Software is window-dressing. Software in itself says nothing about the quality of AML in banks. It mainly offers a way of managing investigations, but the content of the system still needs to be managed by the compliance officer' (ci3). Another example of the critical outlook on these types of software: 'those systems can cost about €2 million but if it is handled wrongly, it actually does nothing' (ci5). The clue is that software in itself cannot protect a bank from money laundering, it depends on the quality of the scenarios, the data that is entered and the way in which the system is fine-tuned.

> The problem is: there are banks that buy software, install it and say: we are finished. But if you start testing it based on a number of money laundering scenarios, it simply passes through the system and there is no alert whatsoever. This really need to be adjusted to the bank, rules need to be created.
>
> (ci5)

On the other hand, both the compliance industry and the compliance officers state that software should allow for an 'acceptable' number of alerts: just enough to be able to follow up on the majority of them – acceptable is therefore related to the resources that are available. This implies that banks need to be able to adjust the parameters of the monitoring system and fine-tune the scenarios, which should allow for an amount of alerts of good quality that is not too much nor too little, providing enough information for the regulator in case of inspections.

> The systems that have been installed still generate a lot of hits. It's trial and error to find the number of hits you can control.
>
> (ci2)

> We need to make sure that the software generates an acceptable number of alerts; the resources are limited and you need to generate a number of alerts that is in relation to the resources.
>
> (ci6)

Some respondents from the compliance industry also point out that current ICT levels in financial institutions are not always oriented towards an AML approach. This implies that the databases that are used in banks are not compatible with AML solutions, which could lead to several problems when trying to combine these databases.

In general respondents are satisfied with the programs and software packages they have at their disposal. Some of them ask for software that can perform name-matching (such as World-Check), which could help them identify PEPs. Furthermore, one of the respondents notes that specific modules regarding market manipulation and insider trading could be very useful. But the general feeling with regard to the availability of software and other tools within their bank is relatively positive. We might therefore suggest that compliance officers are handed a sufficient amount of tools in this respect to enable them to perform their AML tasks.

Supply: advice and expertise

With regard to hiring expertise or consultants with regard to AML and compliance, almost half of the compliance officers that were included in the survey stated that they make very little use of external advisors. These respondents stated that they had never hired these types of services (advice and expertise on the implementation of AML measures, compliance procedures, compliance audits, etc.). Still, slightly more than the majority of respondents say they make use of their services sometimes (the majority) or regularly (just a few respondents). We could not find any connection with the size of the bank for this question.

In the interviews, we asked our respondents which services they are able to provide. These experts can take up several roles, such as consultancy or advisory:

> it starts from setting up a compliance function, helping them define the compliance charter, designing service level agreements with all risk involved functions, how they operate, performing gap analyses with regard to the way they conduct their compliance programme ... and sometimes this can take months. Then you're writing policies, procedures, mechanisms to identify, prevent, manage and report conflicts of interests.
>
> (ci2)

Others also can be hired for testing, fine-tuning or implementing their monitoring systems on the basis of a number of scenarios. 'Sometimes banks are really flabbergasted. They have paid €2 million for their system and it basically does nothing. You need to turn the knobs and then it is fine' (ci5).

In the interviews we also asked the compliance officers for what reasons they decided to hire external advice or why they were reluctant to do so. Most of the respondents that we talked to said that they had not hired forensic auditors or external advisors to date.

> We have not yet worked with forensic auditors, that is a pure internal thing that is investigated by our investigators. I do not know in which cases we could cooperate with them.
>
> (cpl 12b)

> We do not hire advisors in relation to AML, because we are able to test our way of dealing with compliance to other banks. We know perfectly well

how compliance functions in large and small banks: we have regular meetings with compliance departments of smaller banks to discuss specific topics.

(cpl 14)

During the interviews with members of the compliance industry, some explanations were given for the fact that banks are reluctant to hire these services: banks prefer to do these things by themselves, 'to avoid priers, although they sometimes lack the expertise and the means to carry it out in a sound manner' (ci3). According to these respondents, compliance and AML may have an impact on the bank's reputation (and any issues related to this should therefore be sheltered from the outside world) and compliance officers are not willing to show that they cannot cope. Advisors and compliance experts will try to create a 'compliance culture': 'We try to teach compliance officers how they can be added value: not only check the countries on the lists, and legislation, but to really care about this issue' (ci5).

Supply: training and education

Another aspect of the compliance industry relates to training and education, aimed at both bank employees and compliance officers. For compliance officers, a number of trainings are available, provided by Febelfin (the professional organisation for financial institutions). Some of the larger banks also have developed in-house trainings. With regard to AML in specific, Febelfin also organises training for employees, although the majority of the larger banks organise these trainings by themselves; compliance departments are responsible for the organisation and content of these training sessions. One of the examples is a large bank in which employees are given several training sessions when they start their career at the bank. One of the modules in these sessions will be dedicated to AML and compliance (for example one day out of seven). During these sessions, employees are taught about AML legislation, regulation and how to deal with atypical customers or transactions. They are trained in being alert and learn to be watchful with regard to documents and answers by clients. Apart from Febelfin and in-house trainings, external consultants may also be hired for the training of employees and/or compliance personnel. 'We assess compliance functions, perform monitoring of compliance practices, or do a training on anti money laundering by making use of role-playing for the commercial network of banks' (ci1). Although some banks have their own in-house trainings, some also outsource these tasks, mainly small or medium-sized banks, for whom it is not efficient to develop trainings by themselves. Some banks also make note of the fact that they have developed software for online in-house training in cooperation with other external partners, non-AML professionals, such as publishers or ICT developers. In such a cooperation, the latter partner is responsible for developing the program, functionality of the online training and providing technical support, without any input related to content of the training.

Compliance officers say that the number of trainings that is organised is sufficient, although some would like to see a broader offer of these services.

Perceptions of compliance and AML implementation

One of the subjects of discussion with providers from the compliance industry related to their perception of the approach of compliance and AML by banks. Although a number of the respondents were very critical with regard to the thoroughness of AML and compliance by banks, the majority of them had to admit that banks have made a radical change in their attitude towards AML and compliance and that the large majority of banks have adapted a cooperative and professional approach to AML. All banks have invested in AML implementation, are aware of the risks and everywhere 'something is being done', although standards are different and quality diverges. They refer to a 'maturity spectrum' and state that many of the banks are situated at the most professional end of this spectrum. Critics, however, point at small banks, as in those banks the compliance function is still a combined function: many small banks still add compliance tasks to the job description of a legal department or a manager.

> In large financial institutions this is becoming a more professional, very strong sector. The problem is actually in the small institutions, where compliance is still considered as the job of a legal department.
>
> (ci2)

> I think most of the banks are more or less compliant, although I'm not sure about the small banks.
>
> (ci6)

Nonetheless, most respondents of the compliance industry state that compliance officers constitute a new, professional profession. Criticism is therefore mainly directed at the banks, not at the compliance officer's professionalism. Some of the respondents also acknowledge the fact that the position of a compliance officer is not always that easy. 'They are perceived as ruining the game. As costing money, but bringing nothing in, on the contrary' (ci5).

As Belgian banks in general did not start their investment in compliance and AML until after it became a regulatory (and legal) obligation, compliance remains 'relatively weak' (ci1) in comparison with the UK or US approach. Because there are many US influences in the approach of AML (specifically when looking at the monitoring software), standards are also often based on the US regulation. Although not everyone is convinced of the usefulness of these US standards, this is the reality.

As a result of the vagueness of the guidelines in Belgium, compliance and AML is not an easy task for financial institutions. The rules remain ambiguous, which is why banks start making their own assessments of what should be considered as suspicious and what not. 'Banks make their own lists, but this does not always function very well' (ci5). Furthermore, there are some difficulties with regard to legal frameworks that sometimes clash; one of the examples is the privacy legislation. As banks are willing to exchange information within their approach of money laundering, in some cases they are prevented from doing so, as privacy legislation does not allow for this type of information exchange.

Other problems related to AML legislation arise when banks are functioning on an international basis. The way AML is addressed is fundamentally different from country to country. Although there is European regulation, and a lot of general principles are the same throughout Europe, each country has its own specificities and requirements. This may urge banks to develop 'principles' that more or less cover all European regulation, while developing detailed rules for each country. 'There is a big issue for large banks to think about how to develop systems at a world-wide level, it's becoming a nightmare' (ci2). Furthermore, large banks are principally organised on a cross-border level, while the regulators are nationally oriented and supervise on a national level. These different approaches are difficult to reconcile.

As we made clear in Chapter 6, banks follow different procedures for the investigation and reporting of suspicious transactions. This is supported by the compliance industry, which is confronted with different reporting cultures within banks.

> How banks deal with this differs from bank to bank. There are compliance officers who simply refuse to decide in this and report every alert d'office to the FIU. Other compliance officers decide to investigate their transactions before reporting them.
>
> (ci4)

According to the compliance industry, compliance and AML are considered not to be a competitive issue for banks. Banks are willing to make the investments, out of fear for regulatory sanctions and for reputational risk, and in order to do this, they are prepared to cooperate with other banks. After all, apart from these risks, bank have no interest in fighting money laundering. Moreover, reporting suspicious transactions may even put the bank in a very difficult position; there are several risks related to reporting suspicious transactions for banks. It may chase clients away, and not only the malevolent ones.

> Once a bank has filed a report to the FIU, it's out of their control. If the FIU says yes, we're going to investigate this, and it turns out to be a small tax evasion, the judicial authorities have to contact tax authorities. And then the client is going to say: what? My bank is responsible for communicating my tax evasion? And then you're talking about bank secrecy in Belgium...
>
> (ci2)

It is therefore not always self-evident that banks have engaged in this battle against money laundering and we need to be aware of the conflicts between commercial goals on the one hand and rule abidance on the other hand.

> Banks have a true mandate to change something. Otherwise, for a bank, purely fiscally, there is no reason to burden your clients, to burden your ICT, to put such a workload on compliance ... why would you invest in this, in a purely commercial sense? Of course, bank employees are also human, they would not want to sponsor crime, but it's about the bottom line and an external input is needed to motivate these corporations to do so.
>
> (ci6)

> Financial institutions will have the eternal tension between entrepreneurial forces – pass as much money through the systems as possible – and regulation that says: this is not how it works. It will always be a problem.
>
> (ci5)

On the other hand, the compliance industry makes clear that compliance and AML also offer commercial benefits, although not many banks have discovered this side of compliance. Some compliance industry respondents point out that compliance strategies may lead to more effectiveness with regard to costs, as it could have a positive effect on operational management. Banks are forced to monitor their systems and think about their procedures. Furthermore, one of the respondents emphasises the potential of knowing your customers and having insight into their transactions:

> we could make clusters or segmentations based on client behaviour. How often do you use e-banking, how often do you withdraw money, what is your income, who is your employer, how many expenses do you have for your house, have you recently bought a house...
>
> (ci6)

Based on this information, banks could offer and sell better and made-to-measure services. The compliance industry therefore emphasises that banks ought to be more aware of how to turn compliance into commercial advantages, without turning into Big Brother. In our view, it may be clear that this was not the purpose of the AML legislation and we are confident that this kind of approach will result in conflicts with privacy legislation. After all, although banks are allowed to process personal information on the basis of the AML law, commercial use of this information is prohibited (Van Raemdonck, 1996–1997).

The compliance industry and the AML benchmark

We state that the compliance industry has grown as a consequence of the legislation on anti money laundering. Although its services were initially developed as a way to support institutions in its AML obligations, today we see a different influence which nourishes and reinforces the position of the compliance industry within the battle against money laundering. The authorities have contributed to the growth of this industry in several ways.

First of all, as a result of regulatory influence, financial institutions are now obliged to make use of the services of this industry. Instead of taking up a supporting role, the compliance industry has become an imperative part of anti money laundering. By obliging financial institutions to install monitoring systems and failing to provide these systems themselves, the authorities have boosted the growth of the compliance industry. The compliance industry, on the other hand, thrives on increasing regulatory and legal pressure.

Second, by choosing for subjective guidelines in reporting suspicious transactions – based on the principle of 'intelligent reporting' (though this is a principle that is applauded by the banks), the Belgian government has shifted the responsibility for making decisions on which transactions to report onto the banks. This implies that banks will be responsible when they fail to report money laundering cases. The Belgian regulator is perceived as rather strict, based on earlier sanctions that were given to banks who were not AML compliant. As a result, banks will look for ways to protect themselves, by making sure that they are well informed and up to date with regard to AML methods and know-how. They will look for information on how to monitor, how to investigate, and how to report. When authorities fail to provide this kind of information, or only provide small amounts of information, banks must resort to other sources. One of these sources is found in professional AML companies, who are very willing to give advice on money laundering methods, techniques and so on.

Third, we have already established earlier that feedback from the authorities is somewhat minimal (Verhage, 2009d). Banks in general receive very little information on the usefulness of their reports to the FIU or on the quality of their compliance approach. To be able to perform optimally, however, banks and compliance departments want to know how well they perform on the subject of AML. No bank wants to be considered as the leader in AML (because this could chase clients away), but in the same sense, no bank wants to be known as the bank who does nothing against money laundering. Levelling the playing field in AML is important, as it prevents clients from 'shopping around' for the least strict bank. The middle position is the best position in this respect. But how will banks know where the middle is?

As official feedback is lacking, banks try to find out how their AML approach relates to that of other banks. Compliance officers often stay with the same bank for years, so they are not in the position to compare several banks' approaches. In order to get an impression of the AML spectrum and where the bank is positioned on this spectrum, banks can either ask other banks how they function (as they sometimes do), or hire a professional who knows the business and can compare compliance quality as a result of AML expertise.

As a result of the continuous development of new and more advanced AML technologies and expertise, the compliance industry preserves and fortifies its position. After all, banks will be inclined to buy the newest technologies in order to be optimally protected and maximally informed. Consequently, the AML benchmark will be permanently upgraded. The question is, however, when some of the smaller players among the financial institutions will no longer be able to keep up.

Conclusion

The sole existence of the AML complex leads to a rise in demand for services by the compliance industry, while the presence of the compliance industry fortifies the demand and the use of software, technology and knowledge. After all, as the compliance industry keeps evolving and improving the services they offer, a demand for these higher developed instruments will be the result. By upgrading, the compliance industry actually de-levels the playing field in AML, urging other players in the field to raise their standards also.

Dramatisation of risks

One of the inherent dangers of the compliance industry is the fact that this industry of course wants to sell its services. While financial institutions have commercial objectives and have to take on AML activities on the side, the compliance industry prospers as a result of initiatives in AML and higher perceptions of 'danger' or risk. The larger the risk of a money laundering case for a bank, the higher the cost of such a case, the more banks are inclined to appeal to the compliance industry for more support and more protection from reputational or regulatory damage. The compliance industry therefore benefits from higher risk perceptions. By analogy with insurance companies or private security, it is after all not uncommon for professions that are oriented on risk prevention to emphasise the necessity of their services. Many of the rhetorics used in advertisement by the compliance industry emphasise the risk that banks take when they decide to make no use of their services, by pointing out how large the sanction could be and what impact an AML case could have on reputation and market capitalisation or customer loyalty. In the case of private security, the rising sales of security services encouraged feelings of insecurity within the public (Garland, 2001). The existence of the compliance industry and the services they sell may have the same effect, by 'dramatizing the risk of other approaches and making claims about their own ways of seeing and doing things' (Ericson and Haggerty, 2002). Financial institutions and authorities should therefore be aware of this pitfall. One possible way of dealing with this is by assigning quality labels to corporations or products provided by these corporations that should stand for a reliable and, more importantly, high quality AML approach. This would give financial institutions some idea of the quality level of the services they pay for and provide a sense of security when these services are hired. The assignment of these quality labels could be carried out by the regulator of the financial sector, in cooperation with the FIU, who is best informed on the potential of these products. Regular auditing of the actual implementation of these systems can also add to higher quality guarantees and would discourage 'window-dressing software'.

Levelling the playing field

The fact that, by offering services on the AML market, the compliance industry enhances security and protection for financial institutions, results in the conclusion – very comparable to the discussions on private security services – that those who can afford it, will be safer than those who cannot pay for these facilities. With regard to security, however, we refer to the public's fear of crime or their wish to prevent crime. When talking about AML, this is not the case; AML is the government's desire to prevent money laundering as a destabilising factor for the economy at large on the one hand, and for fighting crime on the other. The interests are very different. Banks are simply put forward as instruments for these governmental desires. To what extent can we expect them to make these kind of investments? And, even more importantly, is it fair to allow the level of 'AML security or safety' to be directly linked to what a financial institution can afford to invest? What are the effects of this on competitive positions, specifically for small banks?

AML prevails over privacy?

There are some questions that remain with regard to the blacklists that are used in AML investigations and regular checks of client databases. Although the AML legislation makes an exception for the gathering of information by banks with the aim of investigating potential money laundering or terrorist financing (Van Raemdonck, 1996–1997), this does not mean that all types of information gathering are simply allowed. First of all, we wonder which kind of legal protection there is for people who end up on these lists. The case of Patricia Vinck and Nabil Sayadi has shown that once people are mentioned on one of these lists, it is very difficult to get their names deleted, even though a national court has ruled against it and has acquitted them of any charges. And as Mrs Vinck has remarked herself, even though they may be removed from the lists, it will be very difficult to delete their names in every unofficial trace of these blacklists (*De Standaard*, 7 January 2006). Apart from the difficulties regarding the composition of these lists, and the extent to which these lists are accurate, we also wonder whether we really want commercially oriented companies to offer this kind of private data. As such, confidential and personal data have become one of the commodities within the compliance industry. We are of the opinion that the authorities should take up their responsibility in this respect and offer a complete and all-inclusive 'blacklist' to the financial institutions, which would not only allow for potentially more accurate lists, but also save financial institutions much investment.

Fragmentation of the AML approach

The AML approach represents a good example of the public–private approach in tackling crime. The compliance industry takes up a specific place within this public–private 'cooperation', because of its inherent commercial interests. Although financial institutions of course also strive for commercial gain, they also have much to lose when they do not fully engage in the battle against money laundering. The compliance industry, however, can put its commercial objectives first. This implies that the public–private cooperation in AML is partly governed by and subjected to market mechanisms (Ponsaers, 2000). The compliance industry becomes one of the modellers of the way in which AML is constituted by financial institutions and in consequence partly determines the input at the level of the FIU. This is mainly caused by the lack of clear guidance by the authorities. But how can we assess whether the compliance industry is making use of correct information, providing accurate advice and basing itself on reliable sources? And what impact does this have on the level of coordination between initiatives and who is responsible for attuning governmental policy to commercial tools?

This diversity of actors that is engaged in the fight against money laundering may lead to a fragmented approach towards AML. Is it not necessary that every partner in AML works with the same objectives at heart, or at least a common starting point? The fragmentation that derives from the diversity of services, tools, instruments and corporations, lacking a clear common starting point and/ or transparent working principles (which ought to be provided by the authorities), can have no positive impact on the general battle against money laundering, let alone result in an effective AML system.

In our view, the authorities have an important task in giving guidance and coordination to reduce this fragmentation. As the compliance industry exists merely by the grace of governmental decisions, it is up to the authorities to try to tackle these problems. One of the ways in which this could be done is by providing the blacklists (which is now done by World-Check, among others) to the financial institutions. This would reduce the need for banks to hire services from the compliance industry and at the same time would enhance the quality and reliability of these lists. Any privacy issues could be dealt with more efficiently. In our opinion, composition, supervision and management of these lists is an intrinsic governmental responsibility.

8   The anti money laundering chain in Belgium

Measuring 'effectiveness'?[1]

Introduction

Discussing the effectiveness of the AML approach in terms of amounts or volume of laundered money is difficult because of the lack of conclusive statistics (Harvey, 2004; Van Duyne et al., 2005). In view of the limited information on the statistical results of the AML system (van Duyne and de Miranda, 1999; Levi and Maguire, 2004; Harvey, 2007), we here make some general deductions that can be made on the basis of our research. This, however, does not alter the fact that the problem remains that any result is very difficult to measure. After over fifteen years of AML, and millions of investments by private and public organisations, this is a worrying conclusion.

Efficacy of the AML complex?

First of all, the level of efficacy of the AML system depends on the type of goal that is evaluated. As the AML system combines several interests, each of which is striving for another objective, evaluation is not unambiguous. What is certain is that the battle against money laundering has changed the policing landscape thoroughly, inserting a new type of public–private divide (and not public–private *cooperation*) on a global scale. Statistics on prosecution and conviction, if present, are modest, not only in Belgium, but also in other countries (Levi, 1997; van Duyne and de Miranda, 1999).

Measurement issues

Measuring effectiveness when it comes to AML initiatives or systems is a complicated, if not impossible, task. This conclusion is at the very least striking: after almost twenty years of the AML battle, with millions of euro invested by private institutions and law enforcement, we are not able to make visible whether the system works or not. Two main issues clarify these measurement problems.

First, we lack (valid) instruments to measure the effects of the current framework. Measuring the amount of money laundered has been attempted. Several researchers and authorities provide estimates of the amount of money that is laundered (Europol, 2003; IMF, 2004; Unger, 2006). Some use figures regarding the formal economy, stating that a certain amount of the GDP enters the formal economy as a result of laundering activities. Others try to calculate this by using figures on the proceeds of crime. However, as scholars make clear, these estimations remain attempts (van Duyne, 2006, pp. 35–36). We simply cannot provide conclusive statistics on the amount of money within the illegal and informal economy (precisely because of its illegal or informal status), nor can we measure the exact amount of money that crosses the border between the illegal–informal–formal economy (Harvey, 2004; van Duyne et al., 2005). This provides us with the first reason why measuring effectiveness is very difficult.

Second, in order to assess 'effectiveness', you need to know which goals are being strived for. In the case of money laundering, this also confronts us with some problems: AML activities, as stated above, are carried out throughout the AML chain, by several parties, public and private, in different roles (detection, prevention, repression, sanction, etc.). Each and every one of these actors involved has different motives and expectations in view. This diversity of interests and motives results in a difficult assessment of effectiveness, because: Whose effectiveness are we actually measuring? Which indicators should we use? Do we need to measure the amount of money that was recovered, the amount of suspicious transactions reports, the number of convictions? Furthermore, how do we measure the deterrent effect of the AML system – how do we quantify what did not take place? In other words, we lack a zero setting nor can we determine the current state of affairs.

When looking at the interests of the financial industry, the same problems arise in evaluation: is 'effectiveness' the number of fines that were averted, the strength of the fines, the amount of clients that were not accepted, or the number of newspaper articles that did not get published? This becomes even more difficult since the actors involved in the private contribution to the AML system cannot assess their own effectiveness, as they lack the information to do so (see above). This was confirmed by the Dutch survey: only 11 per cent of the respondents thought effectiveness of compliance could be measured (Nivra-Nyenrode et al., 2007).

When we asked the compliance officers in the Belgian survey which criteria were used for the evaluation of their own performance by their employers, their evaluation criteria did not include the number of money launderers caught, but consisted of qualitative criteria such as efficiency, integrity and accuracy. Quality criteria can be: the observance of compliance rules, the results of internal audits, the results of external audits (by the regulator), or the extent to which goals within the business plan or the annual plan have been achieved. Nevertheless, these criteria are difficult to measure from an outsider's point of view.

An attempt to measure effectiveness

As Harvey (2004) stated, one way to circumvent these difficulties is to take 'second best' criteria in attempting to assess the effects of the AML system, such as the number of suspicious transaction reports, the number of prosecutions and the amount of confiscations. This exercise has been carried out before, for example by Levi and Maguire (2004) and Fleming (2005) for the UK and by van Duyne and de Miranda (1999) for the Netherlands. These studies showed that the impact of the AML chain – assuming that it can be measured – is minimal.

A restriction in this assessment is that we use the official, governmental policy goals of AML as a starting point: making sure that crime does not pay and seeing to it that crime is punished. Keeping in mind that the AML battle requires a large investment by the financial sector (estimations ranging from €9 million in the Benelux countries in 2002 to £19 million in the UK in 2003 (Datamonitor, 2003), and expectations are that these investments will increase in the near future (KPMC, 2007), which partly undermines the financial gain of the battle against money laundering, we need to focus on the other outcomes of the AML investments: outcomes on the level of crime prevention and detection. Determining (approximately) these end results is possible by looking at the outcome of the AML chain.

On each level of the AML chain, measurement is problematic and a number of caveats must be kept in mind. First of all, the statistics at the level of the public prosecutor's office and the courts are not detailed enough and lack reliability (Stessens, 2000), which implies that we need to be cautious in interpreting these statistics. Second, it is difficult to 'count cases' (Levi, 1997), as we cannot be sure that the money launderer's convictions actually result from the AML complex. They may also be the consequence of a financial investigation resulting from a drug offence. And third, the FATF evaluations point out that the statistics on the level of suspicious transaction reporting are not always accurate (FATF, 2005). For the Belgian FIU there is a specific problem, as they transform 'reports' into 'files', which makes counting rather difficult. We will explain this later.

Taking these warnings into consideration, we have attempted to study the annual reports of the Belgian FIU. The figures presented below concern all the private organisations under the AML legislation, as the report of the FIU does not provide us with detailed figures for the financial institutions. However, banks file about 40 per cent of all reports to the FIU, and when looking at the reports that are transmitted to the public prosecution by the FIU, their share becomes even larger (CTIF-CFI, 2004, 2006, 2008, 2009, 2010). These annual reports give us at least some insight into the outcomes of the chain when it comes to reporting suspicious transactions.

The AML chain: data from the FIU

Number of suspicious transaction reports

The first level of the AML chain consists of the investigation and subsequent reporting of suspicious transactions by the private institutions under the AML law. As we can derive from the annual report of the FIU, in general, the number of suspicious transaction reports more than doubled from 1998 to 2009. The transactions reported by the financial institutions have also doubled since 1997 (CTIF-CFI, 2008). However, although the number of total reports keeps increasing steadily, we see that the number of reports by financial institutions has decreased since 2007. In 2009, this meant that financial institutions reported 10 per cent less than in 2008 (CTIF-CFI, 2010).

What this may tell us about the effectiveness of the system, however, is not clear. The increase in the number of reports can probably be attributed to more intensive monitoring by the institutions under the AML legislation. But still, we do not know whether the higher number of suspicious transaction reports also implies a higher amount of prosecutions or convictions.

Investigations and dismissals by the FIU

Between 1993 and 2006, a total of 114,463 reports were sent to the Belgian FIU, reporting potential suspicious or atypical transactions. After receiving these reports from the private organisations and/or their compliance officers, the FIU investigates the reports. These reports are combined by the FIU into 'files', for several reasons. For example, several reports can relate to one and the same suspect (several transactions by the same client) or the same transaction (when several banks are involved in one transaction). As such, 114,463 reports are assembled by the FIU into 25,296 files. After assessing the gravity and legitimacy of these reports, the FIU will investigate the files, making use of police, judicial and other authorities' information. After this investigation, the FIU decides on the necessity of sending the files to the public prosecutor's office. Between 1993 and 2006, 68 percent of all files were dismissed by the FIU: about 8,032 were sent to the public prosecutor's office. These 8,032 files consisted of

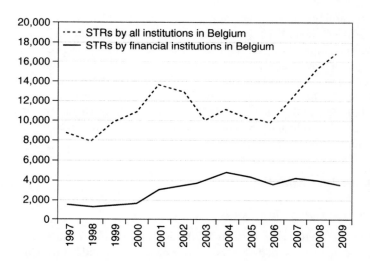

Figure 8.1 Number of STRs by (financial) institutions in Belgium.

55 per cent of all reports to the FIU (CTIF-CFI, 2007). The reasons for dismissing the other 45 per cent are not clarified in its annual reports. We can only conclude here that the FIU does in fact serve as a large filter mechanism.

Public prosecutor's office and courts

On receipt of the files that are composed by the FIU, the public prosecutor's office investigate them. The results of this phase will determine whether or not a defendant will be charged with money laundering.

Ultimately, between 1993 and 2006, of 8,032 files, 939 resulted in a conviction. This implies that about 11 per cent of the files that reached the level of public prosecution (3.7 per cent of all FIU files since 1993) actually result in a conviction of the defendant. 'Conviction' can imply a prison sentence, but also confiscation of criminal assets and/or a fine. In total, after thirteen years of AML in Belgium, 1,766 individuals were sentenced to 3,297 years of prison sentence and about €686 million were confiscated. The fines that were imposed amounted to about €75.9 million (CTIF-CFI, 2007).

Limited results

The caveats we have referred to before, remain. We do not know what part the suspicious transaction reports have played in these convictions, or how many of these convictions actually result directly from the reporting obligation. After all, a money laundering conviction can also be the result of a merging of the reports

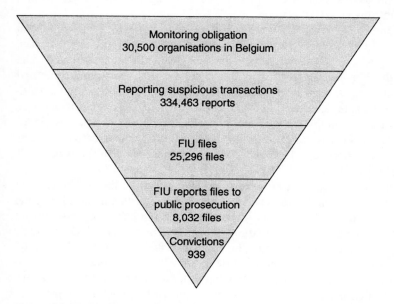

Figure 8.2 The AML chain in figures.

with an existing drug investigation. The number of money laundering convictions can therefore be an overestimation of the impact of the reporting mechanism. On the other hand, the statistics provided above only represent the outcome of the input by the FIU (related to suspicious transaction reports) and do not consider all input on other levels (for example other criminal investigations in which financial investigations are carried out, separated from the FIU reporting mechanism) and as a result cannot provide a conclusive view on the AML system as a whole.

A careful conclusion is therefore called for. The statistics of the FIU suggest a very limited impact of the reporting system with regard to money laundering repression. What these figures do not tell us are the preventive effects of the AML system, which obviously is also relevant. The AML complex is character-ised by a large dropout throughout the process, which however says nothing about the effort that is invested in this process.

About 900 convictions is not very convincing after thirteen years of investing in an ever-expanding AML system. Explanations for this limited effect may be diverse: a low priority on the level of public prosecution for money laundering (as well as for white-collar crime in general) (Croall, 2001), a lack of expertise at the police and judicial level leading to a limited capability or maybe capacity for the investigation of this type of crime, an extensive lead-time of the files, etc. Nonetheless, in the evaluation that was carried out in 2005 by the FATF, it is concluded that the Belgian system can be seen as effective with 800 convictions for money laundering in four years: 'Ces chiffres permettent de conclure à l'effectivité du système répressif belge en matière de lutte contre le blanchiment de capitaux' [These figures allow us to conclude on the effectiveness of the Belgian repressive system with regard to the battle against money laundering] (FATF, 2005, own translation).

To illustrate briefly that this is not only the case in Belgium, we had a look at the statistics found for the USA, after all the cradle of the AML system. Between 1994 and 2001, 9,160 defendants were convicted for money laundering. Although this may seem a low figure, this is not even the most remarkable part of these statistics. Of these 9,160 convicted defendants, 16 per cent (200 defend-ants) were private organisations (banks, casinos, exchange businesses) who were prosecuted for not complying with monitoring and reporting obligations (Moti-vans, 2003). In the UK, where also an increase in suspicious activity reports (SARs) was noted between 1995 and 2005, the number of convictions per SAR stood at 0.13 per cent in 2004 (Harvey, 2007).

A second conclusion we can make is that the effects of the AML chain, at least the visible, measurable effects, seem rather disproportional considering the input. The overview of the Belgian AML chain does not paint a hopeful picture specifically in comparison to the large investments by institutions under AML legislation. We need to keep in mind, however, that the preventive effects of the system also should be taken into consideration. It is therefore important to develop measures to allow for an evaluation of these efforts on different levels. Furthermore, the fact that the relatively low number of convictions in the USA also contains the convictions of non-compliant institutions provided food for thought. As stated above, the surveys in Belgium and France both showed that the perceived risk of non-reporting is very high. When considering the adverse effects of the AML policy (next to, for example, privacy issues as discussed by other authors, e.g. Naylor, 2007), this may be one of them. In spite of a continuous global policy of anxiety on money laundering and the strains that are put on the private sector, the net law enforcement results seem rather low.

Other criteria for efficacy

As we are unable to rely on statistics with regard to efficacy of the preventive system, we are forced to make use of other information on effects. From our interviews we derive that the financial system has indeed closed its ranks and made it much more difficult, if not impossible, to enter a bank with a suitcase of money and deposit it on an account, no questions asked. As a result of the AML system, potential launderers will have to go to more trouble (and pay higher prices?) to get their money cleaned and will therefore either have to take more risks or have less 'clean' money at the end of the laundering phase.[2]

Banks have proven to be loyal reporting institutions: we have seen a steady rise in suspicious transaction reports by financial institutions since 2001, which however has stabilised – and even decreased – since 2007 (CTIF-CFI, 2008). During our research, respondents also stated that if a bank was known for its associations with criminal funds, other banks would react to this (Verhage, 2009b). From this we derive that the financial sector has adopted a self-regulating approach with regard to non-compliant banks (of course, also because these latter banks are unbalancing the competition in the market). The other reporting institutions, such as insurance institutions and leasing companies, seem to lag behind in this respect (FATF, 2005).

However, we do not know how many flows of illicit money are prevented through a general preventive effect of the AML system, nor do we know how many specific clients are prevented from entering the formal financial system by means of exclusion criteria (blacklists, high risk profiles, cash-related corporations, etc.). We assume that the amount of cash that is offered to banks has decreased as a result of AML legislation. We may also assume, that as a result of grown expertise and professionalism within the compliance sector, 'typical' money laundering techniques and schemes are detected. This not only implies that there has been an effect with regard to the soundness of the financial system as a whole, but also suggests that know-how on the subject of money laundering in general has probably increased. The AML system has resulted in the widening of the scope of investigations, not only with regard to financial crime, but also in relation to predicate crimes.

Crime control and hence displacement?

Apart from the discussion on the efficacy of the system, there are some signs of crime displacement with regard to AML. One of the problematic aspects of situational crime prevention is the problem of crime displacement.

The formal financial system, built around the financial institutions, has increasingly fortified AML efforts, making access to the financial system progressively more difficult. As a result, we might suppose that they have succeeded in making money laundering by use of financial institutions more complicated. Specific clients are excluded from financial services (for example people on the so-called politically exposed persons lists) or selected for monitoring based on their 'risk profile', and transactions to particular countries will be either forbidden or followed with prudence. As a result, criminals will have to look for other ways to launder their money. After all, there are no signs that drug markets (or prices) have reduced as a result of AML (van Duyne and Levi, 2005; European Commission, 2009a) – leading to the suggestion that drug crime has not diminished either, although figures on this are not available. Even more, Reuter and Trautmann note in their report for the European Commission that in spite of the fact that the AML system was originally set up with the aim to combat drug crime, the number of seizures related to drugs has been modest in relation to estimations of the volume of the drug trade (European Commission, 2009a).

Apart from drug crime, there is no evidence for a shrinkage of the volume of the informal economy – on the contrary, some authors suggest that the volume is increasing (Schneider and Enste, 2000). Prices in the underground market are said not to have increased (van Duyne, 1997). These findings would imply that the need to launder money has remained unchanged, to say the least. Based on estimations of the extent of the informal economy and the amount of money that needs to be laundered, we might even suggest that the necessity for money laundering has grown.

As a result of the earlier discussed flexibility of money laundering, the displacement effect in money laundering may even be larger. When burglars are deterred by an alarm, they will go to houses with no alarms (Verwee *et al.*, 2007). In money laundering, the same applies: when a certain country or bank has a less strict AML policy, money launderers may turn to these countries for their money laundering acts. However, in contrast with burglary, this is not the only reaction. Another way of dealing with more strict regulations is by developing even more complicated money laundering schemes, which are very difficult to detect. This consequential 'moving up' in knowledge and the investment in more and more profound expertise may be difficult to keep pace with.

Even when we take into account that target hardening may lead to a changing motivation of offenders (according to situational crime prevention theory), the amount of money that needs to be laundered is still sizeable. This entails that those crime entrepreneurs who are in need of legitimate money will try to find other ways of laundering. Some authors point at the use of Hawala systems in this respect (van de Bunt, 2008) or at the techniques of cash transfers by physically carrying it from country to country. The CTIF-CFI report on 2008 notes an increase in reports by exchange agencies and casinos, also institutions under the obligation to report to the FIU in case of suspicious transactions (CTIF-CFI, 2009). The options are virtually endless: offshore financial centres or tax havens still provide lots of opportunities for money launderers, and so do Western

Union or Second Life. It may be clear that in comparison to the financial institutions, the other reporting institutions, such as casinos or exchange offices – although known for a substantial amount of reports to the FIU – have invested less in AML, which will probably result in a higher vulnerability (misbalancing the playing field in AML between institutions). The question is, however, whether we can expect these other (non)financial institutions to invest as much effort, time and means in AML as the banks have done, specifically considering that their interests in AML might be slightly different in comparison to the financial institutions, who have a large interest in complying with AML legislation. This displacement effect is in our view intrinsically linked to crime prevention from a situational point of view, specifically when dealing with a highly flexible and adaptive type of criminal phenomenon. As long as causes of these crimes are not tackled, there will always be new methods and new ways in which this crime can be committed. In the case of money laundering, the cause of the crime is the fact that a lot of money is earned by predicate crimes and the need to make use of this money in the formal economy. Any intervention aimed at the prevention of this use in the formal economy will therefore result in other laundering methods, if the predicate crimes are not tackled.

Summarising, we might state that, while the process effects of the AML system have been very far-reaching – AML has changed the way in which financial institutions work and think – the impact effects with regard to the outcome (in terms of prosecutions or convictions) seem to be modest, although we must note that until today we have had no instrument for measuring the whole outcome that also takes the preventive effect into account (Reuter, 2009).

This is – to say the least – surprising. In order to build a transparent policy, there is a need for data. First and foremost, reliable data should be available and easily accessible, for both researchers and practitioners. In addition, as Van Duyne and de Miranda have already noted (Van Duyne and de Miranda, 1999), international data are indispensible in this respect; money laundering is an international phenomenon, enforced on an international level, which automatically implies that international and comparative research is a condition *sine qua non*. This does not only point at the need of a proper availability of data, but also at a streamlining and harmonisation of data gathering and processing. Different counting units (for example files versus suspicious transaction reports), different registration methods and systems and different criteria for what is considered to be 'suspicious' hinder comparability and hence transparency. This is underlined by the current difficulties of Eurostat in gathering conclusive statistics (Tavares *et al.*, 2010). The awareness of this is a first and necessary step in preventing the AML system from ending like Pygmalion or Narcissus: a system so blinded by the image it has created and by its own reflection that it is no longer able to critically question itself.

9 Conclusion
Policing the money[1]

Introduction

In 2006, our research started with the aspiration to study the fight against money laundering in Belgium, and in particular the position of the private sector (the financial institutions) in this fight.

We started this research from the central hypothesis that two constructions form the basis of the fight against money laundering. First, an AML complex has evolved as a result of regulatory and legislative initiatives. This AML complex consists of both the public and private actors that are engaged in anti money laundering. A second construction consists of the commercial or entrepreneurial approach to anti money laundering. An industry of compliance support has emerged, providing services to the AML complex, such as training, software and advice.

Based on this central hypothesis, we posed three research questions: 1) How does the AML battle function from both a law-abiding (AML complex) and a commercial (compliance industry) perspective? Do we actually see an AML complex and a compliance industry? 2) Second, which interactions do we see between this AML complex and the compliance industry? Are these constructions mutually reinforcing? 3) And third, how does the position of the compliance officer (a bank employee responsible for the implementation of AML legislation) function between these two perspectives? With regard to this last research question, we aimed to expose the commercial versus crime fighting dilemmas and the paradoxical position of the compliance officer – a bank which reports its own customers is bound to have some commercial dilemmas and conflicts with a number of principles of banking. We made clear in Chapter 2 that studying corporations is still a niche in criminology. In Chapter 3, the origins of the fight against money laundering and the specifics of this crime were discussed, showing in Chapter 4 what this implies for the function and position of the compliance officer.

The empirical results of this research, as described in Chapters 3–8, have led to a confirmation of the research hypotheses, and an insight into the 'world of compliance and AML', how compliance is strived for, which kind of obligations banks are supposed to fulfil, how decisions are made during money laundering investigations, what the extent of cooperation between public and private actors in the AML complex is and showed us the role of the compliance industry, trying to push banks further and further into more AML investments to cover as many risks as possible.

On the basis of our empirical results we can state that the three angles involved in the battle against money laundering result in a blurry mixture in which several benefits and concerns are muddled up:

- The AML complex on the one hand serves several goals (both the official goal – repression of crime – and the economic interests of several players).
- The compliance industry, on the other hand, strives for profits based on the implementation of AML measures and benefits immensely from each new kind of regulation or legislation. Moreover, we conclude that legislation has actually strengthened and consolidated the compliance industry by obliging banks to make use of its services. The AML complex and the compliance industry are mutually reinforcing constructions, and in this sense also preserve one another through this interdependence.
- The financial institutions, stuck between both of these angles, have their own concerns and motives for investing in the AML battle: reputational protection, preventing harm to the company and preventing regulatory fines. These interests drive the banks to the implementation of costly and intrusive measures in the battle against money laundering and terrorist financing, the involvement of a rather large amount of new AML professionals and the introduction of high standard instruments, purchased from the compliance industry. The ambiguous function of the compliance officer within the financial institution illustrates the difficulties related to this diversity of interests.

In Chapter 5, we discussed the virtual absence of actual feedback between the parts of the AML complex. This absence of feedback has been confirmed in other European countries as well and is currently recognised as problematic for the AML system.[2] Public and private actors in AML seem to work rather separately, leading to mutual misunderstandings. Compliance officers state that they receive little information on both the way in which they should carry out their AML task, and on their performance of this task (Chapter 6). As feedback from the regulator and the FIU on how AML is carried out within the bank is very modest, and information from the FIU on which criteria to use for monitoring and investigating transactions is virtually absent (apart from the general feedback through the annual report), compliance officers are often forced to make use of their own assessments and criteria. This may lead to a system that continuously confirms its own analyses. As such, we have suggested that the AML system is likely to result in a self-fulfilling prophecy, finding the same usual suspects over and over again.

In Chapter 7, we described the compliance industry. Our research has also shown that there are indeed interactions (even mutually reinforcing interactions) between the AML complex (consisting of the public and private actors in AML) on the one hand and the compliance industry (providing services for AML on a commercial basis) on the other hand. The simple presence of an array of services within the compliance industry promotes the use of these services (Chapter 7). After all, banks are well aware of the AML and compliance 'benchmark' that exists. This benchmark represents both the level of compliance and AML investments by banks and the threshold within banks for money laundering attempts (the level of AML defence). 'The benchmark is what happens in the market', one of our respondents stated (Chapter 5). Banks have stated that they aim to find the mid-position with regard to this benchmark: from an entrepreneurial point of view, it is not interesting to be at the top of AML, nor to be at the bottom. By offering services and promoting AML as a concept in a competitive framework, the compliance industry pushes banks toward more investments in AML and hence raises this AML/compliance benchmark. This is also successful because of the regulator's obligation to make use of the services of the compliance industry. After all, one of the obligations is to have a monitoring system put in place within the bank, allowing for a structural and continuous monitoring of suspicious transactions. As a result, banks are obliged to make use of these types of software, developed by entrepreneurs. This is a mutually reinforcing interaction between the AML complex on the one hand and the compliance industry on the other.

We pointed out in Chapter 8 that there is no substantial proof that the AML system has had huge effects with regard to the amount of money that is laundered – although we must emphasise that there is no proof that it does *not* work, either. This results in the conclusion that the AML system – although implying huge costs for both public and private actors engaged in the AML complex – functions without an accurate view on efficacy or the possibility of making a cost-benefit analysis (Naylor, 1999; Alldridge, 2008). The question is to what extent this results in a system that functions as either a self-fulfilling prophecy or as an alibi. Although it is a system with potential, the danger rests in preserving a system that can no longer be questioned as too many interests are at stake.

In this concluding chapter, we want to take a few steps back in order to gain a more panoramic perspective on the functioning of the AML complex. We hope to do this by paralleling the battle against money laundering with the fight against criminologically more traditional types of crime. By making an analogy with both types of approach, we hope to make clear that the fight against money laundering represents a unique and one of a kind approach to serious types of crime, which has not only resulted in an encompassing international system, but also has shifted the approach to crime and the way in which crime control deals with concepts such as risk, privacy and private responsibilities.

Factors typifying the AML approach

In criminology, attention has long focused on traditional crime, the usual suspects and established crime control organisations. Criminological research has a long tradition of studies on the public police, the judiciary and criminal procedures, and traditional crime such as juvenile crime or petty crime. Corporations as crime fighters, combined with a focus on financial crime, have long stayed out of scope with regard to criminological interest (Ruggiero, 2000; Cools, 2005). We called this focus a 'criminological tunnel vision' (Chapter 2). Times have changed, and criminology has to open its horizon to other fields, phenomena and providers of security. Criminology has been forced to leave the vision of governmental monopoly on crime control as other actors (for example regulatory agencies, private security) have taken up a part of security governance (Hoogenboom, 1994; Bayley and Shearing, 1996). This also implies that more traditional approaches within criminology need to broaden their scope when looking at more recent types of crime and crime control. Conventional instruments of criminology need to expand and adapt in order to grasp these new realities. This implies that when we want to draw parallels between anti money laundering on the one hand, and the approach of traditional crime on the other hand, we need to take into account the differences that may occur. In order to structure this comparison, use can be made of criminological theory on the conceptualisation of crime. One of those theories that is applicable here is the realist school in criminology.

Traditionally, when studying a criminal phenomenon, four central dimensions are emphasised as playing a role in the conceptualisation of crime: offender, victim, state (or formal control), and the public (or informal control) (Young, 1992). These four dimensions, the four corners of the square of crime put forward by the realist school in criminology, represent correspondingly the action and the reaction to a criminal phenomenon. Each of these factors may influence the form and shape of the phenomenon, and interactions between the factors result in changes in the crime rate (Young, 1992).

Not only have the four factors (offender-victim-state-public) changed in terms of appearance and impact (for example, in money laundering, the offender and the victim are not that easy to identify), we also see a number of other dimensions that influence the way we need to deal with money laundering and its combat. We therefore aim to broaden this approach with a number of elements.

Diversity of motives

First of all, the *diversity of motives* underlying the formal control of this phenomenon forces us to adopt a more broad perspective with regard to this dimension of money laundering. Both crime-fighting objectives and financial issues have played a role in the establishment of an AML regime. It may be apparent that Ferguson is correct in stating that behind every important historical phenomenon lies a financial secret (Ferguson, 2008). As we and others have argued before (Levi, 1997; Unger, 2006; Verhage, 2009c, 2009e), in AML, the financial context has not only been influential with regard to the extent to which the phenomenon was criminalised, but has also determined the extent to which control agencies (in this case, banks) are willing and able to control crime. Moreover, it is partly as a result of economic rules of nature that the AML culture has spread this quickly: by excluding banks who are not complying with AML legislation from entering the US financial market or executing transactions in US currency, profit and reputational motives have urged banks to meet these terms (Helleiner, 2000). Furthermore, the financial motive behind anti money laundering has influenced the public perception of the necessity to fight this phenomenon. It may be clear that the public perception of the phenomenon of money laundering has had a huge impact on the attempts to control this type of crime. The fact that policy-makers as well as mass media have portrayed money laundering as a very distressing and threatening crime (with regard to economic stability and integrity), has added to the relatively silent acceptance of this encompassing approach (Alldridge, 2008).

Different interpretation of formal control

Second, the *interpretation of formal control*, traditionally assigned to the state, has seen a remarkable shift in AML. Within AML, private actors are the gate-keepers of the system, controlling and determining the input of the AML system. The government has outsourced its responsibilities to private actors, resulting in a different perspective on formal control and its effects on crime. Although 'new' actors in policing, such as private security services and private investigation, may find a place within the traditional approach, the compliance officer is very difficult to fit into a traditional public versus private scheme. As a result of the diversification in policing actors and the multilateralisation of policing in general (Favarel-Garrigues *et al.*, 2008), combined with the insertion of the compliance officer as one of those actors, the boundaries are no longer as clear as they used to be (Bayley and Shearing, 1996; Jones and Newburn, 2002). Actors of formal control have been privatised and private actors have received 'public' tasks (tasks in a general interest). In our research, we have therefore portrayed the compliance officer as the actor that bridges the world of private interests (the bank and the compliance industry) on the one hand and that of public interest (the AML complex) on the other hand.

Phenomenon

Third, the *specificity of the phenomenon* of money laundering in itself presents the traditional approach with a number of problems. Money laundering is a flexible type of crime. As a result of this flexibility, formal control may influence the manifestation of the phenomenon more than its occurrence, resulting in changed techniques or methods. New legislation and new types of monitoring or control (such as the ever-expanding list of institutions that are obliged to report) will immediately result in modifications in the modus operandi, looking for new lines of least resistance. Furthermore, as Naylor (1999) notes, a rise in formal control may lead to an even higher value of the transactions with regard to money laundering. Whereas in burglary, values may drop as a result of higher risks of getting caught, within enterprise offences, criminal entrepreneurs may choose to insert more 'defensive layers of intermediation' (Naylor, 1999), resulting in higher values associated with the increased risk.

Precisely, this allows for the use of all possibilities and resources that the formal economy provides for; actors of the formal economy (such as lawyers, accountants, etc.) and their expertise are out on the market and can be hired. This results in a very flexible way of not only dealing with new regulation, but also the ability to hire new experts or gather new knowledge on money laundering techniques.

This however also affects the skills that are required with regard to money laundering. As Gottfredson and Hirschi point out, for most types of crime no special skills are required. In crimes of 'personal violence, assault, rape and homicide' (Gottfredson and Hirschi, 1990), all is needed is either strength or weapons. In money laundering, however, special skills are needed; criminals need to know how to access the financial system, how to circumvent controls themselves, or know and hire people that are able to do it for them. The latter may imply the use of representatives of the formal economy, who have access to knowledge and tools to launder money. This difference in skills needed is another reason for the difficulty in studying the phenomenon of money laundering; the complicatedness of a successful, undetected money laundering scheme requires trained professionals with an expertise in money laundering techniques and methods.

Risk orientation

Fourth, the *type of (formal) control* also influences the perspective on money laundering. In AML, a proactive approach is adopted, in contrast with reactive methods that are often used in traditional crime and policing (Ponsaers, 2002b). Anti money laundering is one of the best examples of a risk-based approach and the concept of 'risk' plays a vital and critical role. Although the factor 'risk' is unavoidable in any contemporary crime control method (Ericson and Haggerty, 2002), the risk orientation and the translation of those risks into scenarios within AML demands a different vision on the interpretation of 'formal control'. Risk implies bringing the future into the present (Crawford, 2009). Within AML, compliance officers are proactively detecting transactions based on information from the past, making use of scenarios that are developed with regard to future transactions based on knowledge from earlier transactions.

This risk orientation has effects on the way in which formal control should be democratically supervised, mainly with regard to basic rights such as privacy and due process. Public oversight is difficult, as compliance officers often work behind the scenes and because the public is not informed on the application and content of AML standards and norms. The norms are not communicated which also raises questions with regard to due process and transparency.

To summarise: money laundering is a crime in which a physical victim is absent and in which the mechanisms of control are not the traditional ones. In money laundering, the state is both victim and regulator, and private organisations can act both as instruments for crime, victims of crime and as policing agencies. This all results in the conclusion that the boundaries become very blurred. After all, in comparison with traditional types of crime, where the state's apparatus (one of which is the public police) is given the central role in crime fighting, the AML system shows a striking difference. Whereas in other areas the state is clear in defining its boundaries between public and private crime control (specifically in Belgium, where private security is very strictly regulated – see for example Cools, 2005), within AML, these boundaries are not so clear. AML can be considered as an institutionalisation of a whistle-blowing system for banks with regard to their customers. Although this may seem a paradox, there are some obvious reasons for the engagement of private organisations in this fight against money laundering.

Why private organisations?

By introducing the reporting requirement for suspicious transactions to the FIU, the legislator has chosen for a clear responsibilisation of the private sector. The case of anti money laundering shows that the state has been able and willing to regulate the national financial structure (Sica, 2000). Although regulation of financial institutions is not a new phenomenon (from the earliest days of market economies governments have regulated solvency and integrity of banks (Kay, 2003), AML regulation has introduced a whole new area of banking obligations and a new role for compliance officers in crime control. The involvement of *private* organisations in the fight against money laundering was inspired by a number of motives. First of all, money laundering is an inherent international phenomenon, taking place on international financial markets. As most law enforcement methods are still virtually confined to national borders, in contrast to the financial industry, the engagement of this private sector would allow for a more transnational approach to money laundering, enabling the tracing of cross-border flows of money within the same financial institution. The emergence of money laundering and its recognition as a threat to the financial system has led to the acknowledgement that regular investigation methods were deemed inadequate. As such, anti money laundering has attuned itself to the general trend of globalisation, internationalisation and diversification of crime control (Findlay, 1999; Alldridge, 2008).

Second, as money laundering is often carried out through the use of financial intermediaries, which is almost a condition *sine qua non* for the concealment of funds and the international transferring of money, financial institutions are ultimately qualified to trace these flows of money. Banks are designed to transfer money from A, where the money is, to B, where the money is needed (Ferguson, 2008). Not only are banks the vehicles that are used to carry out the crime, they are also the ones that actually meet the customers and therefore have first-hand information at their disposal. Customers may for example try to use the bank by depositing cash funds in a bank account, by transferring money through several international banking systems, in order to conceal its origins, or by lending money from banks based on illegally earned capital. All charges may be linked to money laundering. Banks may therefore be considered as complicit with these acts if they cooperate – which also reveals their motivation to detect these crimes. From this it follows that financial institutions can also be seen as an appropriate mechanism for preventing and detecting these crimes.

The police services would have more problems in gaining insight into clients' financial background, investments or assets, for two reasons. First, they lack proximity to the client – they would not be able to ask the client questions at the time of disposal of the money in the bank. And second, privacy legislation would probably interdict their access to this kind of information in cases where *knowledge* of a criminal act does not yet exist. Compliance officers have gained an exception to the privacy legislation in their investigations of potential money laundering cases (Van Raemdonck, 1996–1997). We may even wonder whether the instalment of compliance officers to do these types of investigation was not inspired by this circumvention of privacy issues. This becomes even more questionable when we take the modifications of the AML legislation in 2010 into account, allowing banks to exchange client information between themselves on a large scale.[3]

And third, banks have maximum knowledge of their customers, which enables them to distil 'normal', routine activities of these clients from unusual transactions and cash flows, resulting in a fundamental investigation of these activities. Taking these considerations into account, financial institutions are best qualified to monitor transactions and customers. How are police services supposed to monitor all transactions by clients, not knowing their backgrounds or the relation of one transaction with regard to other transactions? Knowing that a large bank processes on average 250,000–450,000 transactions a day, the capacity this would take from a police force, to monitor all transactions by all banks, would be enormous. Furthermore, banks already have a lot of private information at their disposal, and are able to make use of their knowledge of the client in assessing the level of risk that the client or the transaction may represent. After almost eight years of investment in AML compliance in Belgium, we can also state that most banks have gathered expertise on (anti)money laundering. According to our respondents, this acquired expertise of compliance officers sometimes contrasts with the knowledge of the average police officer on financial crime, which may lead to miscommunications.

These observations have resulted in an AML system in which private entrepreneurs (civilians) have become the primary institution in charge of the implementation of public policy goals on money laundering, resulting in a massive and pervasive 'private-public security quilt' (Levi, 2002). Private organisations are the gatekeepers to the preventive AML system and as such determine the input of that system. Within banks, this obligation has been institutionalised by means of the compliance officers, sometimes also referred to as 'banking detectives' (Kochan, 2006). This public–private divide in fighting crime is very specific to the AML approach.

The 'banking detectives': compliance officers and their discretionary powers

The 'intelligent reporting system' that is applied in Belgium has the advantage of a limited number of reports which allows the FIU to make a more thorough filtering of the cases to be sent to the public prosecutor. As the preliminary investigation of suspicious transactions in Belgium is carried out by the bank, a lot of time and effort is already invested in the first phase of the AML chain, implying a serious filter on the cases that ultimately reach the FIU.

Our empirical results have showed that generally, compliance officers are in favour of this system of intelligent reporting; it gives them room for discretion, allows them to know their customers and also represents an intellectual challenge (Chapter 6). However, there are also downsides to this system. After all, it also implies that the centre of gravity of the AML system – the responsibility for monitoring, investigating and reporting, leading to the need for investments in means, tools and expertise – rests with the reporting institutions, who also feel the burden of being sanctioned in case of non-compliance or – even worse – complicity or collusion. In the interviews, the respondents often referred to the possibility of these sanctions and the fact that several compliance officers were accused of complicity with money laundering. We must note, however, that we were not able to find any information (e.g. in the media) to confirm these statements. The FATF evaluation of 2005 mentions that the Belgian regulator had sanctioned at least seven banks (since 1996) for not complying with AML regulation (FATF, 2005).

The implication of this 'intelligent reporting system' is that compliance officers have a specific amount of discretionary powers (room for decision-making) during their activities. We may note that the compliance officer has more discretionary power at his disposal than the regular police in Belgium, where discretionary room has not been officially acknowledged (Ponsaers, 2002b).

This consideration touches upon the main delicacy of this function. Working for a commercial entity while carrying out a public task implies several difficulties. In our survey results, several respondents acknowledged the fact that commercial versus law abidance appraisal may sometimes result in dilemmas. As such, they did not only refer to discussions with commercially oriented colleagues, but also with regard to the decision to report (or not), as both decisions may lead to reputational damage (Chapters 4 and 6). Compliance officers are therefore continuously balancing on a tightrope, trying to assess the potential consequences of their decisions. In addition, within the system of 'intelligent reporting', one of the compliance officers stated: 'Every bank wants to be the most intelligent', referring to the fact that banks are looking for the optimal cost-benefit equilibrium in compliance and AML.

The specificities of the phenomenon of money laundering

There are several reasons why money laundering, as a criminal offence, is difficult to map and detect for governments and police services. First of all, compared to traditional crime where a victim reports a crime to the police, in money laundering, the focus is on *detection* of the crime. Furthermore, the expertise and skills that are needed to recognise transactions as linked to money laundering are rather specific. In comparison with traditional types of crime, the required know-how and expertise of the investigator is of a more specialist nature. Second, adding to this specialist dimension is the fact that fighting money laundering has not grown bottom-up. The fight against money laundering started on an international level. And third, money laundering is a highly flexible crime, making detection and prevention subject to changes in methods and expertise.

(Lack of) historical know-how

Money laundering is a fairly recent crime. It was not until the late 1980s that states started to criminalise the laundering of proceeds of crime. Before this period, governments implicitly 'allowed offenders to enjoy the fruits of their crimes' (Stessens, 2000, p. 3). Although this is far from unique (regularly, new types of crimes are inserted into penal law, such as racism (van den Wyngaert, 2003), in comparison with traditional crime, this recentness of money laundering is a large hindrance, as we have gained relatively little evolutionary knowledge on the phenomenon. In criminology, although fraudsters were always in some way the subject of study, most of the attention went to visible, traditional crime, 'the nuts, sluts and perverts' (Cools and Haelterman, 1999). This is a second explanation for the scarcity of insight into the phenomenon of money laundering. It seems as though the system remains focused on the old stereotypes of crime, in order to protect reputational interests optimally.

Origins of criminalisation

Money laundering is not only more recent than other types of crime, but the way in which money laundering became a criminal act also differs rather fundamentally. In the case of money laundering, an international impetus has forced national states to criminalise the act of money laundering. In most other types of traditional crime, we see that criminalisation has started on the level of the state, in a bottom-up approach, resulting in several states criminalising acts such as theft, robbery or assault at more or less the same time. This implies that while other crimes were internationally considered as impermissible, and therefore internationally seen as 'crime', money laundering became a crime as a result of international – first US, later also European – legislation (Alexander, 2007). Through an international condemnation of this crime, nation states were obliged to adapt their penal laws, inserting the crime of money laundering. The influence of the international and, for Belgium, the European, legislation can be considered as predominant with regard to the prevention and punishment of money laundering.

The autocracy of 'risk' within the AML complex

In Chapter 3, we discussed the application of the rational choice approach in anti money laundering. One of the dangers of the situational prevention approach that is often related to this theory is the high authority that is attributed to 'risk'. 'Situational crime prevention may be understood as quintessentially actuarial (…) Its concern is with crime control as risk management' (McLaughlin *et al.*, 2003). Risk has become a central concept within the battle against money laundering. Not only have regulators and banks decided on a risk-based approach to AML (instead of a rule-based approach (CBFA, 2005)), trying to detect those transactions and clients that may pose the highest risks, we also see a high level risk orientation with regard to the effect of AML on banks in general.

The risk-based approach to AML

Related to the first risk orientation, our empirical results have shown that this risk-based approach to AML unavoidably means the use of criteria and profiles.[4] The risk-based approach results in focusing on the identification of high-risk and/or suspicious categories, scenarios and profiles, potentially impacting basic human rights in view of a higher degree security for all (Zedner, 2003). Clients and client groups are classified into risk profiles (high-medium-low), and their transactions are monitored on the basis of criteria and scenarios. Transactions are screened on 'atypicalities' and 'suspicious' behaviour in relation to or in comparison with previous behaviour, on the destination of the transaction, the country of origin, etc. These scenarios are partly provided by the compliance industry, but are also based on the expertise of the compliance departments. However, the information that is used by both stems from the same sources such as FIU reports or FATF typologies (Chapters 6 and 7). It seems as though this results in the use of rather stereotypical images of money laundering, based on earlier discovered money laundering schemes. The focus is inevitably aimed at the past and at those transactions that are historically linked to money laundering.

The same observation was made by Levi, in 2002: 'although expensive software throws up more sophisticated methodologies to pursue, we note the same criteria of suspiciousness – out of context behaviour largely by the usual suspects – that the police use, only operated this time by bankers' (Levi, 2002). The bias and stereotypes in the system (Naylor, 2007), based on a lack of up to date intelligence, might lead to a fake success of AML. Although some financial institutions try to invest time and effort in proactive projects, this is not feasible for every bank as the means for compliance are often limited. The result is that the AML system functions merely on the basis of previous cases, and might be putting specific clients and transactions under a microscope, looking for the usual suspects, while completely surpassing what is outside the scope of the usual suspects. One of the examples in this respect is the FIU annual report, in which cash transactions, real estate transactions or shell companies are typified as suspicious (CTIF-CFI, 2009). By principally looking at those elements that were found in earlier money laundering cases, the focus remains on traditional types of money laundering which are not likely to lead to the discovery of new money laundering techniques. Even more, it could well be the case that by focusing on these stereotypical cases, looking with a tunnel vision, only the small fishes are caught, while the sharks remain out of scope. The focus on private customers in contrast with corporate clients is one of the many examples of this tunnel vision. Nonetheless, we see the same narrow focus in the reports of the FIU, in which mainly cases of private customers are discussed, very rarely corporations. Broadening the scope possibly will imply that this predisposed view on money launderers and the bias regarding money laundering possibilities could be corrected.

The vagueness of money laundering, the fact that 'dirty' money may look and act exactly the same as 'clean' money makes identification of money laundering very difficult. This contrasts with other types of crime where the good in itself can be identified as illicit relatively easily as is the case in drug crime or prostitution. This fact, in combination with the ambiguity of the legislation trying to prevent money laundering, leads to the fact that detection is rather difficult and that criteria, hence reporting decisions, will always be subjective. Even more, every bank decides on its own criteria and scenarios, which implies a differential and diverse approach to money launderers. The assessment of these criteria is noted as one of the problems within the application of situational crime prevention: there is a danger that success or failure will be determined through 'struggles over the status of criteria' (McLaughlin et al., 2003).

How are banks supposed to choose these criteria? How should they build their scenarios? Is it up to banks to decide which criteria determine whether a client or transaction is suspicious or is this a task for the authorities? After all, it is on the basis of these criteria and the scenarios they are combined in that transactions are screened, on the basis of which alerts go off, client investigations are carried out, and clients are potentially excluded from banking services.

If we compare this approach to the proactive investigation by the police services, we see an enormous difference with regard to suspects' rights of defence and privacy. In case of police proactive investigations, there not only has to be a *'reasonable suspicion' of (future) criminal activity'*, this investigation also has to be approved beforehand by the public prosecutor's office.[5] This implies that there have to be some grounds on the basis of which the public prosecutor can decide to allow a proactive investigation. At the time of the introduction of proactive investigations as a police task in the code of criminal procedure, a number of discussions arose with regard to precisely these issues. Discussions focused on the question of allowing the police this much room for manoeuvre, even though there is no *knowledge* of any criminal fact (yet). What does this imply for basic human rights and how can we prevent abuse of this discretion (Vanderborght, 1999)? In light of this discussion, it seems rather paradoxical for a government to ask banks – citizens – to carry out a continuous and large-scale screening of their clients, based on obscure guidelines, without any democratic control over the process. Apparently, anti money laundering floors these objections, and privacy and legal certainty are considered as subordinate to crime fighting (cf. Levi, 2002).

> Due process is giving way to system rights. That is, suspects' rights are being eroded in favour of surveillance system-rights to obtain knowledge of suspects. Rights are not only shifted away from the suspect, they are disconnected from the centralized, unitary entity of the state.
>
> (Ericson and Haggerty, 2002)

We think that future research should focus on these issues from a more comparative point of view.

AML as a risk for banks

Money laundering has become one of the liabilities for banks in general and compliance officers particularly, resulting in massive investments in compliance staff, tools and systems. There is a large supply of compliance and AML related services on the market (the compliance industry), and banks are very willing to make use of these services, as these promise to cover their compliance and regulatory risk optimally. The compliance officer, who carries responsibility for AML implementation, has to work within this risk orientation. Not surprisingly, the discourse of compliance officers is also highly risk-oriented, focusing on limiting risks for the bank. In this respect, compliance officers are in a dual position; both reporting and non-reporting may pose risks for their financial institution. In case of reporting, a client may file a complaint against the bank if the public prosecutor decides not to prosecute the case,[6] while in case of non-reporting, a regulatory sanction, combined with reputational damage may hang over their heads (Levi and Reuter, 2006; Harvey and Law, 2009). No wonder that compliance officers decide to investigate potential money laundering cases thoroughly, as this may limit their risk, either way. The emphasis on preventing 'bads' (while trying to fight crime and prevent money laundering from a more moral point of view) results from the juxtaposition that each bank and compliance officer finds himself in. Preventing 'bads' (Ericson and Haggerty, 2002) – such as negative publicity, loss of clients, liability – may lead to a negative, defensive impulse when combined with very little information on how to make decisions in specific cases or a lack of support or feedback[7] from the authorities. There is a possibility that in this configuration, risk avoidance (the 'umbrella system') becomes the priority, instead of detecting crime. One of the dangers of this risk-avoidance approach is the fact that every actor shifts responsibility for reporting to a lower rank in the AML chain, while responsibility of the outcome of reporting is shifted upwards in the chain, by a defensive reporting strategy.

This risk orientation is not symptomatic for anti money laundering, however, nor for *private* organisations involved in crime fighting. There is a general tendency, resulting from the pluralisation of policing and the introduction of new actors in the landscape of policing, towards loss prevention and risk minimisation (Garland, 2001). Police also look for ways to cover the risks they are confronted with, by gathering more information, and become information dealers by transmitting this information to other institutions that are trying to assess their risks (Ericson and Haggerty, 2002). This shift in policing results in police services becoming crime risk managers (Ericson and Haggerty, 2002). Garland has characterised this trend as a type of policing that is centred around an 'economic' style of reasoning (in contrast to a social style), built on economic forms of calculation (risk factors, crime costing, cost benefit) that are translated into criminological practice (Garland, 2001). Ericson and Haggerty also warned about the potential dangers that may be inherent to this approach, namely stereotyping, inclusion of the wrong criteria and exclusion of people:

> the concept of risk (...) turns people, their organizations, and their environments in myriad categories and identities that will make them more manageable (...) People, organizations and environments are sorted into whatever categories will fit the practical purpose of the institution that wishes to make them predictable.
>
> (Ericson and Haggerty, 2002)

The merit of this approach however, lies in the evolution from a reactive to a proactive approach of criminal investigations.

AML on a crime control continuum

Here, we aim to discuss the place of the AML complex in relation to the battle against other types of crime, by means of examining its position on a spectrum of crime control, taking into account its characteristics, the public–private divide and its relation to the penal system. We hope to have made clear that the AML system takes up a very specific place in comparison to traditional types of crime control. We will focus on a number of reasons: first, AML is imposed regulation which results in an emphasis on self-protection; second, the public–private divide in AML is no longer clearly delineated; and third, to enhance crime control, AML know-how is needed, but may conflict with privacy interests.

AML as imposed regulation

In AML, financial institutions have been mandated to act as a tool of crime control, involuntarily engaged in a costly fight against crime, of which they are not a victim, but the instrument. Money laundering as such does not harm them, which implies that – strictly speaking – they have no concern in preventing it. Of course there is a moral impetus, and the introduction of AML legislation has resulted in the fact that in cases of non-compliance, there will be (reputational) harm. This does not alter the fact that banks are mandated to fight money laundering in a public interest, without having specific investigative powers or authority, without receiving basic tools, and run the risk of being sanctioned in cases of non-compliance. By consequence, AML is not self-regulation, but imposed regulation. This implies that banks will have their own agendas and strategies in the implementation of this legislation, also related to the threat of sanction that is linked to non-compliance. This contrasts highly with the private security industry, which takes up security tasks out of self-(commercial) interest. Furthermore, while private security shifts the costs of crime prevention towards the victim (either the company that hires private detectives, or the citizen who hires a private guard) (McLaughlin *et al.*, 2003), AML shifts these costs towards the vehicles of crime.[8] Of course, in turn, banks (the vehicles) may shift these costs to their clients.

It may be clear that without AML legislation, and the stick of regulatory sanctions, the appeal of a bank to perform AML monitoring would be very low, which makes the threat of sanctioning a necessary part of the deal. Within AML, the carrot that usually comes with the stick (Braithwaite, 2002), is lacking. An example of a carrot in this respect could be the provision of information to (proactively) handle AML responsibilities or make AML-related decisions with regard to trespassing customers. The AML construction of today, however, implies that the financial institutions' AML policy is not purely aimed at fighting crime, but also – and primarily – at safeguarding themselves from regulatory sanction. Moreover, we also see some elements of private justice in AML, as banks decide on the effect of their investigation for their clients. In a self-protective reflex, financial institutions will get rid of clients who may pose a risk for the bank.

Public–private divide

Financial institutions are obviously not the only private organisations that carry out in-house investigations on rule-breaking or crime. We refer for example to private investigation units, whose existence within large companies has been documented before (Cools *et al.*, 2005). The vastness of monitoring is not exclusive for AML either; there are corporations that monitor cashiers' transactions or telecom use by clients, through software. However, the main difference is that those corporations carry out those monitoring tasks by free will, in their own interest. After all, they are the actual victims of internal fraud or malevolent clients. Private investigation can therefore be considered as a self-imposed regulatory system, based on voluntary initiatives.

Police investigations, carried out in the interest of the general public, mostly investigating crime in which there is a direct physical victim, find themselves at the opposite end of the continuum. They work within a penal context, with a criminal justice objective of fighting crime. They have an official mandate to react to complaints by the public, and have the tools (among which the monopoly on the use of force) to perform their investigations. Although some of our respondents have spoken of an 'outsourcing' of tasks by the government (Chapter 4), AML is strictly speaking not an example of privatisation of law enforcement tasks: there simply never was a public monitoring system. AML is therefore not a task that has been 'taken over' by private corporations (which is the case for guarding services or bodyguarding). As such, the AML complex constitutes a unique example of a public–private divide (or collaboration *nolens volens*) that does not result from a withdrawal by the state, but a proactive involvement of the state that nevertheless has resulted in putting the responsibility for monitoring transactions and identifying customers in the hands of the private sector, the latter not having asked for this responsibility.

Know-how and cooperation

The absence of flexible cooperation (Chapter 5) between the authorities on the one hand, and compliance officers on the other, results in a relatively static AML system, which may get in the way of efficacy. In AML, compliance officers often lack official investigation tools, resulting in the use of criteria in monitoring systems that are mainly based on formerly discovered cases. AML unavoidably has to fall back on historical transactions and atypicalities that were established in the past. One possible way to remedy this static method and the orientation on the past, is by enlarging knowledge and know-how on money laundering. As AML is a system that is obliged to work on the basis of the philosophy of target hardening and rational choice, the increase of expert knowledge is needed to raise the chance of getting caught (Pheijffer *et al.*, 1997) – at least temporarily. Increasing know-how on the way in which crimes are perpetrated is essential to recognise more transactions and perpetrators as suspicious, in any case until the latter have developed new methods. This could be achieved by developing a patrimony of know-how, built on the strategic knowledge of both public and private actors within the AML system, a patrimony that is flexible, up to date and characterised by rapid information exchange on new money laundering methods and techniques. However, a number of remarks need to be made with regard to this type of information exchange. Rules need to be made with regard to the privacy issues in this respect. After all, strategic information on methods does not have to imply that names or identities of suspects are exchanged. They are, after all, still suspects, and banks are not allowed to inform them of this status either. In this respect, the FIU seems to be best qualified to play a pivotal role in this. The FIU is the centre of information gathering and can therefore use this position to communicate its knowledge to all actors in the AML complex. Such an information exchange may also result in a better-founded, more balanced and less arbitrary risk orientation within AML. When banks are better informed of where they need to look and which indicators they need to search for, privacy issues can be dealt with on the basis of knowledge instead of potential risk.

These observations lead us to a continuum, in which private interests are placed against public interests, police investigations against private investigation and self-regulation against the penal system. AML is situated at the right side of the spectrum, leaning towards the penal system and the public interest, but carried out by private actors.

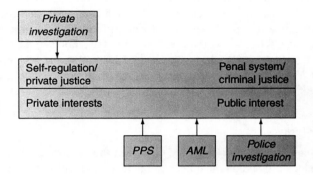

Figure 9.1 The crime control continuum.

Conclusion and directions for future research

Changing banking landscapes

The present study allows for a detailed picture at a given moment in time. In our case, the credit crisis crossed our study at the end of the interviewing phase and has in fact created a different banking landscape. This implies that some of the banks that were interviewed in 2007–2008 either have changed configuration or have dropped out of the picture altogether. In view of these radical changes in scenery, we returned to some of the banks in the spring of 2009 in order to grasp the impact of the credit crisis on the compliance function and the AML task.

We were wondering whether these changes had affected the resources for compliance, the pressure on compliance departments to comply with (AML) legislation and, on a more practical level, the techniques and methods for detecting money laundering. The recent crisis has raised various issues for banks that may be conflicting: the need to ensure effective prevention, detection and response mechanisms (along with the associated resource requirements) against the need to control costs (KPMG, 2009). After all, tougher market conditions may imply that less personnel may be hired – resulting in more pressure on the existing staff, more pressure on compliance departments to allow as many clients as possible, or in contrast, that the bank's priorities are precisely aimed at preventing more damage to their reputation. The latter became clear in the PR campaign of several banks,[9] but also in the public excuses that were made by some bank directors (De Tijd, 18 April 2009). Furthermore, the credit crisis has not only resulted in a low public confidence in banks (*De Standaard*, 28 April 2009), a decrease of the number of transactions carried out through banks and a hold on interbank loans, but may also bring along new opportunities for money laundering. In January 2009, the Belgian FIU (Financial Intelligence Unit) was quoted in the Belgian press, stating that 'Crisis makes money laundering checks peak' (*De Morgen*, 6 January 2009). Apparently, as a result of the financial crisis, criminal money also seeks ways to move around, resulting in more criminal transactions and hence a rise in alerts by reporting agencies. It seems to be very difficult to distinguish criminal flows of money from transactions by worried clients who want to change banks (cf. 'Fortis alerts', Chapter 6). According to the FIU, the financial crisis seems to create opportunities for money laundering. However, different to the media coverage in January, the annual reports of the FIU on 2008 and 2009 show a decrease in reports by banks (cf. Chapter 8: the number of reports has decreased from 2007 to 2009 by almost 600). To be more precise, when looking at the figures more closely, we note that the proportion of reports by banks in relation to the total amount of reports received by the FIU, has been declining gradually (from 44 per cent in 2004 to 21 per cent in 2009) (CTIF-CFI, 2010). A displacement effect therefore seems to have occurred. The heading 'Crime money uses banking crisis as smoke screen' (*De Standaard*, 24 April 2009) may relate to changing techniques in money laundering, but this does not necessarily apply to the financial institutions. The overall rise in the number of reports in 2008 is probably to be explained by the rise in reports by other institutions (mainly the exchange offices, casinos and the customs (CTIF-CFI, 2009)).

As stated, we also confronted some of our respondents with these changes in setting. All three respondents emphasised that the pressure to be compliant has been as high as ever. Some stated that pressure has always been relatively high. A difference, however, is that some financial institutions are obliged to cut costs, resulting in doing the same task, with the same objective, but with fewer people and maybe more challenges. As a result, pressure on staff increases. The respondents stated that the number of reports that they submitted to the FIU has not increased over the past months, although they did witness a rise in cash transactions (often stemming from Fortis or Dexia). These cash transactions were also monitored before the crisis, so this has not changed the operation of AML. They also notice that bank employees have proportionally reported more suspicious transactions to compliance (first-line AML in relation to second line, monitoring by compliance), and state that this is the result of better training and awareness. Overall, compliance respondents state that the crisis has passed AML by completely.

The respondents acknowledged the fact that compliance, in general, has not prevented the crisis from happening, but emphasised the fact that AML compliance is different from, for example, financial risk management. The general expectation at this moment is therefore, that with regard to AML compliance, the credit crunch will not have a specific impact. With regard to risk management and compliance in general, however, respondents expect more regulation and more emphasis on risk management with regard to customers being treating fairly and customer protection. This trend is awaited with some doubt; after all, formal control may be enhanced, but this may not have an impact on the culture and the ethics that rule the world of finance. We concluded that, although the financial landscape has been shaken up, the AML landscape in the banking sector seems relatively stable.

Future research

As research should always raise more questions than answers, we conclude this book by referring to some of the blind spots that were detected throughout this research and hope to give an impetus for further criminological inquiry on this topic. First of all, in the course of our research, the lack of empirical information on money laundering was remarkable. Surprisingly little is known of the phenomenology and practices of money laundering, which makes studying the battle against it a specifically challenging task. Studying the phenomenon could be done in a diversity of ways, e.g. by studying convictions or prosecutions of money laundering cases or by comparing international data on money laundering and its actual manifestation and recent methods. In this respect, focusing on perpetrators, facilitators and methods of laundering money seems an important area for research.

Following the limitations of this study, we suggest a more broad approach by looking at other institutions that have the duty to report suspicious transactions, such as notaries, real estate agents (reporting virtually no suspicious transactions, as well as dealers in diamonds – CTIF-CFI, 2010) or casinos. This would also allow for a more in-depth look at the displacement effect that compliance and AML investments by banks have induced. Furthermore, our research focused on the preventive approach of money laundering, excluding the repressive approach to money laundering (via the follow-the-money strategy). To increase knowledge on (A)ML, it would be highly recommended to study the repressive aspect of anti money laundering.

As a third topic for future research we refer to the AML chain. The functioning, content and decision-making within this chain has not been studied before. Maybe this is due to difficulties in gaining access to information on the contents of this chain, but it does imply that AML has been relatively left to its fate with regard to criminological research. Still, taking into account that AML represents a large investment by a large number of public and private partners, invading personal privacy and due process, and aimed at having an impact on the battle against crime, we think that studying the operation and performance of this system is of great importance. Examining the risk orientation, the decision-making and prioritisation within the several stages of the AML chain is not only vital in view of transparency and accountability, but could assist actors that are engaged in anti money laundering. In a micro approach, this could lead to an examination of the role of public agencies within AML, such as the FIU, the public prosecutors and the police services and the impact that each actor has on the outcome of the money laundering investigation. In a macro perspective, this could give insight as to how the AML chain (as a preventive approach) influences the battle against money laundering as a whole.

In conclusion ...

During this study, we hope to have made clear to you, the reader, that AML is not 'just any crime fighting system'. It does in fact have an impact on a number of basic rights, on our privacy, on our financial transactions and on the way in which institutions are supposed to approach us.

We have concluded that AML takes up a new place in the public–private divide, in which the private sector – by order of the authorities – carries out a large pre-selection, preceding the penal, public selection mechanism. The fact that this pre-selection of cases is based on scenarios of suspiciousness that are centred around a limited amount of information from the past (Crawford, 2009), implies that the AML system runs the risk of resulting in a self-fulfilling prophecy. We have noted that AML constitutes a new and unique position in the landscape of policing and fighting crime. 'Policing the money' has become a new proliferation of the multilateralisation of policing (Favarel-Garrigues *et al.*, 2008). The compliance function can be considered as an extension and an outpost of the traditional police services, with its own deontology, expertise and working methods, and has found its place between private policing and public policing. All this demonstrates that there is all the more reason to broaden the scope of traditional paradigms, within crime control and criminology. Criminological visions and theory need to adapt to the development of 'new' types of crime and crime control, to play a role in the acquisition of knowledge on these new phenomena. We have questioned the non-transparency of the norms and the concepts of 'risk' that are applied in AML. Norms and scenarios on the basis of which transactions and individuals are considered as 'suspicious' are mainly determined by private actors, control or oversight by public actors seems minimal and clients are not informed on the use of these norms. The risk-based approach results in focusing on the identification of high-risk and/or suspicious categories, scenarios and profiles, potentially impacting basic human rights in view of a higher degree security for all (Zedner, 2003). We have cast our doubts with regard to proportionality in this respect. After all, AML illustrates that public and private policing have become interchangeable and intertwined, that victims and perpetrators are not always easy to differentiate, that public and private interests sometimes are entangled and, finally, that while others are policing the money, we need to be aware of the danger that basic rights such as due process and privacy may be violated.

Notes

1 Introduction

1 In 2005, also insurance companies were obliged to install a compliance function (CBFA, 2005).
2 The e-mail was sent by Febelfin to 208 persons; two compliance contacts per bank. In 2007, Belgium counted 104 banks. We do not know whether one or more respondents per bank filled out the survey. The response rate is therefore very difficult to calculate.
3 Most of the interviews were recorded on minidisc, unless the respondent refused recording, which was the case in two interviews. In order to be able to assess the contents of the interviews, and as a preparation for future interviews, most of them were typed out by the researcher herself.

2 Methodology in studying corporations: breaking out of the tunnel vision

1 This is an amended version of Verhage, A. (2009a). With kind permission from Maklu Publishers.
2 'Corporate crime refers to crimes perpetrated by individuals or groups within a respected and bona fide organisation within the framework of the execution of organisational tasks. These entrepreneurs primarily focus on continuing their company, but cross penal boundaries to achieve this' (van de Bunt, 1992).

3 Money laundering and the social reaction: a battle instigated by power motives?

1 This chapter is an amended version of Verhage and Ponsaers (2009) and Verhage (2009b). With kind permission from Springer Science+Business Media.
2 For example, Thony (2002), but also several policy documents relate the battle on money laundering to drug-related organised crime, for example FATF *Prevention of Criminal Use of the Banking System for the Purpose of Money-Laundering*, December 1988.
3 Council Directive 91/308/EEC of 10 June 1991 on prevention of the use of the financial system for the purpose of money laundering.
4 Ibid.
5 From here referred to as CTIF-CFI or FIU.
6 Belgian Senate, 468–1 (B.Z. 1991–1992) Explanatory Memorandum to the draft of Law on the prevention of the use of the financial system for money laundering 22 July 1992, p. 7.
7 Ibid, p. 8.

8 Law of 11 January 1993 on the prevention of the use of the financial system for the laundering of money and financing of terrorism, *B.S.*, 9 February 1993.
9 Article 10 has become article 18 under the current Law.
10 Belgian Senate, 468–1 (B.Z. 1991–1992).
11 In some institutions, there are specific AML officers, working for the compliance department.
12 By article 20 inserted in 2007 in the Law on the statute and supervision of credit institutions, *B.S.*, 19 April 1993.
13 The indicators can be found in the Royal Decree of 3 June 2007 – Royal Decree for the execution of article 14 quinquies of the law of 11 January 1993 on the prevention of the use of the financial system for the laundering of money and financing of terrorism. This article 14 quinquies was changed into article 28 after the adaptation of the AML law in 2010.
14 Belgian Official Journal.
15 Article 30, paragraph 3, Wet van 11 januari 1993 tot voorkoming van het gebruik van het financiële stelsel voor het witwassen van geld en de financiering van terrorisme, en het Wetboek van Vennootschappen, *B.S.*, 26 January 2010. (Law of 18 January 2010 for amendment of the Law of 11 January on the prevention of the use of the financial system for laundering money and financing terrorism, and the Companies Code, *B.S.*, 26 January 2010.)
16 Which was one of the complaints of the banking sector during the interviews, as the address is not noted on passports. The Law now also grants certain professional organisations access to the Public Register, but does not specify which professional organisations this will be (the organisations will be appointed by the King).
17 Article 16, paragraph 3, Belgische Kamer van Volksvertegenwoordigers, 16 juli 2009, Wetsontwerp tot wijziging van de wet van 11 januari 1993 tot voorkoming van het gebruik van het financiële stelsel voor het witwassen van geld en de financiering van terrorisme, en het Wetboek van Vennootschappen Doc 52 1988 (2008/2009), art. 7. Wet van 18 januari 2010 tot wijziging van de Wet van 11 januari 1993 tot voorkoming van het gebruik van het financiële stelsel voor het witwassen van geld en de financiering van terrorisme, en het Wetboek van Vennootschappen, *B.S.*, 26 January 2010. (Article 16, paragraph 3., Belgian House of Representatives, 16 July 2009, Bill for the amendment of the Law of 11 January on the prevention of the use of the financial system for laundering money and financing terrorism and the Companies Code (Doc 52 1988 (2008/2009)), article 7, Law of 18 January 2010 for amendment of the Law of 11 January on the prevention of the use of the financial system for laundering money and financing terrorism, and the Companies Code, *B.S.*, 26 January 2010 (own translation).)

4 The compliance officer: functioning between the hammer and the anvil

1 This is an amended version of Verhage (2009c) and Verhage (2009b). With kind permission from Springer Science+Business Media and Emerald UK.
2 www.bankersalmanac.com, 20 February 2008.
3 Wet van 22 maart op het statuut van en de toezicht op de kredietinstellingen, *B.S*, 19 april 1993.
4 This definition was subsequently included in the Banking Law in 2007.
5 Association for Compliance Officers: http://vco1.nl/.
6 Interview with Dutch compliance expert, February 2008.
7 Regeling melding en regeling transacties in effecten, 1999 (Regulation on reporting and transactions in securities, 1999).
8 In contrast to a decentralised approach. A decentralised approach implies the functioning of compliance units on a regional or local level, for example by use of 'compliance antennas'.

9 After implementation of the Third Directive in 2010, possibilities for (formal) information exchange between banks have increased substantially: they are now allowed to exchange information with other banks – see Chapter 3 or article 30 paragraph 3 of the Wet van 11 januari 1993 tot voorkoming van het gebruik van het financiële stelsel voor het witwassen van geld en de financiering van terrorisme, en het Wetboek van Vennootschappen, *B.S.*, 26 January 2010.

10 This dematerialisation obliges clients to hand in their paper bonds to the banks – the 'dematerialisation' refers to the transformation from paper ('material') bonds to bonds posted in a securities account.

11 Programmawet 27 April 2004, *B.S.*, 8 May 2007. In the current AML law, article 14 quinquies has become article 28.

12 The indicators can be found in the Royal Decree of 3 June 2007 – Koninklijk besluit tot uitvoering van artikel 14 quinquies van de wet van 11 januari 1993 tot voorkoming van het gebruik van het financiële stelsel voor het witwassen van geld en de financiering van terrorisme, 3 juni 2007.

5 The anti money laundering complex: a public–private approach of anti money laundering

1 This is an amended version of Verhage (2009d). With kind permission from Boom Publishers.

2 For more information on methodology and respondents, please see Chapter 1.

3 Quotes of compliance officers will be indicated as 'cpl'. Quotes of respondents with a police background will be indicated as 'pol'. Quotes of respondents with a regulatory background will be indicated as 'REG'. Quotes of respondents from the FIU will be indicated as 'FIU'.

4 Belgian Official Journal.

5 The indicators can be found in the Royal Decree of 3 June 2007 – Koninklijk besluit tot uitvoering van artikel 14quinquies van de wet van 11 januari 1993 tot voorkoming van het gebruik van het financiële stelsel voor het witwassen van geld en de financiering van terrorisme, 3 June 2007.

6 Examples of indicators are: the presence of international transactions (indicator nr. 9) or the absence of documentation to justify bonds or savings (indicator nr. 10).

7 Belgian House of Representatives, *Bill for the reform of the law of 11 January 1993 on the prevention of the use of the financial system for the laundering of money and financing of terrorism with regard to funds and assets that are considered as illegal.* 12 December 2007, DOC 52, 0549/001.

8 ABN AMRO, a Dutch bank, was sanctioned in 2005 by the Dutch and US regulators for a total of $80 million for, among other things, negligence regarding AML procedures, lack of monitoring and failure to report certain transactions.

6 The beauty of grey: the investigation of suspicious transactions

1 This is an amended version of Verhage (2009e). With kind permission of Wolf Legal Publishers.

2 www.world-check.com/overview (accessed 25 November 2010).

7 Supply and demand: anti money laundering by the compliance industry

1 This is an amended version of Verhage (2009f). With kind permission from Emerald.

2 www.compliance-instituut.nl/ (accessed 12 February 2009).

3 The Third European Directive has specified that institutions 'should employ every means to identify actors of money laundering and terrorist financing' – Belgische

Kamer van Volksvertegenwoordigers, 16 juli 2009, Wetsontwerp tot wijziging van de wet van 11 januari 1993 tot voorkoming van het gebruik van het financiële stelsel voor het witwassen van geld en de financiering van terrorisme, en het Wetboek van Vennootschappen Doc 52 1988 (2008/2009), art. 7.and Wet van 18 januari 2010 tot wijziging van de Wet van 11 januari 1993 tot voorkoming van het gebruik van het financiële stelsel voor het witwassen van geld en de financiering van terrorisme, en het Wetboek van Vennootschappen, *B.S.*, 26 January 2010.

4 www.nytimes.com/2005/01/28/business/28riggs.html?_r=1&scp=5&sq=riggs&st=cse (accessed 2 April 2009).
5 http://query.nytimes.com/gst/fullpage.html?res=9B07E4D6103DF937A35750C0A96 39C8B63&sec=&spon=&pagewanted=print (accessed 15 March 2009).
6 Quotes of compliance officers will be indicated as 'cpl'.
7 Quotes of corporations in the compliance industry will be indicated as 'ci'.
8 www.cclcompliance.com/ (accessed 27 February 2008).
9 www.complianceconsultancy.nl/ (accessed 27 February 2008).
10 www.eurogroup.be/en/our_services_expertise.asp#banqueass (accessed 27 February 2008).
11 www.uniskill.com (accessed 27 February 2008).
12 For example, KBC testifies on the Norkom website how well the Norkom software works (www.norkom.com).
13 www.ustreas.gov/offices/enforcement/ofac/sdn/sdnlist.txt (accessed 10 March 2009).
14 www.un.org/Docs/sc/committees/1267/consoltablelist.shtml (accessed 6 April 2009).
15 By means of example, World-Check claims to combine 'over 200,000 different public information sources (such as official governmental, intelligence and police sites) from over 230 countries, multi and global organisations, and international and national media' – e-mail message from World-Check, 2 February 2007.
16 http://diplomatie.belgium.be/en/newsroom/news/press_releases/foreign_affairs/2009/ july/ni_220709_schrapping_vinck_sayadi_vn-sanctielijst.jsp (accessed 25 November 2010).

8 The anti money laundering chain in Belgium: measuring 'effectiveness'?

1 Parts of this text were previously published in Verhage (2009c). With kind permission from Emerald.
2 Figures on this vary from 20 per cent (van Duyne, 1997) to 50 per cent of the original illicit sum (Unger, 2006, p. 145).

9 Conclusion: policing the money

1 This is an amended version of Verhage (2010). With kind permission from Maklu Publishers.
2 Study on 'Best practices in vertical relations between the FIUs and law enforcement services and Money Laundering and Terrorist Financing Reporting entities with a view to indicating effective models for feedback on follow-up to and effectiveness of Suspicious Transactions Reports', Brussels, 2008–2009.
3 Wet van 18 januari 2010 tot wijziging van de Wet van 11 januari 1993 tot voorkoming van het gebruik van het financiële stelsel voor het witwassen van geld en de financiering van terrorisme, en het Wetboek van Vennootschappen, *B.S.*, 26 January 2010.
4 Scenarios are used for monitoring transactions. These scenarios are built on parameters that are derived from previous money laundering cases, parameters such as many international transactions, sudden changes in total assets, etc. (see for more details Verhage, 2009c).
5 Or the federal public prosecutor (article 28 Code of Criminal Procedure).

6 According to Stessens (2000, p. 173), France has introduced a system for banks to cover themselves against prosecutions in this respect. By cooperating with the authorities banks are no longer liable to sanctions. In the case that clients sue the bank for suffering loss as a result of a suspicious transaction report, the bank is able to recover the loss from the state. In Belgium, an analogous proposition was made (Verslag van de commissie voor de financiën van de staat – 1991–1992, 468–2: 35–36) but this has not been implemented.

7 Strangely, although all our respondents mentioned the lack of feedback from the authorities, in the FATF evaluation of 2005 it is stated that feedback to the reporting institutions is considered to be sufficient (FATF, 2005).

8 KPMG calculated in 2007 that costs of AML for banks are high and keep rising (58 per cent in the last three years) (KPMG, 2007).

9 A number of banks have emphasised their trustworthiness and reliability in their marketing strategies. The Banque de la Poste, for example, advertised with the slogan 'Anti-risk Bank' (www.bpo.be).

Bibliography

ABN AMRO (2005). www.group.abnamro.com/pressroom/pressreleasedetail.cfm?Release ID=278325 (accessed 27 January 2008).

Alexander, R. (2007). *Insider dealing and money laundering in the EU: law and regulation*. Hampshire, Ashgate Publishing Ltd.

Algemene Rekenkamer (2008). Bestrijden witwassen en terrorismefinanciering. Den Haag, Sdu Uitgevers.

Alldridge, P. (2008). 'Money laundering and globalization', *Journal of Law and Society* 35(4): 437–463.

Aninat, E., D. Hardy and R. Johnston (2002). 'Combating money laundering and the financing of terrorism', *Finance and development*, IMF 39(3): 44–47.

Ayres, I. and J. Braithwaite (1992). *Responsive regulation: transcending the deregulation debate*. New York, Oxford University Press.

Baldwin, F. (2006). 'Exposure of financial institutions to criminal liability', *Journal of Financial Crime* 13(4): 387–407.

Bartlett, B. (2002). 'The negative effects of money laundering on economic development', The Asian Development Bank, Regional Technical Assistance Project No. 5967, Countering Money Laundering in The Asian and Pacific Region. Available at: www.apgml.org/Index_files/ann_meet_doc_2002_public/pdf/ADB's%20Economic%20Research%20Report%20Final.pdf (accessed on 25 November 2010).

Basel Committee on Banking Supervision (2005). 'Compliance and the compliance function in banks', Basel Committee on Banking Supervision.

Bayley, D. and C. Shearing (1996). 'The future of policing', *Law and Society Review* 30: 585–606.

Bayley, D. and C. Shearing (2001). *The new structure of policing: description, conceptualization and research agenda*. Washington, DC, National Institute of Justice.

BCBS (1988). *Prevention of criminal use of the banking system for the purpose of money-laundering*, p. 4.

BCBS (2005). *Compliance and the compliance function in banks*, p. 16.

Beck, A., M. Gill and A. Willis (1994). 'Violence in retailing: physical and verbal victimisation of staff', in: *Crime at work: studies in security and crime prevention*. M. Gill (ed.). Leicester, Perpetuity Press, pp. 83–101.

Beck, U. (1992). *Risk society: towards a new modernity*. New Delhi, Sage.

Belgian Federal Police, Nationaal Veiligheidsplan 2008–2011, see www.polfed-fedpol.be/pub/pdf/NVP2008-2011.pdf.

Belgian Senate, 468–1 (B.Z. 1991–1992). Explanatory Memorandum to the draft of Law on the prevention of the use of the financial system for money laundering, 22 July 1992.

Bijleveld, C. (2005). *Methoden en Technieken van Onderzoek in de Criminologie.* Den Haag, Boom Juridische Uitgevers.

Billiet, J. and H. Waege (2003). *Een samenleving onderzocht. Methoden van sociaalwetenschappelijk onderzoek.* Antwerpen, De Boeck.

Boon, K. (1993). *De gespecialiseerde private opsporing: een tip van de sluier opgelicht.* Brussel, Politeia.

Bovenkerk, F. (1998). 'Fenomeenonderzoek; of hoe de etnografische criminologie haar onschuld verliest', *Justitiële Verkenningen* 8: 27–35.

Braithwaite, J. (1984). *Corporate crime in the pharmaceutical industry.* London, Routledge and Kegan Paul.

Braithwaite, J. (1985). 'White collar crime', *Annual Review of Sociology* 11(1): 1–25.

Braithwaite, J. (2000). 'The new regulatory state and the transformation of criminology', *British Journal of Criminology* 40: 222–238.

Braithwaite, J. (2002). *Restorative justice and responsive regulation.* New York, Oxford University Press.

Braithwaite, J., J. Walker and P. Grabosky (1987). 'An enforcement taxonomy of regulatory agencies', *Law and Policy* 9(3): 323–351.

Brown, E.D. and J.O.N. Cloke (2007). 'Shadow Europe: alternative European financial geographies', *Growth & Change* 38(2): 304–327.

Button, M. (2007). *Security officers and policing: powers, culture and control in the governance of private space.* Aldershot, Ashgate.

Capgemini (2005). *Turning compliance into competitive advantage.* Capgemini, Paris.

CBFA (1997). Circulaire aan de kredietinstellingen D1 97/10 inzake het voorkomingsbeleid.

CBFA (2001a). Bijlage aan de circulaire D1 2001/13 van 18 december 2001 over 'compliance'.

CBFA (2001b). Circulaire D1 2001/13 aan de kredietinstellingen.

CBFA (2004). Reglement van 27 juli 2004 van de Commissie voor het Bank-, Financie- en Assurantiewezen betreffende de voorkoming van het witwassen van geld en de financiering van terrorisme (Regulation of 27 July 2004 of the CBFA regarding the prevention of money laundering and terrorist financing) B.S., 22 November.

CBFA (2005). Gecoördineerde versie d.d. 12 juli 2005 van de circulaire van de Commissie voor het Bank-, Financie – en Assurantiewezen over de waakzaamheidsverplichtingen met betrekking tot de cliënteel en de voorkoming van het gebruik van het financiële stelsel voor het witwassen van geld en de financiering van terrorisme. (Coordinated version of 12 July 2005 of the circular of the Banking, Finance and Insurance Commission on the duty of diligence with regard to clients and the prevention of the use of the financial system for money laundering and terrorism financing.)

Clinard, M. (1983). *Corporate ethics and crime.* Beverly Hills, Sage.

Clinard, M. and P. Yeager (1980). *Corporate crime.* New York, Macmillan.

Coggan, P. (2002). *The money machine: how the city works.* London, Penguin Books.

Commission of the European Communities (2009). 'Compliance with the anti-money laundering directive by cross-border banking groups at group level', *Commission Staff Working Paper*: 62.

Cools, K. (2005). *Controle is goed vertrouwen nog beter. Over bestuurders en corporate governance.* Assen, Koninklijke van Gorcum.

Cools, M. (1994). *Werknemerscriminaliteit.* Brussel, VUB Press.

Cools, M. (2004). 'In het land van Rembrandt. Groepsportret van een compagnie schutters', *Tijdschrift voor Criminologie* Jubileumuitgave – Een Vlaamse spiegel: 24–29.

Cools, M. (2005). 'Nog een rondje ondernemingen pesten of oude en nieuwe vormen en gedachten inzake criminalisering, inspectie en controle', in: *De suggestie van toezicht en handhaving*. B. Hoogenboom, G. Bakker and M. Pheijffer (eds). Den Haag, SDU Uitgevers, pp. 67–86.

Cools, M. (2006). 'Het kerntakendebat over de politie is nu eenmaal overbodig', in: *Het kerntakendebat continued*. P. Ponsaers, E. Enhus and F. Hutsebaut (eds). Brussel, Politeia, pp. 27–37.

Cools, M. and H. Haelterman (eds) (1999). *Security consultancy. Het actieterrein van de beveiligingsadviseur in België en Nederland*. Diegem, Kluwer.

Cools, M. and K. Verbeiren (2004). *Politie en Privébewaking. Samen Sterk*. Brussel, Politeia.

Cools, M., P. Ponsaers, A. Verhage and B. Hoogenboom (2005). *De andere Rechtsorde. Demonopolisering van fraude-onderzoek*. Brussel, Politeia.

Cornish, D. and R. Clarke (2006). 'The rational choice perspective', in: *The essential criminology reader*. S. Henry and M. Lanier (eds). Boulder, CO, Westview Press, pp. 18–30.

Cowton, C.J. (1998). 'The use of secondary data in business ethics research', *Journal of Business Ethics* 17(4): 423–434.

Coyle, D. (2004). *Sex, drugs & economics: an unconventional introduction to economics*. New York, Texere.

Crane, A. (1999). 'Are you ethical? Please tick yes □ or no □: on researching ethics in business organizations', *Journal of Business Ethics* 20(3): 237–248.

Crawford, A. (2009). 'Governing perceptions of crime and (in)security in an age of uncertainty', paper for the Final Crimprev Conference 'Deviance, Crime and Prevention in a Punitive Age', June.

Croall, H. (2001). *Understanding white collar crime*. Buckingham, Open University Press.

CTIF-CFI (2004). 10e Activiteitenverslag 2002–2003, CTIF-CFI, Brussel.

CTIF-CFI (2006). 12e Activiteitenverslag 2005, CTIF-CFI, Brussel.

CTIF-CFI (2007). Activiteitenrapport, 2006, CTIF-CFI, Brussel.

CTIF-CFI (2008). Activiteitenrapport 2007, CTIF-CFI, Brussel.

CTIF-CFI (2009). 15e Activiteitenverslag 2008, CTIF-CFI, Brussel.

CTIF-CFI (2010). 16e Activiteitenverslag 2009, CTIF-CFI, Brussel.

Dasselaar, C. (2008). 'Register voor compliance professionals', in: *Jaarboek Compliance 2008*. J. de Bruin, P. Diekman and R. Hoff (eds). Nieuwerkerk ad Ijssel, Gelling Publishing, pp. 155–158.

Datamonitor (2003). *Anti-money laundering technology. The risk-based route to compliance*. New York, Datamonitor.

De Baets, P., S. De Keulenaer and P. Ponsaers (eds) (2003). *Het Belgisch Inspectiewezen. De niet ingeloste belofte*. Antwerpen, Maklu.

De Bie, B. and T. Carion (2001). 'Van compliance naar integriteitsmanagement', *Managementjaarboek*: 1–6.

De Morgen (6 January 2009) *Crisis doet witwascontroles pieken* (Crisis makes money laundering checks peak).

De Standaard (24 December 1999). *DRIE. Jo Lernout & Pol Hauspie* (Three. Jo Lernout & Paul Hauspie).

De Standaard (7 January 2006). *Moslimechtpaar uit Putte buiten verdenking financiering terrorisme* (Muslim couple from Putte no longer suspected of terrorism financing).

De Standaard (22 July 2006). *Verdachten Lernout & Hauspie riskeren vijf jaar cel* (Suspects Lernout & Hauspie risk five years in prison).

De Standaard (23 May 2007) *200 nieuwe burgerlijke partijen op tweede procesdag L&H* (200 new civil actions on second trial day of L&H).

De Standaard (18 October 2007) *Dexia en KPMG stellen zich burgerlijke partij in L&H proces* (Dexia and KPMG bring civil action in L&G trial).

De Standaard (3 November 2007). *Indicatoren witwassen zijn bindend* (Money laundering indicators are binding).

De Standaard (20 November 2007). *Banken blokkeren 200.000 rekeningen* (Banks block 200,000 accounts).

De Standaard (2 January 2009). *Eén Belg op drie heeft geen vertrouwen meer in banken* (One out of three Belgians no longer trust banks).

De Standaard (24 April 2009). *Crimineel geld gebruikt bankencrisis als rookgordijn* (Crime money uses banking crisis as smoke screen).

De Standaard (28 April 2009). *Bankiers zweren* (Bankers swear).

De Tijd (9 November 2007). *Banken negeren witwasrichtlijn* (Banks ignore money laundering directions).

De Tijd (12 September 2008) *Criminelen hebben eigen grootbank* (Criminals have their own bank).

De Tijd (18 April 2009). (Without title.)

den Hertog, F. and E. van Sluijs (2000). *Onderzoek in organisaties. Een methodologische reisgids.* Assen, Van Gorcum.

Deruyck, F. (2009). 'Witwassen als nooit tevoren', *Witwassen in Nederland en België* Den Haag, Nederlands-Vlaamse Vereniging voor Strafrecht, pp. 67–130.

Dillman, D.A. (1991). 'The design and administration of mail surveys', *Annual Review of Sociology* 17(1): 225–249.

Dillman, D.A. and D. Bowker (2001). 'The web questionnaire challenge to survey methodologists', in: *Dimensions of Internet Science.* U. Reips and M. Bosnjak (eds). Lengerich, Pabst Science Publishers.

Dowding, K. (1996). *Power (concepts in social thought).* University of Minnesota Press.

Ericson, R. and K. Haggerty (2002). *Policing the risk society.* Oxford, Clarendon Press.

Ernst & Young (2009). *The 2009 Ernst & Young business risk report. The top 10 risks for global businesses.*

European Commission (2008). *Study on 'Best practices in vertical relations between the Financial Intelligence Unit and (1) law enforcement services and (2) Money Laundering and Terrorist Financing Reporting entities with a view to indicating effective models for feedback on follow-up to and effectiveness of suspicious transaction reports',* Brussel, 2008.

European Commission (2009a). *A report on global illicit drug markets 1998–2007.* P. Reuter, F. Trautmann, European Commission.

European Commission (2009b). *Call for comments from the Financial Crime Subgroup on the draft guidelines for the Money Laundering Pilot Project,* p. 7. Brussels, April.

European Parliament and Council (2004). 'Directive 2004/39/EC of the European parliament and of the council of 21 April 2004 on markets in financial instruments directive (Mifid) 32004L0039', Official Journal L, 145: 1–4.

Europol (2003). *Serious crime overviews: counter money laundering: a European Union perspective.* The Hague, Europol.

FATF (2005). '*3ème rapport d'évaluation mutuelle de la lutte anti-blanchiment de capitaux et contre le financement du terrorisme*', available at: www.ctif-cfi.be/doc/en/fatf_eval/37709419.pdf (accessed June 2005).

Favarel-Garrigues, G., T. Godefroy and P. Lascoumes (2006). *Les banques, sentinelles de l'anti-blanchiment. L'invention d'une spécialité professionelle dans le secteur financier*, Paris, CERI.

Favarel-Garrigues, G., T. Godefroy and P. Lascoumes (2008). 'Sentinels in the banking industry: private actors and the fight against money laundering in France', *British Journal of Criminology* 48: 1–19.

Ferguson, N. (2008). *Het succes van geld. Een financiële geschiedenis van de wereld.* Amsterdam/Antwerpen, Uitgeverij Contact.

Fijnaut, C. (2001). '"Polizeiwissenschaft", "police scientifique" en "police science". Enkele impressies vanuit buitenlands perspectief', *Het Tijdschrift voor de Politie* 1/2: 39–41.

Fijnaut, C. and H. Van de Bunt (2000). 'De toekomst van de landelijke bijzondere opsporingsdiensten in het kader van een "goede politiezorg"', in: *De toekomst van de bijzondere opsporingsdiensten.* H. Van de Bunt and J. Nelen (eds). Den Haag, WODC.

Financial Crimes Enforcement Network (19 December 2005). United States Department of the Treasury. www.fincen.gov/abnamro.html (accessed 1 February 2007).

Findlay, M. (1999). *The globalisation of crime: understanding transitional relationships in context.* Cambridge, Cambridge University Press.

Fisse, B. and J. Braithwaite (1993). *Corporations, crime and accountability.* Cambridge, Cambridge University Press.

Fleming, M.H. (2005). *UK law enforcement agency use and management of suspicious activity reports: towards determining the value of the regime*, University College, London.

Freis, J. (2008). *Promoting information sharing in our global anti-money laundering/ counterterrorism finance efforts.* Tenth Anti-Money Laundering and Financing Terrorism International Seminar.

GAO (2008). 'Increased use of exemption provisions could reduce currency transaction reporting while maintaining usefulness to law enforcement efforts.' 08–355.

GAO (2009). Bank Secrecy Act. Suspicious Activity Reports, United States Government Accountability Office, Washington, DC 20548. 09226.

Garland, D. (2001). *The culture of control: crime and social order in contemporary society.* Chicago, University of Chicago Press.

Geis, G. (1993). 'The evolution of the study of corporate crime', in: *Understanding Corporate Criminality.* M. Blankenship (ed.). New York, Garland, pp. 3–28.

Gill, M. (ed.) (1994). *Crime at work: studies in security and crime prevention.* Leicester, Perpetuity Press.

Gill, M. (1998). 'Introduction', in: *Crime at work: increasing the risk for offenders.* M. Gill (ed.). Leicester, Perpetuity Press, pp. 11–24.

Gill, M. and G. Taylor (2004). 'Preventing money laundering or obstructing business?' *British Journal of Criminology* 44: 582–594.

Gottfredson, D. and T. Hirschi (1990). *A general theory of crime.* Stanford, Stanford University Press.

Gouvin, D. (2003). 'Bringing out the big guns: the USA Patriot Act, money laundering, and the war on terrorism', *Baylor Law Review* 55(101): 956.

Grabosky, P. and J. Braithwaite (1986a). 'Corporate crime and governmental response in Australia', in: *The Australian Criminal Justice System.* D. Chappell and P. Wilson (eds). Sydney, Butterworths.

Grabosky, P. and J. Braithwaite (1986b). *Of manners gentle: enforcement strategies of Australian business regulatory agencies.* Oxford, Oxford University Press.

Gray, G.C. (2006). 'The regulation of corporate violations: punishment, compliance, and the blurring of responsibility', *British Journal of Criminology* 46(5): 875–892.

Gummesson, E. (1991). *Qualitative methods in management research.* Newbury Park, Sage.

Harvey, J. (2004). 'Compliance and reporting issues arising for financial institutions from money laundering regulations: a preliminary cost benefit study', *Journal of Money Laundering Control* 7(4): 1–14.

Harvey, J. (2007). 'Just how effective is money laundering legislation?' *Security Journal* 21(3): 189–211.

Harvey, J. and S. Lau (2009). 'Crime-money, reputation and reporting', *Crime, Law and Social Change* 52(1): 57–72.

Hawdon, J.E. (2001). 'The role of presidential rhetoric in the creation of a moral panic: Reagan, Bush, and the War on Drugs', *Deviant Behavior* 22(5): 419–445.

Hawkins, K. (1983). 'Bargain and bluff: compliance strategy and deterrence in the enforcement of regulation', *Law and Policy Quarterly* 5: 35–73.

Hawkins, K. (1984). *Environment and enforcement: regulation and the social definition of pollution.* Oxford, Clarendon Press.

Hazlitt, H. (1979). *Economics in one lesson: the shortest and surest way to understand basic economics.* New York, Three Rivers Press.

Heiskala, R. (2001). 'Theorizing power: Weber, Parsons, Foucault and neostructuralism', *Social Science Information* 40(2): 241–264.

Helleiner, E. (2000). 'The politics of global financial reregulation: lessons from the fight against money laundering', Working Paper no. 15, Centre for Economy Policy Analysis and New School of Social Research.

Henry, S. (1983). *Private justice: towards integrated theorising in the sociology of law.* London, Routledge & Kegan Paul.

Henry, S. (1994). 'Factory law: the changing disciplinary technology of industrial social control', in: *Social Control.* S. Henry (ed.). Aldershot, Dartmouth Publishing Company, pp. 265–284.

Henry, S. and G. Mars (1978). 'Crime at work: the social construction of amateur property theft', *Sociology* 12(2): 245–263.

Heremans, D. (2007). 'Corporate governance issues for banks: a financial stability perspective', KULeuven, Center for Economic Studies – Discussion papers, no. ces0707.

Hoogenboom, B. (1988a). 'Commerciële misdaadbeschrijving. Over de rol van de particuliere beveiligingsindustrie', *Justitiële Verkenningen* 14(2): 83–107.

Hoogenboom, B. (1988b). *Particuliere recherche. Een verkenning van enige ontwikkelingen.* Den Haag, WODC, SDU.

Hoogenboom, B. (1994). *Het Politiecomplex.* Arnhem, Gouda Quint.

Hoogenboom, B. (1999). 'Van oude mensen en dingen die voorbijgaan: criminologie in 2018', in: *Vooruitzichten in de criminologie.* G. Bruinsma, H. van de Bunt and G. Rovers (eds). Amsterdam, Vrije Universiteit Amsterdam, pp. 143–157.

Hoogenboom, B. (2001). *'"t Neemt toe, men weet niet hoe".* *Scenariostudie Financieel-economische criminaliteit 2010.* Den Haag, Vermande.

Hoogenboom, B. (2006). 'Voorbij goed en kwaad van witwassen', *Justitiële Verkenningen* 32(2): 76–86.

Hopkins, M. (2002). 'Crimes against businesses: the way forward for future research', *British Journal of Criminology* 42(4): 782–797.

Huberts, L., S. Verberk, S. Berndsen, H. van den Heuvel, A. van Montfort, W. Huisman and M. Vermeulen (2004). *Overtredende overheden. Op zoek naar de omvang en oorzaken van regelovertreding door overheden.* Amsterdam, Vrije Universiteit.

Huisman, W. (2001). *Tussen winst en moraal: Achtergronden van regelnaleving en regelovertreding door ondernemingen.* Den Haag, BJu.

Huisman, W. and E. Niemeijer (1998). *Zicht op organisatiecriminaliteit; Een literatuuronderzoek.* Den Haag, Sdu Uitgevers.

Hutter, B. (1997). *Compliance: regulation and environment.* Oxford, Clarendon Press.

Hutter, B. (2000). *Regulation and risk: occupational health and safety on the railways.* Oxford, Oxford University Press.

IMF (2004). *The IMF and the fight against money laundering and the financing of terrorism: a fact sheet.*

Johnston, L. (1992). *The rebirth of private policing.* London, Routledge & Kegan Paul.

Johnston, L. (2003). 'From "pluralisation" to "the police extended family": discourses on the governance of community policing in Britain', *International Journal of the Sociology of Law* 31: 185–204.

Jones, T. and T. Newburn (2002). 'The transformation of policing? Understanding current trends in policing systems', *British Journal of Criminology* 42(1): 129–146.

Kagan, R. and J. Scholz (1984). 'The "criminology of the corporation" and regulatory enforcement strategies', in: *Enforcing regulation.* K. Hawkins and J. Thomas (ed.). Boston, Kluwer-Nijhoff Publishing, pp. 67–96.

Kay, J. (2003). *The truth about markets: why some countries are rich and others remain poor.* London, Penguin.

Kellens, G. (1974). *Banqueroute et banqueroutiers.* Brussel, Dessart et Mardaga.

Kempa, M., R. Carrier, J. Wood and C. Shearing (1999). 'Reflections of the evolving concept of "private policing"', *European Journal on Criminal Policy and Research* 7(2): 197–223.

Kennedy, A. (2005). 'Dead fish across the trail: illustrations of money laundering methods', *Journal of Money Laundering Control* 8(4): 305–319.

Kleemans, E. (2001). 'Rationele Keuzebenaderingen', in: *Tegen de Regels. Een inleiding in de criminologie* E. Lissenberg, S. Van Ruller and R. Van Swaaningen (eds). Nijmegen, Ars Aequi Libri.

Kleemans, E., M. Brienen and H. van de Bunt (2002). *Georganiseerde criminaliteit in Nederland. Tweede rapportage op basis van de WODC-monitor.* Den Haag, WODC.

Klerks, P., C. van Meurs and M. Scholtes (2001). *Particuliere recherche, werkwijze en informatiestromen.* Den Haag, ES&E.

Kochan, N. (2006). *The washing machine: money, crime and terror in the offshore system.* London, Duckworth.

KPMG (2007). *Global anti money laundering survey 2007. How banks are facing up to the challenge.*

KPMG (2009). 'Frontiers in finance for decision makers in financial services', March. www.kpmg.com (accessed 8 April 2009).

Lascoumes, P. (1986). *Les Affaires ou l'Art de l'ombre. Les délinquances économiques et financières et leur contrôle.* Paris, Le Centurion.

Law of 11 January 1993 on the prevention of the use of the financial system for laundering money and financing terrorism (Wet van 11 januari 1993 tot voorkoming van het gebruik van het financiële stelsel voor het witwassen van geld en de financiering van terrorisme) (*B.S.*, 9 February 1993).

Levi, M. (1996). 'Money laundering: risks and countermeasures', in: *Money laundering in the 21st century: risks and countermeasures.* A. Graycar and P. Grabosky (eds). Canberra, Australian Institute of Criminology.

Levi, M. (1997). 'Evaluating the "new policing": attacking the money trail of organized crime', *The Australian and New Zealand Journal of Criminology* 30: 1–25.

Levi, M. (1998). 'The craft of the long-firm fraudster: criminal skills and commercial responses', *Crime at work: increasing the risk for offenders*. M. Gill (ed.). Leicester, Perpetuity Press. II: 155–168.

Levi, M. (2001). 'Money laundering: private banking becomes less private', *Global Corruption Report 2001*. Transparency International.

Levi, M. (2002). 'Money laundering and its regulation', *The Annals of the American Academy of Political and Social Science* 582(1): 181–194.

Levi, M. (2005). 'Controlling the international money trail: what lessons have been learned?' *Global Enforcement Regimes. Transnational Organized Crime, International Terrorism and Money Laundering*. Amsterdam, Transnational Institute (TNI).

Levi, M. and V. Maguire (2004). 'Reducing and preventing organised crime: an evidence-based critique', *Crime, Law and Social Change* 41(5): 397–469.

Levi, M. and P. Reuter (2006). *Money laundering*. Chicago: University of Chicago.

Liedtka, J.M. (1992). 'Exploring ethical issues using personal interviews', *Business Ethics Quarterly* 2(2): 161–181.

Lippens, R. (2003). 'The imaginary of ethical business practice', *Crime, Law and Social Change* 40(4): 323–347.

Lynch, M.J., D. McGurrin and M. Fenwick (2004). 'Disappearing act: the representation of corporate crime research in criminological literature', *Journal of Criminal Justice* 32(5): 389–398.

Mars, G. (1972). *An anthropological study of longshoremen and of industrial relations in the port of St John's, Newfoundland, Canada*. London, London University.

Mars, G. (1982). *Cheats at work: an anthropology of workplace crime*. London, Allen & Unwin.

Mars, G. (2001). *Occupational crime*. Aldershot, Ashgate.

Mars, G. (2006). 'Changes in occupational deviance: scams, fiddles and sabotage in the twenty-first century', *Crime, Law and Social Change* 45(4): 285–296.

Marschan-Piekkari, R. and C. Welch (2004). *Handbook of qualitative research methods for international business*. Cheltenham, Edward Elgar Publishing.

Masciandaro, D. (1999). 'Money laundering: the economics of regulation', *European Journal of Law and Economics* 3: 225–240.

McLaughlin, E., J. Muncie and G. Hughes (eds) (2003). *Criminological perspectives: essential readings*. London, Sage.

Micucci, A. (1998). 'A typology of private policing operational styles', *Journal of Criminal Justice* 26(1): 41–51.

Moorman, M. (2005). 'Cutting off the money', SAS, *Banking* pp. 26–29.

Morris, C. (2009). *De meltdown van 2 biljoen dollar*. Amsterdam/Antwerpen, Business Contact.

MOT (2006). Jaaroverzicht 2005 en vooruitblik 2006, Meldingen ongebruikelijke transacties.

Motivans, M. (2003). 'Money laundering offenders 1994–2001', Bureau of Justice Statistics, US Department of Justice, Washington, DC.

Mulkers, J. and H. Haelterman (2001). *Privé-detectives: theorie en praktijk van de private opsporing*. Antwerpen, Maklu.

Naylor, R. (1999). 'Follow-the-money methods on crime control policy', *A study prepared for the Nathanson Centre for the Study of Organized Crime and Corruption*. York University, Toronto.

Naylor, R. (2007). *Criminal profits, terror dollars and nonsense.* Tax Justice NL, Seminar on Money Laundering, Tax Evasion and Financial Regulation. Transnational Institute Amsterdam.

Nelen, H. (2004). 'Hit them where it hurts most? The proceeds-of-crime approach in the Netherlands', *Crime, Law and Social Change* 41(5): 517–534.

Nietzsche, F. (2009). *Voorbij goed en kwaad. Voorspel tot een filosofie van de toekomst.* Amsterdam, Arbeiderspers.

Nivra-Nyenrode, Capgemini and Nederlands Compliance Instituut (2007). *Compliance Survey 2007.* Breukelen, Nivra-Nyenrode Press.

Passas, N. and R.B. Groskin (2001). 'Overseeing and overlooking: the US federal authorities' response to money laundering and other misconduct at BCCI', *Crime, Law and Social Change* 35(1): 141–176.

Patton, M. (2002). *Qualitative research and evaluation methods.* Thousand Oaks, CA, Sage.

Pheijffer, M., J. Kuijl, A. van Dijk and G. Bakker (1997). *Financieel Rechercheren. Theorie en praktijk.* Deventer, Kluwer.

Pieth, M. and G. Aiolfi (2003). 'The private sector becomes active: the Wolfsberg process', *Journal of Financial Crime* 10(4): 359–365.

Pieth, M. and G. Aiolfi (2005). *Anti-money laundering: levelling the playing field.* Basel, Basel Institute on Governance, p. 48.

Ponsaers, P. (1983). Arbeidsinspektie en kapitalisme: strukturalistische analyse van de funktie van een bijzonder strafrechtsbedelingsapparaat in de kapitalistische produktiewijze. *Faculteit Rechtsgeleerdheid, Afdeling Strafrecht, Strafvordering en Criminologie.* Leuven, KU Leuven.

Ponsaers, P. (2000). 'Nieuwe vormen van sociaal conflict: de nieuwe technologische revolutie en de transformatie van de openbare orde.' *Panopticon* 2: 147–160.

Ponsaers, P. (2002a). 'A few considerations by way of conclusion and comparison of an exploratory project', in: *La Criminalité Economique et Financière en Europe.* P. Ponsaers and V. Ruggiero (eds). Paris, L'Harmattan.

Ponsaers, P. (2002b). 'Doorduwen of onderhandelen? De betekenis van sociaal discretionair optreden in het kader van gemeenschapsgerichte politie', in: *Voor verder onderzoek... – Pour suite d'enquête...* G. Duhaut, P. Ponsaers, G. Pyl and R. van de Sompel (eds). Brussel, Politeia, pp. 649–666.

Ponsaers, P. (2009). 'Financieel-economische criminaliteit: stromingen, oorzaken, slachtofferschap en de relatie tot Community (Oriented) Policing', in:. *De criminologische kant van het ondernemen.* G. Vande Walle and P. Van Calster (eds). Den Haag, Boom Juridische Uitgevers, pp. 129–140.

Ponsaers, P. and R. De Cuyper (1980). Arbeidsinspektie: Overheidszaak of privé-aangelegenheid? *Interuniversitaire reeks Criminologie en Strafwetenschappen.* Antwerpen.

Ponsaers, P. and B. Hoogenboom (2004). 'Het moeilijke spel van wortel en stok – organisatiecriminaliteit en handhaving-strategieën van bijzondere inspectie- en opsporingsdiensten', *Tijdschrift voor Criminologie* 46(2): 165–181.

Ponsaers, P. and L. Pauwels (2002). 'De methodestrijd in de criminologie', *Criminologie in Actie. Handboek criminologisch onderzoek.* K. Beyens, J. Goethals, P. Ponsaers and G. Vervaeke (eds). Brussel, Politeia, pp. 55–72.

Ponsaers, P. and S. Snacken (2002). 'Privatisering en nachtwakersstaat', *Panopticon* 23(2): 97–101.

Ponsaers, P., S. De Keulenaer and K. van Altert (2003). *Bijzondere inspectiediensten: empirisch onderzoek naar hun verbaliseringsgedrag.* Gent, Academia Press.

PricewaterhouseCoopers (2002). *Regulatory compliance: a review of future trends.* PricewaterhouseCoopers, London.
PricewaterhouseCoopers (2005). *Compliance: finance's bridge to the enterprise.* PricewaterhouseCoopers, London.
PricewaterhouseCoopers (2007). *Economic crime: people, culture and controls. The 4th biennial Global Economic Crime Survey.*
Programmawet 27 April 2007 (B.S. 8 May 2007).
Punch, M. (1996). *Dirty business: exploring corporate misconduct – analysis and cases.* Thousand Oaks, CA, Sage.
Regeling indicatoren ongebruikelijke transacties (2005). Regeling tot hernieuwde vaststelling van een indicatorenlijst voor ongebruikelijke transacties 19 augustus 2005. No. FM 2005–00241 M. (Regulation on indicators for unusual transactions (2005) Regulation on the renewed assessment of the list of indicators for unusual transactions, 19 August 2005 (own translation))
Reuter, P. (2009). *Assessing money laundering controls.* Presentation for the AML/CTF conference, Sydney, April.
Robertson, D.C. (1993). 'Empiricism in business ethics: suggested research directions', *Journal of Business Ethics* 12(8): 585–599.
Rosenthal, R. (1995). 'Critiquing Pygmalion: a 25-year perspective', *Current Directions in Psychological Science* 4(6): 171–172.
Rosenthal, U., J. Van Riessen, L. Schaap, P. Ponsaers and A. Verhage (2005). *In elkaars verlengde? Publieke en private speurders in Nederland en België.* Zeist, Uitgeverij Kerckebosch.
Ruggiero, V. (2000). *Crime and markets: essays in anti-criminology.* Oxford, Oxford University Press.
Ruggiero, V. (2007). 'It's the economy, stupid! Classifying power crime', *International Journal of the Sociology of Law* 35: 163–177.
Russell, S. and M. Gilbert (1999). 'Truman's revenge: social control and corporate crime', *Crime, Law and Social Change* 32(1): 59–82.
Schneider, F. and D.H. Enste (2000). 'Shadow economies: size, causes, and consequences', *Journal of Economic Literature* 38(1): 77–114.
Shapland, J. and P. Ponsaers (2009). 'Potential effects of national policies on the informal economy', in: *The informal economy and connections with organised crime: the impact of national social and economic policies,* J. Shapland and P. Ponsaers (eds), Den Haag, Boom Juridische Uitgevers, Reeks Het groene gras, pp. 1–21.
Shearing, C. and P. Stenning (1980). 'The quiet revolution: the nature, development, and general legal implications of private security in Canada', *Criminal Law Quarterly* 22: 220–248.
Shields, P. (2005). 'When the "information revolution" and the US security state collide: money laundering and the proliferation of surveillance', *New Media Society* 7(4): 483–512.
Sica, V. (2000). 'Cleaning the laundry: states and the monitoring of the financial system', *Millennium – Journal of International Studies* 29(1): 47–72.
Simpson, S. (2003). 'The criminological enterprise and corporate crime', *Criminologist* 28(4): 1–5.
Skolnick, J. (1975). *Justice without trial: law enforcement in democratic society.* New York, John Wiley & Sons.
Spreutels, J. and C. Grijseels (2001). 'Interaction between money laundering and tax evasion', *EC Tax Review* 10 (1): 3–12.

Stessens, G. (2000). *Money laundering: a new international law enforcement model.* Cambridge, Cambridge University Press.

Suendorf, U. (2001). *Geldwäsche: eine kriminologische Untersuchung.* Neuwied, Luchterhand.

Sutherland, E.H. and D. Cressey (1992). *Principles of criminology.* Lenham, AltaMira Press.

Sutherland, E.H. (1940). 'White-collar criminality', *American Sociological Review* 5(1): 1–12.

Sutherland, E.H. (1945). 'Is "white collar crime" crime?' *American Sociological Review* 10(2): 132–139.

Sutherland, E.H. (1949). *White-collar crime.* New York, Holt, Reinhart and Winston.

Sutherland, E.H. (1983). *White-collar crime: the uncut version.* New Haven, Yale University Press.

Tavares, C., G. Thomas and M. Roudaut (2010) *Money laundering in Europe.* Report of work carried out by Eurostat and DG Home Affairs, Eurostat.

Thierens, F. (2004). 'De compliance functie in België', *Tijdschrift voor Financieel Recht* 3: 778–794.

Thony, J. (2002). 'Money laundering and terrorism financing: an overview', IMF. www.imf.org/external/np/leg/sem/2002/cdmfl/eng/thony.pdf.

Trends (16 October 2008). *Geen verklikkers meer* (No more tattlers).

US Department of State (1998). *1997 International Narcotics Control Strategy Report.* Washington, DC, released by the Bureau for International Narcotics and Law Enforcement Affairs.

Unger, B. (2006). 'The amounts and effects of money laundering', *Report for the Ministry of Finance.* Den Haag.

van de Bunt, H. (1992). *Organisatiecriminaliteit.* Arnhem, Gouda Quint.

van de Bunt, H. (1993). 'De verlokkingen van de georganiseerde misdaad', *Criminele Inlichtingen: de rol van Criminele Inlichtingendiensten bij de aanpak van georganiseerde misdaad.* A. van der Heijden (ed.). Den Haag.

van de Bunt, H. (2008). 'The role of Hawala bankers in the transfer of proceeds from organised crime', *Organized Crime: Culture, Markets and Policies*: 113–126.

van de Bunt, H. and W. Huisman (2004). 'Organisatiecriminaliteit', *Tijdschrift voor Criminologie* 2(46): 106–120.

van de Bunt, H. and W. Huisman (2007). 'Organizational crime in the Netherlands', in: *Crime and Justice in the Netherlands.* M. Tonry and C. Bijleveld (ed.). Chicago, University of Chicago Press, pp. 217–260.

van de Werdt, E. and P. Speekenbrink (2008). 'Witwassen, een koud kunstje', *Jaarboek Compliance 2008.* J. De Bruin, P. Diekman, R. Hoffet *et al.* (eds). Nieuwerkerk aan de IJssel, Gelling Publishing, pp. 201–216.

van den Heuvel, G. (1993). *Onderhandelen of Straffen: Over organisatie-criminaliteit en overheidscontrole.* Arnhem, Gouda Quint.

van den Heuvel, G. (1998). *Collusie tussen Overheid en Bedrijf – een vergeten hoofdstuk uit de organisatiecriminologie.* Rede uitgesproken bij de aanvaarding van het ambt van hoogleraar in de Criminologie, Universiteit Maastricht.

Van den Wyngaert, C. (2003). *Strafrecht, strafprocesrecht en internationaal strafrecht in hoofdlijnen.* Antwerpen, Maklu.

van Dijk, J. and G. Terlouw (1996). 'An international perspective of the business community as victims of fraud and crime', *Security Journal* 7: 157–167.

van Duyne, P. (1997). 'Money laundering. Pavlov's dog and beyond', *European Regional Fraud Conference.* Amsterdam.

van Duyne, P. (2006). 'Witwasonderzoek, luchtspiegelingen en de menselijke maat' *Justitiële Verkenningen* 32(2): 34–40.

van Duyne, P. (2009). 'Serving the integrity of the Mammon and Compulsory Regulatory Conduct Disorder', *Crime, Law and Social Change*, Springer, 52(1): 1–8.

van Duyne, P. and H. de Miranda (1999). 'The emperor's clothes of disclosure: hot money and suspect disclosures', *Crime, Law and Social Change* 31(3): 245–271.

van Duyne, P. and M. Levi (2005). *Drugs and money: managing the drug trade and crime-money in Europe.* London, Routledge.

van Duyne, P.C., M.S. Groenhuijsen and A.A.P. Schudelaro (2005). 'Balancing financial threats and legal interests in money-laundering policy', *Crime, Law and Social Change* 43: 117–147.

Van Heuckelom, C. (2004). 'Het tot stand komen en de krachtlijnen van de Wet van 19 december 2002 tot verruiming van de bijzondere verbeurdverklaring', in *Follow the money: De jacht op crimineel geld.* J. Denolf and E. Francis (eds). Brussel, Politeia, p. 13.

Van Outrive, L., R. Bas, T. Decorte and W. van Laethem (1995). *Private opsporing en bewaking: onderzoek naar methoden van private opsporing en bewaking en de grondrechten van de mens.* Brussel, DWTC.

Van Overtveldt, J. (2007). *The Chicago School: How the University of Chicago assembled the thinkers who revolutionized economics and business.* Chicago, Agate.

Van Raemdonck, K. (1996–1997). 'De verwerking van persoonsgegevens in de banksector. De invloed van de Wet van 8 december 1992', *Jura Falconis* 33(4): 649–690.

van Steden, R. (2007). *Privatizing policing: describing and explaining the growth of private security.* Den Haag, Boom Juridische Uitgevers.

Vande Walle, G. (2002). 'La salle de jeu des criminels en col blanc raffinés. Criminalité financière et économique en Belgique', in: *La Criminalité Economique et Financière en Europe.* P. Ponsaers and V. Ruggiero (eds). Paris, L'Harmattan, pp. 77–98.

Vande Walle, G. (2005). *Conflictafhandeling of risicomanagement? Een studie van conflicten tussen slachtoffers en ondernemingen in de farmaceutische sector.* Brussel, VUBPress.

Vande Walle, G. (2008). 'A matrix approach to informal markets: towards a dynamic conceptualisation', *International Journal of Social Economics* 35(9): 651–665.

Vanderborght, J. (1999) 'Het doel heiligt de middelen? Proactieve recherche in de strijd tegen georganiseerde criminaliteit', *Custodes*, Politeia, 1: 13–32.

Veblen, T. (2007). *The place of science in modern civilization.* New York, Cosimo Classics.

VERBI Software (2007). Consult. Sozialforschung. GmbH MAXQDA [Computer software]. Berlin: Available from www.maxqda.com/maxqda-eng/start.htm.

Verhage, A. (2009a). 'Corporations as a blind spot in research: explanations for a criminological tunnel vision', *Governance of Security Research Papers Series I, Contemporary Issues in the Empirical Study of Crime.* M. Cools, S. De Kimpe, B. De Ruyver, M. Easton, L. Pauwels, P. Ponsaers, G. Vande Walle, T. Vander Beken, F. Vander Laenen, G. Vermeulen. Antwerpen, Maklu, pp. 80–108.

Verhage, A. (2009b). 'Between the hammer and the anvil? The anti-money laundering complex and its interactions with the compliance industry', *Crime, Law and Social Change*, Springer, 52(1): 9–32.

Verhage, A. (2009c). 'Compliance and AML in Belgium: a booming sector with growing pains', *Journal of Money Laundering Control*, Emerald UK, 12(2): 113–133.

Verhage, A. (2009d). 'The anti money laundering complex: power pantomime or potential payoff? Perspectives on practices, partnerships and challenges within the fight against money laundering', in: *The informal economy and connections with organised crime: the impact of national social and economic policies*. J. Shapland and P. Ponsaers (eds). Den Haag, Boom Juridische Uitgevers, Reeks Het groene gras, pp. 79–111.

Verhage, A. (2009e). 'The beauty of grey? AML as a risk factor for compliance officers', in: *Crime, Money and Criminal Mobility in Europe*. P. van Duyne, S. Donati, J. Harvey, A. Maljevic, K. von Lampe (eds). Nijmegen, Wolf Legal Publishers, pp. 205–242.

Verhage, A. (2009f). 'Supply and demand: anti-money laundering by the compliance industry', *Journal of Money Laundering Control*, Emerald, 12(4): 371–391.

Verhage, A. (2009g). 'Compliance in de Belgische financiële sector. Of hoe zelfregulering en overheidsregulering in elkaar verstrengeld raken', in: *De criminologische kant van het ondernemen*. G. Vande Walle and P. Van Calster (eds). Den Haag, Boom Juridische Uitgevers, pp. 87–98.

Verhage, A. (2010). 'The anti money laundering complex on a crime control continuum: perceptions of risk, power and efficacy', in: *Governance of Security Research Papers, Topical Issues in EU and International Crime Control*. M. Cools, B. De Ruyver, M. Easton, L. Pauwels, P. Ponsaers, G. Vande Walle, T. Vander Beken, F. Vander Laenen, G. Vermeulen and G. Vynckier (eds), Antwerpen, Maklu, pp. 141–166.

Verhage, A. and P. Ponsaers (2009). 'Power-seeking crime? The professional thief versus the professional launderer', *Crime, Law and Social Change*, Springer Netherlands, 51(3–4): 399–412.

Verslag van de commissie voor de financiën van de staat – 1991–1992, 468–2: 35–36.

Verwee, I., P. Ponsaers and E. Enhus (2007). '*Inbreken is mijn vak'. Textuur en praktijk van woninginbraak*. Den Haag, Boom Juridische uitgevers.

Wet van 22 maart op het statuut van en het toezicht op de kredietinstellingen (*B.S*, 19 april 1993). (Law of 22 March on the statute of and supervision on the credit institutions (*B.S*, 19 April 1993))

Wikström, P.-O. (2006). 'Deterrence and deterrence experiences: preventing crime through the threat of punishment', in: *International Comparative Handbook of Penology and Criminal Justice*. S.G. Shoham (ed.), Eastbourne, Sussex Academic Press, pp. 345–378.

Willemsen, F., F. Leeuw and B. Leeuw (2008). 'Toezicht en inspectie in maten en soorten', *Tijdschrift voor Criminologie* 50(2): 96–113.

Williams, P. (1994). 'Transnational criminal organisations and international security', *Survival* 36(1): 96–113.

Wright Mills, C. (1956). *The power elite*. New York, Oxford University Press.

Young, J. (1992). 'Ten points of realism', in: *Rethinking criminology: realist debate*. J. Young and R. Matthews (eds). London, Sage.

Zedner, L. (2003) 'Too much security?' *International Journal of the Sociology of Law* 31: 155–184.

Zedner, L. (2006). 'Liquid security: managing the market for crime control', *Criminology and Criminal Justice* 6(3): 267–288.

Zimiles, E. (2004). 'KPMG survey: banks accept more costly money laundering laws, expect heightened cooperation with regulators', *The Journal of Investment Compliance*: 26–30.

Index

Page numbers in **bold** denote figures.